# SWORD OF ZEN

# Sword of Zen

*Master Takuan and His Writings
on Immovable Wisdom and the Sword Taie*

PETER HASKEL

University of Hawai'i Press
Honolulu

**Library of Congress Cataloging-in-Publication Data**
Haskel, Peter.
  Sword of Zen : Master Takuan and his writings on immovable wisdom and the
sword Taie / Peter Haskel.
     p.  cm.
  Includes bibliographical references and index.
  ISBN 978-0-8248-3543-9 (cloth : alk. paper)—ISBN 978-0-8248-3678-8 (pbk. : alk.
paper)
  1. Takuan Soho, 1573–1645.  2. Takuan Soho, 1573–1645. Fudochi shinmyoroku.
3. Takuan Soho, 1573–1645. Taiaki.  4. Zen Buddhism—Doctrines.  5. Swordplay—
Japan—Philosophy.  6. Yagyu, Munenori, 1571–1646. Hyoho kadensho.  I. Takuan
Soho, 1573–1645. Fudochi shinmyoroku. English.  II. Takuan Soho, 1573–1645. Taiaki.
English.  III. Title.
  BQ9399.T337H37 2013
  294.3'420427—dc23

                                                              2012010497

University of Hawai'i Press books are printed on acid-free
paper and meet the guidelines for permanence and
durability of the Council on Library Resources.

Designed by inari
Printed by Sheridan Books, Inc.

*For my parents*

# Contents

# Preface

I was introduced to Takuan Sōhō's writings on Zen and swordsmanship not long after enrolling as a graduate student in the East Asian Languages and Cultures department of Columbia University. My advisor, Yoshito Hakeda, had translated excerpts from Takuan's *Record of the Marvelous Power of Immovable Wisdom*, and these had been published in *The Buddhist Tradition*,[1] an anthology of Buddhist texts included in the department's curriculum. I was immediately taken with Takuan's essay, which struck me as the most practical and direct explanation of Zen I had ever come across. It is rare to find in the writings of early Japanese Zen masters such a detailed, accessible discussion of the mind and its workings, or such a straightforward description of how to realize and manifest Zen mind in daily life. Professor Hakeda was pleased that I shared his enthusiasm for Takuan's instruction on Zen and the sword, and suggested that at some point we translate the material together in its entirety, a project regrettably forestalled by his untimely death.

During this same period I was undertaking studies of a very different sort with Charles Nelson, an old marine who ran what he called the School of Self-Defense, on West 72nd Street, a short subway ride downtown from Columbia. A grizzled veteran of the Pacific War, Charlie had evolved a personal system of "dirty street fighting" that combined techniques from jujutsu, boxing, tai chi, and karate. His instruction focused on actual instances of urban violence gleaned from tabloid crime reports and the personal histories of his students, primarily cops, bouncers, mugging victims, and the merely curious, like myself.

Charlie's school was a shabby, second-floor loft, littered with an assortment of plastic knives, guns, bats, and machetes that he used to demonstrate his methods. These emphasized keeping the body balanced at all times and, in contrast to traditional martial arts, avoiding any fixed forms or stances in order to maintain maximum flexibility, to shift easily to meet an attacker's next move.

Charlie knew of my interest in Buddhism and one day confronted me in the middle of our workout. "Isn't this Zen just a bunch of baloney?" he demanded.

"Well," I said, thinking immediately of Takuan and *Record of Immovable Wisdom*, "You always teach not to let the body take any fixed stance so you're free to respond according to the situation. Zen just says to do the same thing with the mind." I don't think Charlie was wholly convinced, but he shot me a grin and we went on with the lesson.

Now, some thirty years later, after delays for several intervening projects, I have finally completed my translations of the two classics on Zen and swordsmanship by Takuan Sōhō (1573–1645): *Record of Immovable Wisdom* and *On The Sword Taie*. In assembling my introduction to these works I have tried to concentrate on the major themes underlying both, especially Takuan's emphasis on the dynamic function of Zen mind. The introduction also incorporates passages from Takuan's other prose writings that highlight or expand on the master's theory of mind, along with a brief discussion of the New "Shadow" sword school (Shinkageryū), stressing the manner in which Takuan's ideas are reflected in *Art of the Sword* (*Heihō kadensho*),[2] by his student Yagyū Munenori (1571–1646). My primary focus in the introduction has been the Zen-related aspects of Takuan's teachings on swordsmanship, and I have dealt only cursorily with the influence of Neo-Confucian metaphysics, Han cosmology, and such on Takuan's writings here and elsewhere. Deserving as the topics may be, I felt they lay beyond the scope of the present work.

The two translations that form the core of this book follow the text in volume 5 of *Takuan oshō zenshū* (Complete Works of Master Takuan).[3] Although both works are undated, *Record of Immovable Wisdom* has been placed first following the practice in most modern Japanese collections of Takuan's writings. The texts have been translated into English numerous times, beginning with D. T. Suzuki, who included portions of each in his 1959 *Zen and Japanese Culture* in the Bollingen series.[4] Why then did I feel the need to undertake a new translation of the material? Having read and reread Takuan's sword writings over the years, I have always been left with a nagging sense that the existing translations, while competent, failed to convey the full character and vitality of Takuan's original. And the works themselves are so unusual, so compelling, that I felt they merited another attempt, with an eye to eliciting Takuan's distinctive voice. It is for the reader to judge whether I have succeeded in this regard.

Two additional factors impelled me to undertake the project. I've now spent over forty-five years struggling with Zen practice as a resident student at the First Zen Institute of America, and while I can't claim these efforts lend me any special authority or expertise—at best, as Bankei Yōtaku would say, I've become something of "an expert in delusion"—they have made me appreciate the uniquely vivid presentation of Zen and Zen mind offered by Takuan in his two works on the sword. Such basic, plain-language explanations to lay people are highly unusual for Zen masters in premodern China or Japan. Indeed, the mind and how it actually operates are difficult things to speak about for anyone, ancient or modern, including Zen masters and master swordsmen.

Lastly, my research and translation work since my days at Columbia with Professor Hakeda has concentrated on the history of Japanese Zen in the Tokugawa, or Edo period (1600–1867). In particular, my attention has been drawn to those masters who tended in one way or another to "buck the system," mavericks like the freewheeling and popular teacher Bankei, the loner and roadside vinegar seller Tōsui, and the beloved beggar-poet Ryōkan. Takuan, with his independent, outspoken approach to Zen and authority, seemed to me fitting company for these figures, and his essays on swordsmanship, like Bankei's sermons, are among the vernacular treasures of Tokugawa Zen.

Takuan is remembered today not merely for his writings but for his place in the history of Japanese Buddhism, in particular for his leading role in the so-called Purple Robe Affair, and for his close relationship with the third Tokugawa shogun, Iemitsu (1604–1651), and with Iemitsu's sword master Yagyū Munenori. Takuan is also among the last illustrious Zen masters linked with the great Kyoto headquarters temple Daitokuji, being an esteemed spiritual descendant of the temple's founder, Daitō (1282–1337), and of the wildly eccentric late medieval poet-priest Ikkyū Sōjun (1394–1481). Takuan's biography is thus of more than casual interest, and the latter portion of the book presents the principal elements of the master's story as we know it, hoping to suggest something of the context in which his works on Zen and the sword were composed. In describing Takuan's eventful life, I have relied wherever possible on contemporary sources, particularly Takuan's own extensive correspondence and the twin biographies by his student Takeno Munetomo: the 1648 *Account of the Life of Master Takuan* (*Takuan dai-oshō gyōjō*) and the largely identical but expanded 1650 *Biographical Record of the Master of Tōkaiji* (*Tōkai oshō kinenroku*).[5] Like all such premodern Japanese Buddhist works in which a disciple records the events of his teacher's life, Takuan's biographies are, by twenty-first-century standards, hagiographies rather than critical studies and as such reflect the traditional views of Takuan's story accepted in his Zen line. In setting forth the particulars of Takuan's career and their interpretation, I have therefore relied greatly on Funaoka Makoto's fine 1988 biography *Takuan*. It is among the few modern Japanese books to address the master's life seriously, and it is the source of many of the quotations I have included from Takuan's letters and other works.

Takuan stands out in Tokugawa religious history as a remarkable individual, perhaps the most well-known Japanese Zen master of his day, and it seemed to me regrettable that as yet no university press book had been devoted exclusively to him and his distinctive works on Zen and the sword. It remains my hope that this volume will be a modest first step in remedying that situation.

# Acknowledgments

Many people have contributed to the preparation of this book. Along with Professor Hakeda, who first inspired me to take up Takuan and taught me the theory of "no fixed mind," and Charlie, who taught me its practical application, I owe a special debt of gratitude to Ryuichi Abe, Edwin O. Reischauer Institute Professor of Japanese Religions in Harvard University's Department of East Asian Languages and Civilizations. A fellow graduate student under Professor Hakeda, Professor Abe has generously shared with me his wisdom and expertise, helping with countless questions that arose in the course of the translation and associated research. Maria Collora, Michael Hotz, and John Storm read the manuscript through at various stages, offering many helpful suggestions, while Peeter Lamp and Ian Chandler were always ready to untangle ticklish computer-related problems. Hiroaki Sato kindly made available his personal copy of Yagyū Munenori's *Heihō kadensho,* and Haruo Watabe helped procure Japanese print and internet materials relating to Munenori and the New Shadow school. Haruo also arranged for me to visit the New York City New Shadow school dojo, where I was able to observe American men and women, armed with both wooden and "live" swords, training in the time-honored traditions of the Yagyū school. My sincere gratitude to the current head of the school, Yagyū Koichi, and to Hamada sensei of the New York Yagyū-kai.

For information on the Baize and its connections with Chinese Zen, I am indebted to Professor Don Harper of the University of Chicago, who kindly shared with me portions of the research for his forthcoming book on occult texts and popular culture in China from the fourth century BCE to the tenth century CE. I was also unusually fortunate in my peer review reader for the manuscript, who had a compendious knowledge of not only Takuan and his writings but the history of Japanese swordsmanship in the sixteenth and seventeenth centuries, and directed me to a wide variety of sources and issues that otherwise might have been overlooked. While academic publishing protocol prevents me from knowing the reader's identity, I am very much indebted to his many apt and detailed suggestions, which contributed greatly to the introductory portion of the work. Thanks also to my editor at University of Hawai'i Press, Patricia Crosby, for once again finding such skilled readers and for her seemingly endless patience in seeing the book through to completion, and to Susan Stone, the press's copy editor extraordinaire.

Finally, I would like to acknowledge the First Zen Institute of America for graciously making available to me its library and computer facilities, and Sachie Noguchi, Kenneth Harlin, D. John McClure, Chengzhi Wang, and the other staff members of Columbia University's Starr East Asian Library for their help over the course of the present project.

# 1 An Introduction to Takuan's Writings on Zen and Swordsmanship

LIKE MANY ZEN PRIESTS of his day, Takuan was a literary as well as a religious figure. Besides extensive correspondence and quantities of poems in both Chinese and Japanese, the master produced a number of independent prose works in *kana majiri* (mixed kana and Chinese characters), the majority, according to Tsuji Zennosuke, probably composed for particular daimyo patrons.[1] The most widely read of these writings, apart from the two works on swordsmanship, are *Night Talks at Tōkaiji* (*Tōkaiji yawa*) and *Knotted Cords* (*Ketsujōshū*), and a third work, *Tinkling Gems* (*Reirō-shū*).[2] While occasionally touching on Zen, all three are essentially miscellanies, random collections of Takuan's thoughts on a range of topics, Buddhist and non-Buddhist. By contrast, Takuan's writings on swordsmanship focus from first to last on a single purpose—illumining the principles of Zen through the exigencies of the warrior's art. Indeed, of all Takuan's surviving writings, only *Record of the Marvelous Power of Immovable Wisdom* and *On the Sword Taie* (hereafter generally abbreviated *Record of Immovable Wisdom* and *The Sword Taie*) deal so directly, thoroughly, and exclusively with Zen, and in particular with the practice and function of Zen mind. The texts are also to my knowledge the earliest surviving examples of a Rinzai master's written instruction on Zen and the martial arts.[3] Of the two, *Record of Immovable Wisdom* is overall the more lively and detailed; but *The Sword Taie* retains a distinct character and flavor that make it a valuable companion piece to its more celebrated cousin.

It is not known if the title *Record of the Marvelous Power of Immovable Wisdom* was assigned to the work by Takuan or—as seems more likely—attached to the text posthumously. (Takuan's mid-nineteenth-century biographer Kudō Yukihiro remarks that the work went by a variety of titles.)[4]

The text is organized under thirteen headings, which Takuan comments on, some at length, others with only a sentence or two. Many of the headings are or allude to phrases and concepts derived from Buddhist and specifically Zen sources. Obviously directed at a layman, Takuan's language throughout is simple and straightforward, and technical Buddhist or Zen terms are explained clearly, using examples from both dueling and common experience.

While ostensibly Takuan's thoughts on Zen and the Way of the Sword, *Record of Immovable Wisdom* also constitutes a sort of "owner's manual" for the Zen mind—what it is and how one can use it not only in combat but at all times and in all circumstances. Thus, although much of Takuan's discussion draws on aspects of swordsmanship, his work is above all an introduction to Zen, regarded not as a formal system of practice and study but as a reality that is central to and inseparable from daily life, from one's intimate functioning at every moment. "The Way is simply our daily activity," Takuan observes in *Knotted Cords*. "Apart from our daily activity, no Way exists. It's not as if there's something called 'enlightenment,' which you realize. What you call 'being enlightened' is delusion. Unless you're deluded, there is no enlightenment."[5] In conformance with this view, Takuan's presentation of Zen in *Record of Immovable Wisdom* is consistently down to earth, compelling yet matter of fact; or, as one modern Japanese scholar puts it, "powerful, matter-of-fact explanations of something itself matter of fact [i.e., Zen]."[6]

At the very start of his teaching, Takuan sets out the essentials of mind and how they apply to swordsmanship. When confronting an opponent, the swordsman must above all avoid "stopping" or "attaching" the mind (*kokoro o tomeru*). Whether it is his adversary's movements or his own movements, his fears, thoughts, or expectations, whatever traps his attention, the instant the mind stops, it becomes confined, constrained, losing its freedom to respond; and once his mind is captured in this way, the swordsman can be killed. "The moment your attention is drawn to the slashing blade of your opponent, you rush to meet his attack at that place, with the result that your mind becomes attached there to your opponent's blade, so that you lose your free functioning and can be slain. This is what is meant by attachment."[7] This stopping, attaching mind, Takuan says, is what Buddhism refers to as delusion. It is the cause of all suffering and ignorance, the fetters of birth and death. By contrast, the enlightened, non-stopping mind is like water, never staying in one place but always fluid, free to flow wherever it is needed. This is the original, true mind with which everyone is endowed, the mind that is the heart of both swordsmanship and Zen. "Not keeping the mind in any one place is what practice is all about," Takuan sums up. "Not attaching the mind anywhere at all is the main matter, what really counts."

For the swordsman, this means confronting each adversary directly, without deliberation or hesitation: "When you see the opponent's blade strike, just see it and don't attach your mind there, parrying the attacking blade without any thought or calculation. The instant you see your opponent's blade raised, without attaching to it for even a moment, move right in and capture his blade, seizing the sword that was about to kill you so that it becomes instead the sword that kills your opponent."

Part of the problem with the stopping mind is that it creates an "interval" or "interruption" (*ma, sukima*) in the mind's flow, a potentially deadly gap between the opponent's attack and the swordsman's riposte. By contrast, both Zen and swordsmanship prize immediacy and directness of response. As in the lightning give and take of Zen dialogue, or *mondō*, what matters here, Takuan emphasizes, is not speed as such but naturalness and spontaneity, signaling the mind's resilience and freedom from attachment. Takuan offers the example of a swordsman successfully battling a quick succession of opponents, meeting each attack on its own terms, unhindered by lingering thoughts of the previous encounter. If, however, the swordsman's mind becomes trapped anywhere, even momentarily, his contact with the present moment is severed, leaving him unable to counter his next attacker effectively. As soon as the mind stops in any particular place, it misses all the other places. By not attaching the mind anywhere, it permeates everywhere.[8]

This is the principle, according to Takuan, embodied in the image of the Thousand-Armed Kannon,[9] the popular bodhisattva whose myriad arms wield a variety of weapons and other implements, symbolizing the limitless responsiveness of original mind. Precisely because Kannon is never "fixed" on any single arm or implement, all one thousand can function smoothly and simultaneously. This is a metaphor for the operation of the human mind. When the mind is attached in any particular place, Takuan says, it becomes "biased" (*hen*); while by remaining unbiased (*shō*) it is always supple and free, just as a wheel kept loose on its axle can turn but if fastened at any point immediately becomes stuck. Using several other examples, Takuan in *Night Talks at Tōkaiji* articulates this flexibility of the nonattached, "empty" mind:

> When you direct the mind to take some particular role, no matter what it is, there's no way the mind can then respond to the things that [actually] happen. Just leave the mind without any particular role and you can let it respond to

whatever comes along. As an example, the eye is the actor that sees; the ear, the actor that hears; the nose, the actor that smells; the tongue, the actor that tastes; the body, the actor that knows by touching; the hand, the actor that grasps; the foot, the actor that walks.[10] And despite all these varied roles, the mind smoothly manages each and every one without missing anything. So if you avoid fixing the mind in one particular role, you won't be lacking in all the various roles. That's why we say that leaving the mind *without* any particular role is emptiness [*komu*]. In employing a soldier, for example, a common soldier should be able to fight with each of various weapons—a bow, a gun, a spear, a halberd. But if the general who commands all the soldiers fixes on a particular weapon—the bow, the gun, or whatever—he'll be deficient in everything else. A general, by not taking any single role, acts in all capacities. Not to be distracted by any single activity is what is meant by emptiness.[11]

This mind that is never fixed but always in play, effortlessly shifting in response to circumstances, is what Takuan refers to as immovable, or un-moving, wisdom (*fudōchi*). Moving, here, indicates attachment to any-thing—to one's hand wielding the sword, to one's opponent's attack. Immovable means that whatever presents itself, the mind doesn't "move" and attach to it. In Takuan's interpretation, immovable does not signify standing still but rather never moving from the mind's intrinsic flexibility and freedom. "Immovable wisdom," Takuan observes, "means the mind moving as it wants to move—forward, left, right, in all directions, without ever being attached."

Takuan's notion here contrasts with that of Mencius (372–289? BCE), for whom the immovable mind (Ch. *budongxin*) is also of key importance and whose teachings were among the "Four Books" (Ch. *sishu*, J. *shisho*), the four classic Confucian texts revered in Takuan's Japan.[12] The mind (Ch. *xin*), Mencius held, has an innate tendency to righteousness (Ch. *yi*), but it can be disturbed by the fluctuations of one's vital force, or *qi*. The mind, therefore, must be nourished through cultivation of a "floodlike breath," or "energy" (*haoranzhiqi*), an inner moral power that directs the mind to righteousness in all situations and lends one the fortitude to remain un-swayed, unmoved (Ch. *budong*) by whatever contravenes ethical behavior. Unlike Takuan's insistence on a mind that is wholly free-flowing and un-fixed, for Mencius' unmoved mind, as one modern scholar observes, "*qi* needs to be tightly constricted to serve moral ends."[13]

Use of the term "immovable" (J. *fudō*) is not confined to Mencius and Confucianism. It is widely used in Indian and Chinese Mahāyāna Buddhism to connote various states of transcendence, and its meanings include a state that does not violate or go contrary to reality.[14] Takuan, as a cultivated Zen monk of his time, was thoroughly conversant with Confucianism, its classics, and its metaphysics, much of which he elsewhere discusses at length.[15] It is in this general Buddhist context, however, that the master seems to speak of the unmoved mind, as when, near the opening of *Record of Immovable Wisdom* he invokes the familiar image of Fudō Myōō, the Immovable King of Radiance.

In his discussion of Fudō Myōō, Takuan emphasizes that this mind of immovable wisdom is not something alien but our existing, original mind (*honshin*). As such, it does not need to be learned or acquired but merely allowed to operate. The task of both the swordsman and the Zen student is simply to refrain from obstructing the mind's natural freedom and fluidity. Like the swordsman distracted by his opponent's movements or by his own strategy or stance, it is only when we are preoccupied, attached, or stuck in some particular place that the original mind turns into deluded mind (*mōjin*). Takuan compares this to water and ice. Water, like original mind, is formless, always changing but always the same. When it turns to ice, however, water congeals into particular forms and loses its fluidity, just as mind, when it stops or becomes frozen at some point, is no longer free to flow and accommodate itself to circumstances. The object for the swordsman, Takuan says, is to "melt" the mind whose response has been frozen by attachment, to let it flow unhindered through the body, returning deluded consciousness to its original, enlightened state.

Attachment, which impairs the mind's freedom, is also a function of intention (*ushin*), literally, "having mind," by which Takuan means harboring some particular thought. A Nō dancer intent on displaying his skill will find this very concern an impediment to his art, and the same is true of a dueling swordsman's obsession with victory, speed, or the avoidance of defeat. What the accomplished swordsman as well as the Zen student must cultivate is the mind of nonintention (*mushin*), or "no-mind," a familiar Zen expression that Takuan elsewhere pairs with the similar term "no thought" (*munen*). "By 'thought,'" he explains in *Knotted Cords*, "we mean going back over what is past, thinking about it again and again without letting it go. By 'mind' we mean pondering this way and that about what is happening here in the present. You may imagine that as human beings we're unable to keep from thinking about what is past or to refrain from thinking about what is happening in the present, so that no-thought and no-mind are not really possible; but such things exist all the same. What is called no-mind is something one needs."[16]

Similarly, the Buddhist concept of emptiness (*kū*) is interpreted by Takuan as having nothing in the mind, as the absence of all attachment or intention. Emptiness and nonintention, however, should never be confused with inertia. Quite the reverse, Takuan argues: inertia occurs when something is *in* the mind, blocking its spontaneous response. Nonintention is really noninterference with the mind's natural free-flowing activity, and emptiness describes the state in which this occurs, a state where the mind remains fluid and wholly unattached, even to distinctions of subject and object. This, Takuan explains, is not only the core realization of Buddhism and Zen but the key to mastering swordsmanship. In the midst of combat, from one moment to the next, the swordsman must put the teaching of emptiness into practice by never allowing the mind to become mired or trapped at any point but leaving it always unconstrained, like a hollow gourd bobbing on a stream. In concrete terms, unconstrained means "You don't attach the mind to the hand that is wielding the sword. Completely forgetting the hand wielding [the sword], strike and kill your opponent, [but] don't fix the mind *on* your opponent. Realize that your opponent is empty, that you are empty, that both the hand wielding the sword and the sword being wielded are empty. Don't even let your mind be captured by emptiness!"

In *Night Talks at Tōkaiji*, Takuan elaborates his view of emptiness as the absence of deliberate thought or calculation, the ground for the marvelous power of original wisdom. Whatever the changing situation, Takuan says, only emptiness can meet it appropriately because nothing is in one's mind, nothing in the way, interposed between the immediacy of events and one's response.

> In whatever you do, it's in the present moment that the marvelous reveals itself. You should not prepare for things in advance. By preparing for things in advance, you cannot respond to the actual situation before you. Emptiness alone can accurately respond in all circumstances; long, short, round, square, it's always right on the mark. When you make the heart empty, holding nothing in your mind, whatever comes your way you'll respond accordingly. [Whereas,] if you plan things out in advance, you'll have what you planned for in your mind, and instead of responding to what comes along, the thing you planned to do gets in the way. With your mind already occupied, there's no way it can receive what actually presents itself.[17]

Takuan goes on to compare the function of emptiness, its dissolution of subject and object in the present moment, to the movement of a cloud across the heavens or the flawless working of a mirror:

Before the cloud appears, the sky is perfectly clear and serene, without a trace of anything at all. Then the cloud arrives and drifts across the sky. But whether it drifts to the east or the west, once it's gone, the sky remains as it was. Before the cloud appears, no place has been prepared for it; and similarly, after it's gone, no trace of it is retained.

. . . Mind is also like a mirror. A mirror reflects the things that come before it. When nothing comes before it, it remains absolutely clear. Just so, if no things are kept in the mind, we call that emptiness. If there are things [kept] in the mind, its functioning is lost.[18]

Like the sky and the mirror, which retain no traces, original mind is endlessly responsive precisely because it is empty of thought or intention. However, empty mind is not to be realized simply by stilling or stifling mental activity. Deliberately trying to get rid of thought, Takuan cautions, only becomes another thought, another intention. To empty the mind by suppressing thoughts or keeping them in check only results in constraining the mind, interfering with its natural flow. Instead, Takuan calls on the swordsman to free the mind, to let the mind go, as if releasing a cat on a leash. For the warrior who is confronting an opponent to focus his mind anywhere—inside or outside himself—can be a deadly mistake, a dangerous narrowing and weakening of his awareness. Takuan is critical of any attempt to forcibly control or manipulate the mind, including concentrating attention in the *tanden*, or lower abdomen, a familiar training technique in both Zen and the martial arts and one closely associated at times with Daoism.[19] Takuan identifies such mistaken approaches to the mind with certain Neo-Confucian techniques for self-cultivation centering on the practice of moral seriousness, or reverence (Ch. *jing*, J. *kei*). For the most part, such practices are extensions of Mencius' "unmoving mind" and "floodlike breath," referred to earlier, concepts revived in the Song by theorists such as the Cheng brothers and Zhu Xi as a basis for Neo-Confucian meditation. Single-minded concentration on reverence within, the Chengs assert, will lead to righteousness without, a humane interaction and oneness with all things that avoids what they allege to be Buddhism's moral ambiguity.[20] A century later, a similar concept was elaborated by Zhu Xi: "The task of reverence is the first principle of the Confucian school," Zhu Xi avers. "From beginning to end, it must not be interrupted for a single moment. . . . Seriousness merely means the mind being its own master. . . . It is merely to be apprehensive and careful and dare not give reign to yourself. In this way, both body and mind will be collected and concentrated as if one is apprehensive of something."[21]

While conceding some role for such practices as expedients for beginners, ultimately Takuan views them as forms of stopping the mind, when what is needed is to set it free. "In using the mind," he instructs, "let it go where it wants. If you tightly restrain it, it becomes inflexible. Keeping the mind tightly reined in is strictly for beginners."

The swordsman can let the mind go anywhere freely because it is originally pure, like a smoothly polished crystal that remains clear even if it falls into the mud. Accordingly, the way to deal with thoughts—with perceptions, intentions, notions, feelings—is by what Takuan calls "forgetting the mind" (*kokoro o wasuru*), being natural, free, and unselfconscious. The problem, after all, is not thoughts but our attachment to them by stopping the mind. The difficulty, says Takuan, is automatically resolved by allowing the mind to resume its natural nonstopping state, "flowing like a raging torrent." Then, as he observes elsewhere,

> Even though you don't deliberately *seek* to keep things from lingering in the mind, to give them up or let them go, they'll cease naturally, of themselves, and nothing will linger in the mind. That way, without cutting off or transforming your evil mind, you'll simply occupy yourself with whatever is right before you: when happy, you'll smile; when sad, you'll sigh; when things from the past come to mind, you'll just let them come. Since things in the world are always changing, [you recognize that these are] temporary thoughts, leaving no traces, so you don't linger in these thoughts. . . . Just as when the wind blows, waves arise and splash, and when the wind ceases, the ocean is quiet and the water calm, so when the winds of one's mind have ceased, no trace remains of the waves of mind, and the waters of mind are serene. Imagining you musn't think, you try not to think about things so that whatever you encounter leaves no trace. [But] when you neither deliberately try *not* to think nor try to get rid of your thoughts, your mind will instantly find itself at peace.[22]

What interferes with this practice of letting go and freeing the mind to operate spontaneously is the very stubborness of attachment. For the swordsman, whose opponent can instantly seize on any imbalance or lapse in attention, the "mind that attaches to things and is then pushed about and deluded by them" is a matter of life and death. In *Record of Immovable Wisdom*, Takuan offers a general approach to this problem but outlines no definite technique for untethering the mind from its particular anxieties and fixations. According to Buddhism, everything in the universe, our selves included, is in flux, impermanent, and therefore empty and insubstantial so that any attachment is deluded. But actually unblocking the mind, overcoming its powerful tendency to "stop" and become mired in things in the passing stream, is clearly no easy matter. In *Knotted Cords*, discussing how to deal with nagging feelings such as anger or grief, Takuan suggests a practical way to shake oneself free of attachment and return to original, empty mind, flowing in the moment:

> When you are mired in your anger, shut away in your gloom, your *ki*[23] has no way to expand. What happens when you get angry about something is that your mind sticks to that thing and won't let go. And the harder you try to make it go, the worse things get. When that happens, you should look at something, a cloud or a mountain; the mind that had been stuck in whatever you were angry about will then be able to detach itself, shifting to the cloud or mountain.
>
> Take a man trying to seize a biting horse. To get the horse away from its set of mind, he thrusts a flower in front of it, and, when it sees the flower, the horse is freed from the state of mind it was stuck in. Even the horse is then in the state of no-mind, and without any bother the man can seize it. . . . This is the expedient of using things to relieve the mind. The principle behind chanting *dharani* or mantra[24] is to avert misfortune, to turn perversity into reasonableness, to order the wayward mind, and to free the mind stuck in some thing. Even magic spells and such have some reason behind them.
>
> There was a woman whose *ki* was stuck in her chest, who was feeling ill with no inkling of why. A certain doctor declared, "This woman is lovesick. She is an adulteress."
>
> The woman immediately flew into a rage. "I'd never be guilty of such a thing!" she protested. "This doctor's accusation is simply outrageous!"
>
> As her fury rose like a black cloud, the *ki* lodged in her chest suddenly dispersed, and her illness was cured. The doctor cured her illness without using any medicine. He had a device by which, with just one word, he snatched away the gloom in her heart.[25]

Takuan's advice on grief and anger accords with the instruction in *Record of Immovable Wisdom*, where the swordsman is exhorted to "melt" the mind that has become attached, to let it flow throughout the body without being trapped or constricted at any point. Freedom of mind is Takuan's pivotal message, the principle that underlies these teachings and, he insists, the key to all religion and art, including the Way of the Sword. Whether in Zen, swordsmanship, or any other endeavor, the path to realization lies not in contracting and holding back the mind but in "just leaving it alone and freeing it to go anywhere at all."

The insistence on freedom also dominates Takuan's other work concerning Zen and the sword, *The Sword Taie*. The sword Taie (J. *tai'a*) of the title is a fabulous weapon drawn from Chinese legend, a sword that can penetrate anything and renders its owner invincible. As Takuan explains: "The sword Taie is the name of a famous sword without equal anywhere on earth. It freely cuts through [all] hard [substances], from gold and iron to gems and rocks. Nothing under heaven can resist its blade."

The original story appears in the "Record of Precious Swords" chapter (Waichuanji baojian) of *The Glory of Yue* (*Yuejue shu*), a famous second-to-third-century compilation of texts concerning the rival Chinese kingdoms of Wu and Yue during the period 771–221 BCE. According to the account, the King of Chu dispatched his retainer Master Feng Hu to Wu with various treasures to gain that king's permission for the acclaimed sword smiths Gen Jing and Ou Ye to make several swords for his personal use. On obtaining the King of Wu's consent, the sword smiths produced three wondrous iron swords, among them the sword Taie (Great Riverbank). When the King of Chu asked about the sword's curious name, Feng Hu explained, "Its patterning is majestic and vigorous, like the waves of a flowing river." The King of Jin, hearing of these swords, demanded them for himself, and when the King of Chu refused to yield them, sent three armies to besiege a city in Chu. The siege continued for three years till all weapons and food in the city were exhausted. The King of Chu's generals and ministers were unable to break the siege. Finally the king himself unsheathed the sword Taie, and brandishing it mounted the city walls. The three investing forces were defeated, "blood ran everywhere . . . and the King of Jin's hair turned white." Overjoyed at this victory, the King of Wu asked Master Feng, "Is this a result of the power of the sword or of my own strength?" Feng Hu replied, "It is the power of the sword, but this depends on Your Majesty's spiritual power." "The sword is only iron," declared the king. "How can it have such spiritual power?" Feng Hu observed that earlier blades had been made of other materials such as jade. "Jade too is a substance with divine properties," Feng explained, "but it only becomes so when it meets a sagelike ruler. . . . At this time we make iron weapons, whose might can defeat three armies. When the world knows of this, no one will fail to submit. This is the spiritual power of iron weapons and Your Majesty's sagelike virtue."[26]

The sword Taie is a kind of supersword, but the sword as such was itself an object with potent symbolism for Takuan's Japan. For the Tokugawa samurai it was emblematic at once of his personal honor and his warrior caste, signaling his membership in Edo society's hereditary elite. Besides being synonymous with weaponry and combat (the expresion "sword fight" [*tachiuchi*] signified any form of combat from archery to stone throwing), prized swords served as valuable gifts to and from the shogun, and ownership and display of such swords imparted power and prestige. The sword, moreover, had a long history in Japan as an object of reverence at shrines, a sacred vessel in which Shinto deities might manifest themselves.[27]

The sword was also an important metaphor in Buddhism and in the Zen school in particular. The bodhisattva Manjusri (J. Monju), whose image dominates the meditation hall (*zendō*) of many Japanese Zen temples, holds a naked sword representing *prajñā*, the intuitive wisdom that spontaneously annihilates attachments. In turn, the head monk who monitors meditation in the *zendō* is considered the personification of Manjusri, while the *keisaku* (also *kyōsaku*), or "warning stick," he carries to rouse drowsy monks with a sharp thwack on the shoulders is conceived as Manjusri's sword.[28] The theme of the sword appears as well in many of the medieval Chinese phrases and expressions employed in koan study:

Where a sharp sword cuts, no wound remains. . . .

Two heads simultaneously lopped off: one terrible sword supported by heaven.

The keen-edged sword sweeps all away, heaven and earth are still; raise the chilling blade and even the constellations shiver.

Even the precious sword Taie started out as raw iron.[29]

Similarly, Takuan gives the sword Taie his own interpretation, identifying it variously as mind, buddhahood, one's original face, seeing one's nature, and so forth. The sword represents that which is intrinsic, possessed innately, "what is original to all persons." It is what Takuan calls the "self of true self" (*shinga no ga*), one's actual being as distinct from the false, ego-centered "self of self-and-other" (*ninga no ga*). Unlike his false self, which is readily apparent, the swordsman's true being, originally empty and unattached, is without shape or form, invisible to his opponent. In the same way, the opponent is said to be invisible to the realized swordsman, who, transcending the false, limiting self, sees past his opponent's ego-bound strategy focused on strength or weakness, victory or defeat.

A somewhat similar understanding of the sword of Zen was offered by the master Imakita Kōsen (Kōsen Sōon, 1816–1892), a leading reformer and modernizer of the Rinzai school during the Meiji period (1868–1911). Kōsen criticized as insufficient Confucius' goal of realizing humanity by "overcoming the self," a goal that, Kōsen asserts, can be attained permanently only by "killing" the self with the sharp sword of the Zen koan.[30] Kōsen's lineage descendant Sokei-an (Sasaki Shigetsu, 1882–1945), the first Rinzai master to settle permanently in the United States, offers a more extended explanation of the sword metaphor in Zen in comments on the following passage from the *Record of Linji*: "When a man tries to practice the Way, the Way does not function / And ten thousand evil circumstances vie in raising their heads. / But when the sword of wisdom (*chih chien*) flashes forth, nothing remains; / Before brightness is manifest, darkness is bright. For that reason a man of old said, 'Ordinary mind is the Way.'"[31] Sokei-an observes to his American audience:

> When the sword of wisdom comes forth, there will be nothing at all. . . . This sword, this diamond sword, will annihilate everything: time and space, beginning and end, true and false, good and bad. The negative and positive are aspects seen from the human angle, but from the universal angle there is just one aspect, and that is absolute. There is no negative or positive. . . . When this sword shines alone in heaven, all is reduced to nothingness. The sword of wisdom, the absolute sword, cuts out all relative conceptions. It is in silence that one attains this sword. When you reach this view, you have the sword of wisdom. Do you have that sword in yourself? . . . You must take the sword from its scabbard and cut the dust away. Then you will see the original sword.[32]

Because it flows naturally from the true self, Takuan says, the free functioning embodied by the sword Taie is spontaneous and easy, an expression of original, everyday mind. As such, it is not to be experienced in some remote or mysterious realm but in "all one's ordinary activities."[33] This is what Takuan intimates when he speaks of never departing from the "ordinary" (*jinjō*) and when he exhorts the swordsman to "neither take one step forward nor one step back but secure victory remaining right where you are."

All that prevents the unhampered operation of the true self on the field of combat is the swordsman's clinging and calculating consciousness, his persistent attachment to intention. By contrast, Takuan says, the sword Taie is "the power of the marvelous function of acting without intention," and, as in *Record of Immovable Wisdom*, Takuan cautions the swordsman confronting an adversary against attaching even momentarily to thoughts or movements. Similarly, the swordsman must dispense with all rules, forms, and models, meeting reality head-on. "Laws and regulations that are like molds have nothing to do with the great function manifesting before you. . . . One for whom this great function is immediately manifesting is free and without obstruction, whether he goes this way or that."

This unobstructed activity of mind, Takuan reiterates, is not only the secret of great swordsmanship but the very essence of Zen, the special transmission outside the scriptures that was passed down from the Buddha to his disciple Mahākāshyapa and preserved across the generations of awakened teachers. It is a principle whose mastery not only transforms the swordsman's awareness but, according to Takuan, renders him invulnerable. Because his mind is always open and empty, like the polished surface of a mirror, the enlightened warrior assesses each situation instantly and intuitively, without betraying any intention of his own, without, as modern boxers might put it, "telegraphing" his moves. With no thoughts to slow or distort his response, such a swordsman, we are told, is able to act with lightning speed and matchless skill, immediately lopping off his opponent's head. However, should two realized swordsmen join in combat and unsheathe their Taie swords, the result in both military and spiritual terms will be a "draw," a true meeting of minds. This is compared to the encounters of enlightened teachers and disciples pictured in the Chinese Zen records, epitomized by the legend of Mahākāshyapa's smile when the Buddha held up a flower before his assembly of followers, the genesis of Zen's wordless transmission.

Even faced with an ignorant adversary, the enlightened swordsman, although he possesses the means to kill outright, no longer has the necessity to do so. At one with original mind, he naturally assumes command of any situation. And confronted with this principle manifesting in the master swordsman, the opponent's false self perishes, freeing his own intrinsic wisdom and vitality. This, Takuan indicates, is the true working of the sword Taie, the reason the sword that kills is also the sword that brings to life. In turn, it reflects the Daoist-inspired views of early Tokugawa period military writers such as Munenori, who conceived the samurai not as killers but as protectors of the peace and regarded the enlightened avoidance of bloodshed and combat as ultimate manifestations of the warrior's skill and virtue.[34]

While it obviously shares many themes with *Record of Immovable Wisdom*, *The Sword Taie* is a far shorter work with a more traditional and restrictive format, that of a textual commentary, specifically, Takuan's remarks on a Japanese text of unknown origin concerning Zen and the art of the sword. The text Takuan addresses is recorded in *kanbun*, or Sino-Japanese,[35] and incorporates standard Buddhist terms, occasional references to Chinese history, philosophy, and culture, and numerous phrases from the *Blue Cliff Record* and other medieval Zen classics. Takuan's comments, composed in a mixture of *kana* and Chinese characters, are presented in clear and simple language and seek to explain the text in terms of the nature and function of Zen mind.

There is no indication for whom *The Sword Taie* was prepared, but it can be assumed from the work's subject matter and basic, simplified approach to Zen that it was intended for a warrior, presumably one of Takuan's samurai patrons, such as Munenori or his son and heir Jūbei Mitsutoshi (1607–1650).[36] There has even been speculation that the *kanbun* text itself was composed by Takuan,[37] and a passage like the following recalls Takuan's treatment of nonattachment in *Record of Immovable Wisdom* and elsewhere: "The point of such a man's sword is never revealed. It is swifter than a streak of lightning, faster than a sudden storm. Lacking this sort of skill, the moment you attach anywhere, or intentionally direct the mind toward anything, you ruin the point of your weapon and injure your hand and will never be fit to achieve victory." One possibility is that the *kanbun* text was written by Takuan as a transmission document (*densho*) for the martial arts of the type the master is reported to have furnished during his years in exile in Dewa to his host Toki Yoriyuki (1606–1684) and to Yoriyuki's lance teacher Matsumoto Sadayoshi (n.d.).[38] Conceivably, Takuan could later have been asked to explicate the often opaque *kanbun* text of *The Sword Taie* by way of a vernacular commentary, leading to the present document. Lacking further evidence, however, the source of the *kanbun* text and the background of the work as a whole are likely to remain obscure.

On the origins of *Record of Immovable Wisdom*, by contrast, we find ourselves on firmer ground. Until recently, there seems to have been general agreement that the text, together with the addendum, was addressed to Yagyū Munenori, the shogun Iemitsu's sword master and one of Takuan's principal champions at the shogunal court. However, recent research by Japanese scholars indicates that the work in its earliest form may have been prepared by Takuan specifically for Iemitsu at the latter's behest, following a discussion of swordsmanship (*heihō*) that Iemitsu convened in autumn 1636. The meeting is mentioned by Takuan in a letter,[39] which notes that besides himself and Munenori the participants were Iemitsu and his senior retainer Hotta Masamori (1606–1651). Iemitsu pronounced himself delighted with the meeting and asked Takuan to compile a record of the discussion, a document that the master completed and presented to the shogun several days later. This is arguably the original source for *Record of Immovable Wisdom*, and, as it was intended for Iemitsu, it did not include the addendum section, plainly addressed by Takuan to Munenori, who was presented with a copy of his own the following day. In a later, undated letter to Munenori, Takuan reports compiling for him a clean copy of the treatise originally given to Iemitsu and says he intends to deliver it to Munenori when they meet at the shogun's castle. Presumably, Munenori would then have passed on the final version to Iemitsu after having gone over the text.[40] The addendum to Munenori would thus have been added later by Takuan along with the reference in the main text to "Mataemon," Munenori's early given name.

The issue is further complicated by the survival of different versions of *Record of Immovable Wisdom*. In an attempt to determine the ordering of these and the development of the work, Satō Rentarō has surveyed the various versions, dated and undated, hand-copied and printed.[41] Of these, he has published three, which he considers key to understanding the text's transformations.[42]

(1) The Kunaichō, or Imperial Household Agency, manuscript, the most simplified of the versions. It is written in formal style, probably with the title *Fudōchi*, "Immovable Wisdom," abbreviated from *Mumyō jūji bonnō shobutsu fudōchi*, "The Ignorance of Attachment as the Ground of Delusion and the Immovable Wisdom of the Buddhas." Satō judges this to be a handwritten copy of the original text compiled by Takuan for Iemitsu following the fall 1636 discussion of the principles of swordsmanship referred to earlier. Consisting of eleven sections, it contains some differences from the text of the *Takuan oshō zenshū* (the basis for the present translation and for most postwar published versions and translations). Specifically, it lacks both the addendum and the headings that accompany the various sections.

(2) The Tōhoku Library manuscript, an 1808 copy of a 1774 text. It contains thirteen sections with headings and is titled *Fudōchi*. There is some difference in wording from the Kunaichō text, of which it appears to be an expanded version, mentioning, for example, the fifty-two stages and Munenori's childhood name Mataemon.[43] Although it lacks the addendum, a colophon placed at the end states, "This was composed by Master Takuan and presented to Yagyū Tajima no Kami [i.e., Munenori]."[44]

(3) The Kokuritsu Komonjo Naikan Bunko (National Cabinet Library for Ancient Documents) manuscript, bearing the title *Takuan oshō Yagyū Tashū heihō mondō* (Discussion on the Art of Swordsmanship [by] the Zen Master

Takuan [compiled for] Yagyū Tajima no kami [Munenori]). Clearly directed to Munenori as a work of instruction, this version of *Record of Immovable Wisdom* contains the addendum;[45] addresses not simply the "art of swordsmanship" but "Your Lordship's art of swordsmanship" (*kidono no heihō*); contains the reference to "Mataemon" in section 4; and refers to the practice of "No-Sword" (*mutō*), a technique important to Munenori's New Shadow (Shinkage) school of swordsmanship and one that Munenori terms "the exclusive secret of this school."[46] The addendum itself refers to the Yagyū valley (Yagyūdani), the ancestral Yagyū lands in what is today Yamato Prefecture, and to "Your Lordship's son . . . the court steward," court steward (*naizen*) being the honorary title conferred by the shogun on Munenori's son Munefuyu (1615–1675). A hand-copied manuscript of the late Tokugawa period (1830s–1860s), the document contains thirteen sections and is composed in *sōrōbun*, the polite epistolary style of the age. Because this manuscript marks the first appearance of the addendum, it seems to have served as a model for later versions of *Record of Immovable Wisdom*. Interestingly, the manuscript omits the curious Chinese poem at the end of the work, indicating that the poem may have been added at a later stage.

Altogether, however, Satō admits that the form of the original text of *Record of Immovable Wisdom* is uncertain. The *Takuan oshō zenshū* version, commonly used today, could be a faithful transmission of some no longer extant manuscript, even with seemingly extraneous elements like the poem and story at the close of the text, but given the surviving evidence it is impossible to be certain.[47]

The addendum, which in many respects appears to be a separate document, takes the form of a memo upbraiding Munenori for various types of selfish and overbearing behavior. Beyond the fact that it, too, is obviously addressed to Lord Yagyū, it has little apparent connection with the preceding text, apart from its perfunctory iteration of the symbolism of the Thousand-Armed Kannon and the closing poem on mind misleading mind. Instead, the addendum is largely given over to Confucian-morality-laced invective and advice, similar in tone to Takuan's missive rebuking his younger brother Hanbei and to his 1634 letter to Munenori, which calls on the sword master to avoid extravagance in the administration of his realm and even takes him to task for smoking.[48]

Among the more serious shortcomings noted by Takuan in the addendum is Munenori's poor choice of retainers. He accuses Munenori of favoring samurai who are ignorant and depraved, so long as their company is congenial, while ignoring those who are sober-minded and virtuous. Takuan attributes this to Munenori's arrogance and denounces it as the ultimate disloyalty to his lord, the shogun. Takuan also implicitly accuses Munenori of abusing his access to Iemitsu to solicit bribes from various daimyo and urges Munenori to set a better example for his sons.

There is a distinctly formulaic character to much of Takuan's censure, and perhaps in the context of the times such pointed remarks would have been regarded as a kind of reverse reproof, more a testament to Takuan's intimacy with Munenori than evidence of the feudal lord's actual failings. Takuan's criticisms may also be the master's attempt to inject into his work on Zen and the sword an ethical dimension, subtly prevailing on Munenori to extend his attainments in Zen and the martial arts into the sphere of his public activities.

Munenori's close relationship with Takuan is nowhere more apparent than in his own *Family-Transmitted Book on the Art of the Sword* (*Heiho kadensho*, hereafter abbreviated *Art of the Sword*).[49] Munenori's work incorporates numerous elements that appear to have been transposed almost verbatim from *Record of Immovable Wisdom*. Takuan's influence on *Art of the Sword*, especially conspicuous in the latter part of the text, has been widely noted by modern scholars,[50] and it is tacitly acknowledged by Munenori himself, who observes at the close of the work's part 2, "I have recorded here the instruction I received from my Dharma teacher."[51] Writing several years later, Munenori's son and heir Mitsutoshi adds that his father, having studied koans under a teacher and realized their inner meaning, employed Zen phrases to elucidate the similarities between Zen and the art of the sword.[52]

Unlike *Record of Immovable Wisdom*, *Art of the Sword* is clearly dated, inscribed by Munenori for the ninth month of the ninth year of Kan'ei (roughly, October 1632), some two months after Takuan's return to Edo from exile. Watanabe Ichirō concludes that in this period of no more than and perhaps much less than eight weeks following his return to the capital, Takuan, at Munenori's request, inserted his own instruction into the draft of *Art of the Sword* as well as making assorted suggestions, revisions, and corrections.[53] Because so many elements from *Record of Immovable Wisdom* are incorporated virtually wholesale in Munenori's book, some scholars have suggested dating Takuan's work to the period just before the compilation of *Art of the Sword*.[54] While it is impossible to assign a firm date for *Record of Immovable Wisdom*, the many borrowings in *Art of the Sword* indicate that Takuan's work, or at least some early form of it, may have been in existence by late 1632, available to be cannibalized by Munenori or to be used by Takuan himself to augment Munenori's text.

*Art of the Sword* thus provides a rough dating for *Record of Immovable Wisdom*. But it also sheds a fascinating light on the manner in which Zen, and specifically Takuan's teaching of mind, was integrated by the New Shadow sword school under Yagyū Munenori.

Munenori had received the teaching of the New Shadow school from his father, Yagyū Sekishūsai Munetoshi (1527/1529–1607), who had himself received the sanction of the teaching's founder, Kamiizumi Ise no kami Hidetsuna.[55] A master of both the lance and the sword, Hidetsuna had studied in his youth under a number of different teachers, among them Aisu Ikōsai Hisatada (1452–1538), progenitor of the Kageryū, or Shadow sword school. Hisatada is said to have formulated the principles of the Shadow school while observing a spider spin its web across the top of a folding fan and watching a swallow flit from willow to willow along a riverbank.

Hidetsuna's family had been vassals of the powerful Uesugi clan of Kōzuke, an old province northwest of present-day Tokyo; but buffeted by the disordered conditions of the period, Hidetsuna found himself shifting allegiances and serving under various warlords, among them the Uesugi's archrival, Takeda Shingen (1521–1573).[56] Munetoshi, who was already an accomplished swordsman, was anxious to test his skill against Hidetsuna. But, when the two finally met in summer 1563, Munetoshi discovered he was no match for either Hidetsuna or the members of his entourage, and begged to become the master's disciple. Impressed by Munetoshi's sincerity, Hidetsuna accepted the feudal lord as his student and instructed him at the Yagyū domain until he left for Kyoto early the following year. Before departing, Hidetsuna asked Munetoshi to work on a problem that had interested him for some time. Once, Hidetsuna explained, he was at a temple in Owari (Aichi Prefecture) drawing Chinese characters in the sand of the temple's garden, when suddenly he heard a loud shout and turned to find a madman bearing down on him with a drawn sword. Using his bare hands, Hidetsuna managed to stop the sword's blade and subdued the man. Since then, however, he had been pondering the best strategy for disarming an attacker slashing with a sword when one is oneself unarmed. Munetoshi readily agreed to take on the assignment.

In Kyoto, Hidetsuna's swordsmanship was praised by the Ashikaga shogun Yoshiteru (r. 1546–1565), who in recognition awarded Hidetsuna a higher court title, Musashi no Kami. A year later, in 1565, when Hidetsuna returned to the Yagyū domain, he asked Munetoshi to demonstrate his progress in mastering the "No-Sword" technique and watched in amazement as Munetoshi, weaponless, repeatedly bested one of Hidetsuna's senior students in a series of duels. In acknowledgment of Munetoshi's achievement, Hidetsuna awarded him his *inka*, or formal sanction, designating Munetoshi a master of the New Shadow school, together with a certification titled *Shadow Catalog* (*Kage mokuroku*), documenting the history and essentials of Hidetsuna's teaching.[57]

Writing in the *Catalog*, Hidetsuna states that he formulated the New Shadow technique by extracting the essence of his masters' teachings, emphasizing above all the ability to "shift in response to one's opponent . . . just as, observing the wind, one unfurls the sail; and, seeing the hare, one releases the hawk."[58] In this regard, Hidetsuna is credited with originating the concept of *marobashi* (also *korogashi* or *ten*). Literally, "rolling," or "tumbling," the term expresses the realized swordsman's perfect naturalness and fluidity, a state compared to a smooth, round gem rolling in a tray or a boulder falling off a mountain.[59] Munetoshi articulates the notion in a poem included in his *Hundred Verses on the Art of the Sword* (*Heihō hyakushu*):

> The art of combat is the sword in the depths of the mind
> The blade that responds shifting with the moment.[60]

The notion of *marobashi* may well have been adopted from Zen. There is a similar Zen expression, "rolling, rolling along" (*ten roku-roku*), a variant of which, "turning freely" (*ten rokurokuji*), appears in case 39 of *Blue Cliff Record*, "Yunmen's 'Flowering Hedge.'"[61] The concept also figures in a well-known poem traditionally held to be the enlightenment verse of Zen's twenty-second Indian patriarch, Manorhita:

> My mind shifts in accordance with the myriad circumstances
> And this shifting, in truth, is most mysterious
> Recognizing my nature while according with the flow
> I've no more joy, nor any sorrow.[62]

Munenori even cites Manorhita's poem's first two lines toward the end of *Art of the Sword* as demonstrating the essence of both Zen and swordsmanship: the principle of letting the mind shift freely without attaching anywhere. In swordsmanship, Munenori explains, "myriad circumstances" refers to "the countless moves your opponent makes. Your mind shifts at each of these moves"; while "most mysterious" indicates that "your mind should not tarry here and there. If it tarries in one spot, you will lose the sword fight. If it stays rather than keeps shifting, that would be a disaster. . . . If you intently watch your opponent's move and allow your mind to tarry there, you will be defeated. The purpose of my quoting this verse has been to say, 'Don't let your mind tarry.'"[63]

Like Zen, Hidetsuna's New Shadow style of swordsmanship claims mind as the pivot of its teaching, a conviction shared and amplified by the Yagyūs, Munetoshi, Munenori, and Mitsutoshi, who, following Hidetsuna's death, became the school's leading exponents.[64] All seem to concur that a swordsman who masters only forms and techniques but fails to grasp the underlying importance of mind will never realize the essence of the art of the sword. As Munetoshi observes in another poem:

> What use is there in any teacher's *inka*
> Without transmitting the art of the sword in the depths of the mind?[65]

The term "shadow" (*kage*) in the name of Hidetsuna's school underscores the teaching's emphasis on the yielding, ever-responsive mind. The character generally employed in the school, read *yin* in Chinese and *in* in Sino-Japanese, is the ideogram for the female or passive principle that offsets the male principle, or *yang* (J. *yō*), in yin-yang cosmology.[66] Here, it indicates the central role of intuition, the primacy of mind over mere physical strength, of the natural and resilient over the forced, studied, and contrived. Thus, a shadow instantly follows a moving form, just as a mirror or the still surface of a pool registers an object's reflection. "The shield [i.e., defensive technique] of the New Shadow [Shinkage] school," Mitsutoshi writes in his work *Notes on the Moon* (*Tsuki no shō*), "is the stance that has no fixed stance but follows the opponent's movement."[67]

It is often observed that the particular blending of spirituality and swordsmanship that emerged in early modern Japan reflected the samurai's need to adapt to the new conditions of the postmedieval world and in particular to dramatic changes in the nature of Japanese warfare during the period. Earlier armed conflict had frequently centered on battlefield encounters between individual samurai or small groups of warriors, mounted on horseback, circling and shooting at each other with bows and arrows in a series of disorganized "galloping archery duels."[68] But by the sixteenth century, emphasis had shifted to the deployment of large formations of low-ranking foot soldiers, or *ashigaru* (literally, "light infantry").[69] The samurai's role was further altered with the introduction of firearms by Portuguese traders in the mid-sixteenth century. While never displacing earlier samurai weapons such as the bow or lance, guns were a formidable asset to any warlord's army, and strategically arrayed harquebuses, fired in volleys by common infantry-men, could decisively turn the tide of battle.[70] Samurai identity was also affected by the stability and regularization of Japanese government and society following Ieyasu's 1600 victory at Sekigahara and the inauguration of the new shogunate. In the largely peaceful conditions that accompanied consolidation of Tokugawa authority, the warrior class had little opportunity to employ its skills in actual warfare. With pitched battles between contending armies a thing of the past, swordsmanship became an end in itself, transformed, so the oft-heard argument goes, from a practical technique (*jutsu* or *gei*) for the battlefield to a "Way" (*dō* or *michi*), a path to perfection that was at once an art, a spiritual discipline, and even a form of moral cultivation. As revealed by recent scholarship, however, the actual history of the sword in Takuan's Japan was considerably different, the facts both more revealing and more complex.

To begin with, the sword itself—hoary tales, military romances, war-time propaganda, and countless samurai films to the contrary—never occupied more than a minor combat role in medieval and early modern Japanese warfare.

In common with his medieval European counterpart, the Western knight, the samurai was mounted on horseback and protected by a helmet and body armor. But unlike the late medieval French or English knight, the samurai's preference, from the twelfth century on, was for long-distance weapons, particularly the bow and arrow, and he saw no shame but rather considerable advantage in avoiding close combat with his foe on the battle-field. As it turns out, the redoubtable Japanese sword of legend, the "soul of the samurai" that has been cast as the principal weapon of countless wild, blood-soaked battles (J. *chanbara*), is essentially a myth.

The evidence derives from the age of samurai warfare itself, which extended roughly from the Middle Ages through Takuan's lifetime. Warriors were rewarded by commanders according to their individual "deeds of valor" (*kōmyō*), recorded meticulously in documents known as "Records of Loyal Military Service" (*gunchūjō*). These documents detailed samurais' battlefield performance, including ranks and names of enemies captured or killed—or, if the victims' identities were unknown, whether they were on horseback or wore helmet and armor, all indications of warrior status. Also recorded were the precise circumstances in which deeds of valor occurred, including any eyewitnesses present and a list of all wounds inflicted or sustained.[71]

Suzuki Masaya, who examined hundreds of such reward petitions from the fourteenth through the seventeenth centuries,[72] determined that the overwhelming number of wounds in battle were caused by projectiles and missiles. Even in the fourteenth century, in the wars pitting the forces of the Ashikaga shoguns against those of the Southern Court, sword wounds, by Suzuki's reckoning, constituted only 8 percent of casualties. Roughly 90 percent of injuries were from projectiles, principally arrows (68.6 percent), but including rocks rolled down from hills or fortifications, stones hurled from slings, and spears. Overall, hand-to-hand combat with swords seems to have been rare.[73]

The same essential pattern, Suzuki found, continued through the sixteenth and early seventeenth centuries, despite the new reliance on massed infantry, noted above. With the widespread deployment of firearms from about 1560, guns replaced arrows as the leading cause of casualties (44 percent), wounds from arrows being followed, in descending order, by those from lances, rocks and stones, and finally swords, the last constituting only 3.8 percent of the total.[74]

With warfare now centered on long-distance weaponry—guns or bows manned by unmounted subordinates—the sword was, for the samurai, at best a weapon of last resort. If he himself was compelled to close with the enemy in combat, the samurai preferred the lance, or *yari*. The lance could lend a greater extension to his thrusts than a sword and could even be used to knock an adversary to the ground and then pierce him beneath his helmet or through a gap or suture in his armor. As was generally recognized, a sword was simply no match for a spear. A modern contest between two eminent prewar masters of the spear and sword, respectively, resulted in a series of swift victories for the former over the latter in thirty consecutive matches. Indeed, among the lists of wounds and exploits for individual warriors examined by Suzuki, the lance is mentioned continually, the sword scarcely at all.[75]

It is true that the sword was a standard article of male attire in sixteenth- and seventeenth-century Japan, worn even by commoners (and occasionally Buddhist priests). Visiting Portuguese missionaries noted as early as 1562 that Japanese men, including youths, carried swords at all times and even when sleeping kept the weapon beside their pillows.[76] Samurai carried both a long sword (*katana* or *tachi*) and a short sword (*wakizashi*),[77] and in war swords were apparently worn even by servants such as sandal-carriers and coolies. Nevertheless, a number of structural factors made the sword essentially unsuitable for most battlefield combat. Often brittle and always subject to rust, bending, and breakage, the samurai sword was virtually useless against an opponent clad in helmet and armor. Even so-called prized swords (*meitō*) fashioned by famous sword smiths were liable to fracture after one or two encounters. And if sword blades failed to break outright on contact with helmets or with other weapons such as spears or even wooden staffs, they quickly became dull. (Conscientious samurai were known to carry their own whetstones onto the battlefield.)[78] While presumably of service in close-quarter fighting and urban combat, in general lethal use of the sword in Takuan's day was reserved for specific *non-battlefield* situations. These included murder, duels, assassinations such as revenge killings, the execution of criminals and of offending samurai retainers (the latter a not uncommon occurrence), and the capture and killing of fugitives holed up in warrens.[79]

On the battlefield itself, the sword in medieval and early Tokugawa Japan was identified with one function above all: the taking of enemy heads, or *kubi tori* (from *kubi,* "head," and *tori,* the noun form of the verb *toru,* "to take"). Taking of heads in combat was central to the military reward system and figures prominently in surviving warrior records of the period. Such documents, like those for other deeds of valor, included the victim's name, rank, and any corroborating testimony, along with rewards subsequently received for the head, or heads, rewards that might include land, armor, and even valuable swords. For midlevel samurai, such certified lists of heads taken, termed "accountings of heads" (*kubi no reki*), served as a kind of warrior curriculum vitae. As such, they could be presented to a prospective employer should a samurai move on to another army or domain, or could be submitted to one's present lord in petitioning for a promotion in rank. For daimyo and higher-level warriors, the taking of heads served to considerably burnish their own reputations for leadership and battlefield prowess. As a rule, quantity was outweighed by quality in the feudal reward system, and the taking of a general's or warlord's head in battle was a signal accomplishment. Enemy heads were taken during or after combat, frequently severed with one's short sword, and prepared for display by specially trained women who cleansed the gore, arranged the hair, reblackened the teeth, and applied powder to the face.[80]

Since heads were a kind of currency for warriors, the scramble for prize heads in the midst of combat could be intense and might even impede the successful prosecution of a battle so that leading generals like Ieyasu had on occasion to issue sudden orders to suspend the activity.[81] Abuses, too, seem to have been common, and the warrior clan house rules of the 1500s are replete with injunctions against a variety of shameful practices associated with head taking. These include samurai quarreling over heads and stealing heads from one another, and even adding to their toll of enemy trophies the head of a comrade in arms who had died in battle. This last was a grave offense that reflected badly on one's commander and was punishable by the death of the offender's wife and family, or, if he were unmarried, the execution of his parents.[82] The deeds-of-valor system, as might be expected, placed a premium on heads taken in actual combat and discouraged taking the heads of those who had already expired from their wounds or the heads of women, children, or people who had died from disease—all apparently common contrivances.[83]

By the time the samurai of Takuan's generation had passed on—samurai of the generation that had witnessed and participated in actual battlefield combat—such aspects of the history of the sword tended to be forgotten, re-placed by the eighteenth century with popular war tales that glorified the sword as the principal weapon of the samurai of old. This was attributable not so much to willful amnesia and romanticism about the past as to the fact that mid-Tokugawa Japan was essentially a nation at peace. The only in-stances of samurai violence the urban citizen was now likely to observe were brawls, duels, assassinations, executions, or vendettas, all of which involved the use of swords, reinforcing the notion that swords and sword fighting had always been crucial to samurai warfare.[84]

At the same time, Tokugawa Japan saw a vogue for schools of swords-manship representing different sword traditions, or *bugei ryūha*, each with its own secret techniques passed on from master to student. By the close of the seventeenth century, such schools, often under hereditary headship, had increased in both number and popularity, largely, but not exclusively, among the samurai class. These schools evolved elaborate curricula, charged for instruction, and issued diplomas and teaching licenses.

Among the most famous of these organizations was the Yagyū clan's New Shadow school. Like many other prominent contemporary sword schools, such as the Ono and Ittō, by the eighteenth century the New Shadow school came under attack from military scholars for its emphasis on choreog-raphy, its stress on the mastery of set postures and routines. Such a curricu-lum struck many of the school's critics as effete and wholly unrelated to the exigencies of actual combat. Scholars like Ogyū Sōrai (1666–1728) argued that this sort of instruction, often mixed as it was with mystical and ethical ele-ments borrowed from Chinese religion, philosophy, and cosmology, consti-tuted a distortion of samurai training as it had existed in the now-legendary age of warfare.[85] As such, it was alleged, traditions like the New Shadow school contributed to the weakening of the spiritual and moral fiber of the entire samurai class, which in an age of peace had degenerated into a warrior caste with no wars to fight. Often consumed as they were with bureaucratic duties, the Tokugawa samurai, it was charged, were reduced to justifying their continued military status by participating in what were essentially finishing schools for gentlemen warriors. In addition, critics bemoaned the fact that sword schools like the New Shadow school were wont to emphasize the avoidance of bloodshed and injury, and to champion the sort of mind training that made confrontation between "realized" opponents wholly unnecessary.[86] Swordsmanship, critics contended, had been fatally compromised, transformed into an art, a "Way," at once a form of realization and a kind of aesthetic display, like calligraphy or the performance of Nō. The only means to reverse this degradation of the true warrior spirit, it was maintained, was to return to the allegedly original, purely pragmatic sword techniques of the fighting samurai of the sixteenth and early seventeenth centuries.

This sort of argument can still be heard, denigrating martial arts swordsmanship as a form of spiritual exercise or leadership training and calling for a revival of combat-proven sword-fighting techniques from the classic age of samurai warfare. The argument, however, fails to take into account the fact that the samurai sword, as has been seen, was at best a minor asset on the battlefield. More important, such negative views of the Tokugawa schools of swordsmanship arose from ignorance of their origins in the age of warfare itself. Scholars now estimate that already by around 1500 such schools had begun to take form, propounded by individual and often eccentric itinerant masters like Aisu Ikōsai and Kamiizumi, men who regarded themselves as artists rather than combat technicians. These schools of swordsmanship, from the start, incorporated spiritual elements, and their curricula were neither derived from methods of battlefield combat nor intended in any way for use on the battlefield. As such, they were at times distinguished as "naked" (kyōha) styles, as opposed to those styles involving helmet and armor, which focused on such rough-and-tumble tactics as devastating blows with the side of the sword along with slashing cuts to the opponent's sword hand, carotid artery, windpipe, or even legs. The celebrated swordsman Miyamoto Musashi, for example, began his career as a helmet and armor warrior, garnered combat experience, and later became a master in his naked two-sword style (nito-ryū).[87]

The naked sword styles were generally reserved for controlled exhibitions and demonstrations, which stopped just short of injuring one's opponent. Thus, the martial arts schools of swordsmanship existed as an alternate form of sword training, developing separate from and parallel to the evolving modes of practical combat in late medieval Japan.[88] Even as battlefield use of the sword further declined in the sixteenth and early seventeenth centuries, as individual combat played an increasingly minor role and large-scale battles became the norm, the martial arts sword schools grew in popularity and prestige, not in spite of the spiritual elements they incorporated but precisely because of them. Swordsmanship was an accomplishment for any aspiring gentlemen and particularly for members of the rising warrior classes who sought the veneer of refinement associated with other aristocratic practices like Nō, Zen, and tea. It was this aspect of the sword schools that their later critics so badly misconstrued. While far more numerous, structured, and in-stitutionalized in their Tokugawa period manifestations, organizations like Munenori's New Shadow school represented not transformations of or devia-tions from the helmet-and-armor techniques of the samurai of old but a natu-ral extension of the martial arts schools' own sixteenth-century counterparts, blending the physical and the spiritual, and distinct from actual battlefield techniques. Sword schools like Munenori's were no more intended to trans-mit practical modes of killing and combat than the tea ceremony was in-tended to convey utilitarian procedures for the brewing and consumption of powdered tea.

This sort of approach is evident in *Record of Immovable Wisdom*, where Takuan invokes both Zen and Confucianism to convey the true meaning of swordsmanship,[89] and it is also a prominent feature of the Yagyūs' expositions of the New Shadow teaching. Confucian elements are notable in Munetoshi's verses on the martial arts, and numerous direct and indirect references to Zen characterize Munenori's *Art of the Sword*. Another intellectual influence on the Yagyūs' teaching of the sword may be the classical Japanese dance-drama Nō, particularly the Konparu school, with which both Munetoshi and Munenori were associated.[90] As a kinetic art that combined elaborate and often demanding postures with a Buddhist-tinged philosophy and vocabulary, Nō may have provided a tem-plate for Munenori's synthesis of Zen and swordsmanship.

To modern sensibilities, *Art of the Sword*'s conjunction of religion and fighting techniques aimed at eviscerating or maiming one's opponent may appear odd if not downright sinister. But the incorporation of a Buddhist teaching like Zen in a manual like *Art of the Sword* would not have seemed at all out of place in Munenori's Japan. From the time of its introduction in the Kamakura period (1192–1333), the Zen school had been closely linked with successive Japanese military dynasties and with the powerful clans and individual warlords who were often the nation's actual power brokers. Zen priests served Japan's warrior elite in a variety of secular and spiritual capacities, and Zen temples were the beneficiaries of often lavish patronage bestowed by the shoguns and leading warrior houses. While the teaching itself was unconnected with warfare or the martial arts per se, certain aspects of Zen would have made it attractive to a professional swordsman like Munenori: its stress on directness and instantaneousness of response, on immediately "sizing up" others' capacities; and its insistence on flexibility, on meeting each situation free of preconceptions and expectations, even in the face of death. Moreover, the combat arts in Munenori's day, as in our own, involved not only strength and agility but also psychology—an awareness of the mind's moment-to-moment functioning in any encounter. In premodern Japan matters concerning mind were generally the province of religion, and a Buddhist school like Zen, which made mindfulness and mind practice the basis of its teaching, was in this respect naturally suited to the swordsman's art.

While borrowing freely from *Record of Immovable Wisdom, Art of the Sword*, unlike Takuan's informal instruction, is primarily a secret transmission document for the New Shadow school of swordsmanship.[91] As such, much of the content is technical, detailed if occasionally elusive descriptions of methods of combat in Munenori's sword tradition. However, philosophical elements also figure prominently, in particular the Zen-influenced mind practices and theories in which Munenori seems to have tutored his sons and Tokugawa Iemitsu.[92] Such materials, at times recalling or simply paraphrasing passages in *Record of Immovable Wisdom*, occur especially in the latter half of chapter 2, "The Blade That Kills,"[93] and in Munenori's third and final chapter, "The Blade That Brings to Life."[94] (Chapter 1, "Shoe Presentation Bridge,"[95] is a catalog of sword postures and techniques handed down by the New Shadow school's first and second patriarchs, Hidetsuna and Munetoshi.)

A distinctive feature of Munenori's discussion of mind is his frequent reference to the diseases or illnesses[96] that impair the swordsman's functioning. Among these are the swordsman's straining after victory, his desire to display the full extent of his skill, and his impetuosity, his eagerness to go on the attack.[97] All, Munenori explains, are diseases of the mind, and underlying each is the primary disease of attachment,[98] the false mind that stops or becomes stuck at any point. Like Takuan in *Record of Immovable Wisdom*, Munenori admonishes the swordsman not to let his mind stay where he has struck: to do so leaves him vulnerable, his attention arrested at its temporary destination, like a servant dispatched on an errand who remains where he is sent and never returns.[99] Attachment is the swordsman's deadliest adversary because as soon as the mind fixes anywhere it loses its freedom to shift with the moment. "Swordsmanship," Munenori declares, "agrees with Buddhism and is in accord with Zen in many ways. It abhors attachment, the state of tarrying with something. This is the crucial point. Not tarrying is of vital importance.... No matter what secretly transmitted technique you may use, if you allow the mind to tarry on it, you will lose your fight. Be it your opponent's move or your own, in slashing or in thrusting, the important thing is to train your mind so that it may not tarry in anything."[100] The disease of attachment is experienced as a disabling self-consciousness, an artificial tensing of the mind that cripples and distorts the warrior's response so that the archer will miss his target and the swordsman's attack falter. "If you are conscious of swordsmanship while employing it," Munenori warns, "that is a disease. If you are conscious of shooting an arrow while doing so, you are diseased with archery."[101]

How, then, is the warrior to eliminate the disease of attachment? At first,[102] he practices forcibly regulating his mind, keeping it from becoming stuck at any point or being lost in distraction. But eventually he realizes that the attempt to rid oneself of disease is itself a disease, another form of attachment. Rather than trying to control or concentrate the mind, therefore, the experienced swordsman, Munenori says, releases it and sets it free. This plainly resonates with Takuan's views on freeing the mind, articulated in *Record of Immovable Wisdom*. Describing the final stage of the swordsman's cultivation, Munenori even borrows Takuan's metaphor of turning loose a cat that has been restrained on a leash.[103] Ultimately, the key to attacking the disease of mind, Munenori claims, is to "let yourself go *with* the disease and relinquish the mind; then you can let the mind go wherever it wants."[104] Instead of a frontal assault that aggressively seeks to extirpate the disease, Munenori counsels an absolute resilience: "Let yourself go with the disease, be with it, keep company with it: that is the way to get rid of it."[105] The warrior advanced in his practice does not seek consciously to banish disease but, as one Japanese scholar sums it up, just lets the mind take its own way and be as it is—attachment and all.[106]

This yielding, pliant response is not simply a technique but the expression of the warrior's intrinsic being, which Munenori calls "natural mind" or "the mind in a natural state."[107] The term, like "disease," part of Munenori's special vocabulary in *Art of the Sword*, is described as the Way (Dao) and ultimate reality,[108] the mind that is originally fluid, free, and unattached, "the state where you mingle with disease while remaining free of disease."[109] Natural mind, in Munenori's conception, is a kind of default mind that is at once the warrior's "original face"[110] and the key to perfection in all his activities. Throughout *Art of the Sword*, Munenori stresses the importance of always using one's natural, unself-conscious mind and defines a master as "someone who does everything with his mind in a natural state."[111] Such a person's mind is said to be immovable because it never "moves" out of its natural state, never departs from its authentic, spontaneous response. To illustrate this, Munenori points to the blinking reflex, challenging the stereotype of the unflappable samurai in total mental and physical control:

> Thrust your fan in front of someone with his eyes open, and he will blink—that is a natural state of mind. Blinking doesn't mean the person is upset. Repeat your thrust twice, three times to surprise him. If he doesn't blink at all that shows he is upset. Not to blink, refraining from doing so, trying hard not to do so, means that the mind has moved. . . . Someone with an "immovable mind" remains natural, and when something comes before his eyes,[112] will blink, unthinking. That is the state where you are not upset.
>
> The point is not to lose your natural state of mind. When you try not to move, you have already moved. . . . To move is not to move. Turning is the natural state of the waterwheel. If the waterwheel does not turn it has gone against its nature. For someone to blink is natural. Not to blink shows his mind has moved. Not to change your natural state of mind . . . is good.[113]

Because the true mind is natural, Munenori instructs, it accomplishes everything easily, without straining or difficulty.[114] The warrior has only not to alter it, not to assert a "new" mind by deviating from his original, intuitive response. Any attempt at control or manipulation betrays the mind's natural state and engenders a false mind that noticeably impairs the swordsman's movements. This false mind contrasts with no-mind, or mindlessness, the state in which all attachments are, as Munenori puts it, "slashed away,"[115] leaving the mind empty, like a mirror, receiving whatever comes without hesitation or bias.

Rather than concentrating on strategy or technique, or struggling to focus his errant thoughts, the accomplished swordsman locked in combat with an opponent must abandon any sort of calculation and simply refrain from interrupting the mind's spontaneous functioning. Munenori refers to this as "becoming one with original mind."[116] The warrior must be able to ground himself in the mind's natural wisdom, which without any added prompting or direction is always available, always on the mark. This cannot in the end be realized through deliberate effort, but only by a complete letting go.

> Someone with nothing in his mind is a man of the Way. If you have nothing in your mind you can easily do whatever you do. . . . No matter what you do, if you do it single-mindedly, trying to control your mind correctly and not allowing it to be distracted, you will end up becoming muddleheaded. . . . When you are not aware of yourself, and your arms and legs do whatever they are supposed to without your mind contriving things—that is when you do right whatever you do ten out of ten times. Even then, if you allow your mind to interfere if only slightly, you will miss it. If you are mindless you hit it every time. "Mindlessness" does not mean having no-mind whatsoever; it simply means the mind in a natural state.[117]

Given the many similarities between *Art of the Sword* and *Record of Immovable Wisdom,* and the fact that Munenori was Takuan's devoted pupil and patron, can it be inferred that the Zen-related portions of Munenori's work offer additional examples of Takuan's teachings on Zen and swordsmanship? In all likelihood, yes, in view of Munenori's acknowledgment of Takuan as his Zen teacher and of Takuan's assistance in composing the Zen-related portions of the manuscript. Of course, except where elements are borrowed directly from *Record of Immovable Wisdom,*[118] it cannot be claimed with certainty that those parts of the text dealing with Zen are attributable to or inspired by Takuan. Nevertheless, it is reasonable to recognize Takuan's influence and voice in various aspects of *Art of the Sword* that cannot be traced literally to *Record of Immovable Wisdom,* such as Munenori's constant emphasis on the mind's free functioning, identified with Buddhist concepts like no-mind, original mind, and immovable mind. One can hear Takuan, for example, in a passage like the following, which dismisses a "supernatural" interpretation of Buddhist terms for a Zen-type reading that extols freedom of mind: "The marvelous divine power of transformation," Munenori writes of the Buddha's power to change and shift at will, "has nothing to do with gods and demons dropping from the sky to perform miracles but means that in whatever you do, you act with complete freedom."[119]

It may never be possible to verify the full extent of Takuan's impact on *Art of the Sword,* to document conclusively every instance of his influence on the text. Yet Munenori's work, in its attempt to apply certain of Takuan's principles to the practices of the New Shadow school, provides at the least a valuable perspective on the Zen master's versatile teaching. Observing how Munenori restates, amplifies, and elaborates ideas presented in *Record of Immovable Wisdom* and *The Sword Taie* enlarges our frame of reference for Takuan's works and broadens our appreciation of these two singular classics that merge the art of the sword and the wisdom of Zen.

Enthusiasm for Takuan's two sword writings was not limited to his contemporaries and later Tokugawa readers but was rekindled in Japan during the modern period, albeit for at times questionable purposes. In the late nineteenth and early twentieth centuries, the country's rulers promoted an extreme nationalism in which the alleged uniqueness and racial superiority of the Japanese were expressed through worship of the emperor and commitment to the nation's imperial destiny. Although inspired in part by the West and the West's own versions of jingoism, the government tended to employ elements of traditional Japanese culture to justify its efforts. Among these was *bushidō*,[120] the Way of the samurai warrior, or *bushi*, whose legendary fighting spirit was constantly held up as a paradigm of the enduring "soul of Japan," *yamatodamashii*. Linked with this cult of the premodern warrior was a stress on the importance of the samurai sword, both constituting vestiges of a storied past resurrected on the basis of often dubious history to serve the state's propaganda campaign as Japan sought to claim a larger role on the world stage.

Every part of society, from Buddhist sects to public schools, was expected to absorb and impart such official indoctrination unquestioningly, and generally these institutions and their leaders readily acquiesced in the government's program.[121] A spate of books concerning Takuan and his works on the sword appeared at this time, culminating during the period leading up to and during the Pacific War.[122] While "hijacked" may be too extreme a term to describe the fate of Takuan's sword writings under the successive waves of ultranationalism that engulfed Japan in the early part of the twentieth century, "distorted" would surely characterize the manner in which Takuan's teachings were exploited to advance the government's wartime agenda.

As the 1937 invasion of China gathered steam, the tone of official propaganda grew increasingly strident. One egregious example is that of Ishihara Shunmyō, a Sōtō priest who was publisher of the popular Buddhist magazine *Daihōrin*. Lending his hand to the government's efforts at whipping up patriotism on the eve of war, Ishihara invoked Takuan and his writings on the sword to rouse patriotic Japanese to sacrifice themselves in the name of the nation and the emperor:

Zen is very particular about the need not to stop one's mind. As soon as flint-stone is struck, a spark bursts forth. There is not even the most momentary lapse of time between these two events. If ordered to face right, one simply faces right as quickly as a flash of lighting. This is proof that one's mind has not stopped.

Zen Master Takuan taught . . . that in essence Zen and Bushidō were one. He further taught that the essence of the Buddha Dharma was a mind which never stopped. Thus, if one's name were called, for example "Uemon," one should simply answer "Yes," and not stop to consider the reason why one's name was called. . . .

I believe that if one is called upon to die, one should not be the least bit agitated. On the contrary, one should be in a realm where something called "oneself" does not intrude even slightly. Such a realm is no different from that derived from the practice of Zen.[123]

Sadly, such sentiments, emphasizing the "oneness of Zen and the sword," were hardly unique but were echoed by many prominent Zen masters, Rinzai and Sōtō, during this turbulent period in Japan's modern history.

Even after Japan's surrender, books on Takuan and his writings on swordsmanship continued to proliferate, soon outnumbering those published during the war years. This was particularly true of the 1970s and 1980s, the pinnacle of postwar Japan's economic boom.[124] This was a period when the Japanese businessman was sometimes regarded as an "economic soldier," when subordination of individual needs to corporate identity recalled to some the old samurai virtues of selfless loyalty and dedication to one's clan— though even at the time such parallels were seriously questioned.[125]

Each subsequent period in Japanese history seems to have discovered some message in Takuan's writings on Zen and the sword, often reflecting its own needs and the prevailing ethos of the moment. Yet, across the centuries, something in these two works has transcended the particular circumstances of the age in which they were written and the manner in which they were received by each succeeding generation. The heart of *Record of Immovable Wisdom* and *The Sword Taie*, after all, is Takuan's striking presentation of the problems of mind and its functioning, problems that today remain unanswered and will likely continue to intrigue students of the human condition, East and West.

# 2 Translations

*Record of the Marvelous Power of Immovable Wisdom*
(*Fudōchi shinmyō roku*)

*The ignorance of attachment as the ground of delusion (mumyō jūji bonnō).* The term "ignorance" is made up of the characters for "no light"—that is to say, delusion. The term "attachment" is made up of characters meaning "to stop" and "stage." In the practice of Buddhism, there are the fifty-two stages,[1] among which attachment indicates the way the mind stops at things. "To stop" refers to attaching the mind to things, of whatever sort. Applied to Your Lordship's[2] art of swordsmanship,[3] [this means that] the moment your attention is drawn to the slashing blade of your opponent, you rush to meet his attack at that place, with the result that your mind becomes attached there to your opponent's blade, so that you lose your free functioning and can be slain. This is what is meant by attachment.

When you see the [opponent's] blade strike, just see it and don't attach your mind there, parrying the attacking blade without any thought or calculation. The instant you see your opponent's sword raised, without attaching to it for even a moment, move right in and capture his blade, seizing the sword that was about to kill you so that it becomes instead the sword that kills your opponent. In the Zen school we call this "seizing your opponent's lance and turning it against him."[4] What's meant here is the idea of snatching away the sword wielded by your opponent and using it instead to kill him. This is what Your Lordship refers to as No-Sword.[5]

If you stop your mind for even a second, a moment, an instant—whether it's at [the thought of] being attacked by an opponent or of attacking [an opponent], of the person who is attacking or of the sword that is being wielded—your free functioning will be completely lost and you can be killed by your adversary. If you become fixed on your opponent, your mind is captured by your opponent, so you should not even fix your mind on yourself. To fix your mind on yourself may be [appropriate] when you are a beginner and just learning, [but] your mind will [then] be captured by your sword. [In the same way,] when you fix your mind on meeting your [opponent's] attack, your mind is captured by the meeting of that attack; when you fix your mind on your sword, it is captured by your sword. In all these instances the mind attaches to things and you become preoccupied. I am sure Your Lordship is well acquainted with [such matters]. And [they] apply to Buddhism [as well]. In Buddhism, this stopping mind is called delusion. That's why we speak of "the ignorance of attachment as the ground of delusion."

*We speak of the immovable wisdom of the buddhas.*[6] The term "immovable" (*fudō*) consists of the characters for "not" (*fu*) and "moving" (*dō*). The term "wisdom" (*chi*) signifies the wisdom of *prajñā*.[7] But even though we speak of not moving, that doesn't mean insentient like stone or wood! Immovable wisdom means the mind moving as it *wants* to move—forward, left, right, in all directions, without ever being attached.

Fudō Myōō[8] clutches a sword in his right hand and a snare in his left, gnashing his teeth, eyes glaring, [feet] planted firmly, ready to subdue evil spirits who would obstruct the Buddhadharma.[9] Yet, however [terrifying] Fudō's appearance, he is not hiding in some [other] world. Outwardly, he manifests the form of a defender of Buddhadharma, but his substance he reveals to sentient beings as this immovable wisdom. Terrified [by this], ordinary unenlightened people resolve never to harm the Buddhadharma. But those whose minds are near to enlightenment realize [Fudō's] manifestation of immovable wisdom, dispelling all delusions. In other words, when you illumine immovable wisdom, this very body is none other than Fudō Myōō. Those who thoroughly carry out this practice of mind are Fudō Myōō [manifesting himself] in order to lead [sentient beings] to realize that even evil sprits cannot disturb them.[10]

Thus, Fudō Myōō signifies the mind's not moving. He also signifies remaining steadfast. Remaining steadfast means not being disturbed by things. Immovable means that when you notice something, your mind doesn't attach to it. The reason is that when your mind attaches to something, all sorts of discriminations appear in your breast, where they move about in all sorts of ways. When the mind attaches to something, that attaching mind moves, but it doesn't function freely.[11]

As an example, let's say you're attacked by ten swordsmen, one after the other. If you parry each attack without your mind remaining fixed to it, leaving it behind and going on to the next, then you won't lose your free functioning, even while fighting ten different opponents. Confronting the ten different opponents, your mind responds ten different times, but if you never attach your mind to any one of the attackers, [simply] confronting them one after another, your free functioning will never waver. In contrast, if your mind is fixed on one of the swordsman, even if you're able to parry *his* attack, when it comes to the next one, you're sure to lose your concentration.

Consider the Thousand-Armed Kannon: It has a thousand arms, [but] if its mind becomes fixed on the one arm that holds the bow, the other 999 arms won't work. It's just because its mind doesn't become fixed at any one place that all its arms work. How can Kannon have a thousand arms on a single body? It manifests this form in order to demonstrate to people that when immovable wisdom is revealed, even if one's body has a thousand arms, all of them will function.

Let's suppose you're looking at a [maple] tree [in autumn]: If your eye becomes fixed on one particular red leaf, you miss all the rest. When you don't fix on any *one* leaf, but look at the tree without any intention, you see all the myriad leaves. If your attention is captured by a particular leaf, you miss all the others. If your mind isn't attached to any one leaf, you see all the hundreds and thousands of leaves.

One who realizes this is himself a Kannon with a thousand arms and eyes. Yet ordinary, unenlightened persons believe blindly that it's a marvel having a thousand arms and eyes in a single body; while those who are know-it-alls deride the whole idea, saying, "How can there be a thousand eyes in one body? What nonsense!"

When you come to understand things better, neither the unenlightened person's belief nor denial is the point. Those who revere the principle behind [the image of Kannon] manifest this principle as the single, underlying truth of Buddhadharma. This is the case in all the religions. You see it particularly in Shinto.[12] One who takes [the image of Kannon] literally is an unenlightened being. One who derides it is worse still! Within this [image] there is a principle. This or that religion may assume various different forms, but ultimately all arrive at the selfsame truth.

After starting as a beginner and through practice attaining the stage of immovable wisdom, one needs to come back and stay in the beginner's stage. I can describe this using Your Lordship's art of swordsmanship. The beginner, since he knows nothing about how to hold the sword, isn't attached to a particular stance. When someone attacks him, he just spontaneously meets the attack without even thinking about it. However, you [eventually] learn all kinds of details—how to hold the sword, where to focus your attention—and having been taught all sorts of things, you acquire all sorts of notions; then when you go to attack someone, you find yourself debating this or that approach and completely lose your freedom to respond. As you practice over the days, years, and months, you finally arrive at the point where you cease to be conscious of either your stance or your manner of holding the sword so that you become just like you were when you started out and didn't know anything at all—completely unschooled. This is a state of mind in which beginning and end become seemingly identical. It's like when you count over and over from one to ten, so that one and ten both end up side by side. Or like the musical scale,[13] where you progress from the lowest tone to the highest, [but when you begin the next octave] the lowest and the highest are side by side. The very high and very low end up alike.

With Buddhadharma, too, when you gain real mastery, you become like someone who knows nothing at all about either Buddha or Dharma, someone without any outward signs of accomplishment that could be noticed by others. That is why the initial stage of ignorance and evil passions becomes one with the final [stage of] immovable wisdom, so that all sense of your own cleverness and skill disappears, and you abide serenely in the realm of no-mind and no thought.

When you arrive at the ultimate, you reach the stage where arms, legs, and body know of themselves, and the mind becomes completely unnecessary. A poem by National Master Bukkoku[14] says:

> Even though it has no thought
>> of protecting the fields
> The scarecrow
>> doesn't fail in its task

Everything [I have been saying] is like this poem. A scarecrow is made in the shape of a person, and a bow and arrow is placed in its hands. Birds and beasts flee at the sight of it. This mannequin has no mind whatsoever; and yet deer are scared by it and run away, so that it accomplishes its purpose and doesn't fail in its task. This is a metaphor for the naturalness of someone who attains perfection in all the various Ways.[15] One who, in all the movements of his hands, legs, and body, never allows his mind to become attached, remaining unaware even of where his mind is, abides in no thought and no-mind and attains the rank of a scarecrow in the field.

The usual run of ordinary ignorant person has never possessed any wisdom, so there's little chance of wisdom manifesting. The same with one whose wisdom is far advanced: because it's already deeply ingrained, it never outwardly manifests itself. By contrast, those who are know-it-alls can't help making a show of their wisdom, which is ludicrous. Your Lordship must find the practice of monks nowadays to be just such a ludicrous business. What an embarrassment!

There is the practice of principle, and there is the practice of action.[16] As for principle, as I've stated above, when you have real attainment, you don't attach to anything, as if you were simply discarding the mind, as previously described. But if you fail to practice action, you'll only have principle in your mind, and then neither body nor hands will function.

In discussing the practice of action in terms of Your Lordship's art of swordsmanship, the five kinds of bodily stance[17] all come down to one truth, which is learned as various techniques. Even if you understand principle, you still have to [be able to] function freely in the realm of action. [By the same token], even if you can expertly wield your sword, so long as you remain in the dark about the ultimate meaning of principle, you'll be unable to achieve perfection. Action and principle must become like the two wheels of a cart.

*There is an expression "Not space to insert even a hair."*[18] I can describe this using as an example Your Lordship's art of swordsmanship. Space, here, means that two things are placed [so closely] together that not even a hair can be inserted between them. For instance, when you suddenly clap your hands, at that moment a sharp sound is produced. There isn't so much as a hairsbreadth between the hands coming together and the sound being produced. It's not that the sound is produced *after* clapping your hands [because] you deliberately leave an interval for it. The instant you clap, right then and there the noise is produced. When your mind attaches to an attacker's sword, an interval appears. And in that interval you lose your freedom to respond. But if there isn't even a hairsbreadth between the opponent's attacking sword and your own response, then your opponent's weapon will become *your* weapon.

This same mind is to be found in Zen dialogues. In Buddhism we have no use for this stopping mind that mires itself in things. That's why we say that stopping is delusion. What we value is the never-stopping mind, flowing like raging torrent on which a ball hurled in is simply swept along by the rushing waters.[19]

*There is the expression "A response instantaneous as a spark struck from flint."*[20] This expression has the same sense as the one before. At the very instant you strike together [two pieces of] flint, a spark appears. And since the moment the flints are struck, the spark is produced, there's no interval or gap anywhere between. So this, also, expresses the idea of there being no interval in which the mind can attach [to anything]. It's an error to understand this solely as a matter of speed. It's a matter of not attaching the mind to things, a matter of the mind not even attaching to speed. When your mind attaches to something, your mind will be captured by your opponent. So if you act quickly with the deliberate *intention* to act quickly, your mind will be captured by that deliberate intention.

Among Saigyō's[21] collected poems is the following verse composed by a courtesan of Eguchi:[22]

> I had heard that you were one
>      who loathed the world
> Do not, then, I pray, let your thoughts abide
>      in this temporary lodging

The final line, "Do not, then, I pray, let your thoughts abide . . . ," can be said to correspond to the ultimate mastery of the art of swordsmanship. The main thing is not attaching the mind.

In the Zen school, if someone asks, "What is Buddha?" you should raise your fist.[23] And if someone asks, "What is the ultimate significance of Buddhadharma?" before the words are even out of his mouth, you should reply, "The plum flowers on the branch"[24] or "The cypress tree in the garden."[25] The point is not to pick and choose between these answers but to revere the mind that isn't attached. The mind that isn't attached isn't caught up in either color or smell. The substance of this mind that isn't caught up in things we worship as the *kami*, revere as the buddhas; we speak of it as Zen mind and ultimate mastery. However, when you have first to form your thoughts and then afterward speak them, even golden words and marvelous phrases will be [nothing more than] the ignorance of attachment as the ground of delusion.

The expression "A response instantaneous as a spark struck from flint" describes the swiftness of a flash of lightning. For example, when someone calls, "Mataemon!"[26] and you instantly answer, "Yes!" that's what's meant by immovable wisdom. In contrast, if someone calls, "Mataemon!" and you start to think, "What does he want?" and so forth, the mind that then wonders, "What does he want?" and so forth is the ignorance of attachment as the ground of delusion. The mind that attaches to things and is then pushed around and deluded by them is called delusion arising from attachment. This is the mind of ordinary beings. In contrast, when someone calls, "Mataemon!" and you answer, "Yes!" that's the wisdom of all the buddhas. Buddhas and sentient beings are not different. Nor are *kami* and humans. That which accords with this mind we call *kami* or Buddha. The Way of the *Kami*, the Way of Poetry, the Way of Confucius—there are many different Ways, and yet all express the brightness of this one mind.

If you are capable only of interpreting the mind using words, then that's the kind of mind in which you and others [like you] will live, day and night. And then, following your karmic destiny, whether you do good things or bad things, you'll end by abandoning your family and destroying your country. Good things and bad things both result from the karmic activity of mind. And yet no one realizes just what this mind is; so they all remain deluded by the mind.

In the world, people who don't understand the mind are the norm, while those who understand it well are almost impossible to find. And one hardly ever comes across people who both understand and practice it. Just because you're able to talk about this one mind doesn't mean you're able to realize it. Explaining about water won't wet your lips, and even speaking vividly about fire won't burn them. Without coming into contact with actual water or actual fire, you won't be able to know what they are. Just because you can interpret *books* doesn't mean you know. If someone tells you all about food, it's not going to cure your hunger. You can't realize [the mind] from someone else's explanation.

Buddhism and Confucianism both teach about the mind. But if people don't practice those teachings themselves, the mind isn't going to be realized. Unless you thoroughly penetrate and realize the one mind originally existing in each and every person, it's going to remain unclear to you. That even the minds of people studying Zen remain unclear [shows that] although there are lots of people studying Zen, it doesn't mean a thing, since the attitude of every one of them is false. The only way to illumine this one mind is from your own profound understanding.

*Where to focus the mind.* Where should you focus the mind? When you focus on your opponent's movements, the mind is captured by your opponent's movements. When you focus on your opponent's sword, the mind is captured by your opponent's sword. When you focus on trying to kill your opponent, the mind is captured by trying to kill your opponent. When you focus on your sword, the mind is captured by your sword. When you focus on not being killed, the mind is captured by not being killed.

When you focus on your opponent's stance, the mind is captured by your opponent's stance. All in all, there *is* no particular place to focus the mind.

Someone said to me, "If you have a tendency to let your mind go elsewhere, your attention will be captured at the place your mind goes and you'll be defeated by your opponent. So keep your mind below the navel,[27] not allowing it to go anywhere else, and let it respond according to your opponent's movements."

This makes sense so far as it goes. But in terms of advancing in your study of Buddhism, to keep the mind below the navel and not let it go elsewhere constitutes an inferior stage, not a way to advance. It's the stage of a beginner just learning to practice. It's the stage of reverence, of Mencius' words "Recover the lost mind."[28] It is not a stage from which one can advance but the state of mind of reverence. I have written of this "lost mind" in other places and can refer Your Lordship to these discussions.

When you keep [your mind] below the navel and don't let it go elsewhere, your mind is captured by the thought of not letting it [stray], so that you lose your ability to immediately respond and become quite inflexible in your movements.

Someone asked me, "If keeping the mind below the navel leaves one unable to function and inflexible, without the ability to respond, then where in the body *should* one focus the mind?"

I told him, "If you focus on your right arm, your mind will be captured by your right arm, and your body will lose its ability to function freely. If you focus on your eye, your mind will be captured by your eye, and your body will lose its ability to function freely. If you focus on your right leg, your mind will be captured by your right leg, and your body will lose its ability to function freely. *Wherever* it is, when you focus your mind in one place, you completely lose your free functioning everywhere else."

"So, where *should* one focus the mind?" [he persisted].

My answer: "Don't focus it anywhere at all. Then the mind will spread to fill you completely, extend throughout your body. That way, when you need your arm, your mind is there to let it do its work. [The mind] flows to wherever you need it so that whatever part [of the body] you need, the mind will be there to let it do its work."

When you focus the mind on one particular place, that's called being biased. Biased means having fallen to one side. *Unbiased* means [a mind that] pervades everywhere. Unbiased mind means to spread the mind through the whole body without attaching to any one part. To be stuck in *one* place and absent in *another* is what we call biased mind. I have no use for being biased. To be stuck in any particular thing is to be biased, something of no use at all in the Way.

If you're not thinking, "Where shall I focus [the mind]?" the mind will spread to fill your whole body. Without focusing your mind anywhere at all, you should deploy it according to your opponent's movements from one moment to the next, wherever he is. Since [the mind] is pervading your whole body, when you need your arm, you should use the mind in your arm; when you need your leg, you should use the mind in your leg. If you focus the mind so that it's fixed in one spot, when you go to transfer it [someplace else], it becomes attached *there*, and your free functioning in the earlier place will be gone.

When you treat the mind as if it were a cat on a leash, keeping it confined within your body, your mind will be imprisoned by your body. But if in your body you just turn the mind loose, it won't go anywhere else! Not keeping the mind in any one place is what practice is all about. Not attaching the mind anywhere at all is the main matter, what really counts. When you don't focus the mind anywhere, it will be everywhere. Even when you direct the mind outside, if you focus it in one place, you'll miss all the rest. But when you don't focus the mind in any one place, it permeates every place.

*We speak of original mind and deluded mind.*[29] Original mind is mind that doesn't attach to any one place but spreads to fill the entire body. Deluded mind is mind that, preoccupied by something, is *stuck* in one place. So when original mind is stuck in one place, it becomes what we call deluded mind.

When original mind is lost, your free functioning everywhere is lost, so you must strive above all not to lose [original mind]. Let me give you an example. Original mind, like water, never stays in one place. Deluded mind is like ice in that you can't use ice to wash your hands and face. [But] when you melt ice, you turn it to water, so that it flows everywhere and you can then wash your hands, your feet, and anything else. When mind is stuck in one place or attached to one thing, it congeals like ice and can't be freely used. Just as you can't use ice to wash your hands and feet, you should allow the mind to function by melting it and letting it flow through your whole body like water. You just let [the mind] go to wherever you want it and use it there. That's what's meant by original mind.

*We speak of the mind of intention and the mind of nonintention.*[30] The mind of intention is the same thing as deluded mind. The characters for intention read literally "having mind," [that is,] being preoccupied with any particular thing. Once a thought is present in the mind, discriminations and calculations arise, so we speak of the mind of intention. The mind of nonintention is the same thing as original mind, referred to before. The mind that isn't fixed, that is without discrimination or calculation, the mind that spreads to fill you completely, that pervades the whole body, is what we speak of as [the mind of] nonintention. It's the mind that isn't focused anywhere at all. Yet it isn't like stone or wood. *Never* being inert is what's meant by nonintention. When there's inertia, there's something in the mind; when there's constant free-flowing activity, there's *nothing* in the mind. Having nothing in the mind is what's called the mind of nonintention. It's also called "without intention and without thought." When you've thoroughly mastered this mind of nonintention, you don't attach to anything and you don't lack anything. Like water continually brimming over, it fills your body so that whenever you need to use it, it's there at hand and does its work.

The mind that's become fixed and attached in one place isn't able to function freely. The wheels of a cart can turn because they're kept loose on the axle. When they're too tight anywhere, they're unable to turn. The mind, too, won't function once it's stuck [in some place]. When there's anything you're thinking about in your mind, you hear what people say but you don't [really] hear them. That's because the mind is attached to what you're thinking. With the mind stuck in those thoughts, it becomes sidetracked in one place; and being sidetracked in one place, even if you hear something, you won't hear it, and even if you see something, you won't see it. That's because you have something in your mind. By "have," here, I mean you have some thought. When you get rid of those thoughts you have, your mind will be without intention and will simply function when you need it, just as you need it. [However,] deliberately trying to get rid of these thoughts in your mind only becomes something *else* in your mind! When you're not trying to do so, [these thoughts] go away on their own, and you'll spontaneously realize [the mind of] nonintention. Always have your mind like this, and you'll naturally arrive at this stage. [But] if you try to do it in a hurry, you'll [never] get [there at all]. As an old poem says:

> Trying not to think of a thing
>   One still thinks of it
> So even though I tell myself I won't
>   Can I help thinking of you, my beloved?

*Plunge a hollow gourd into a stream, try to hold it down, and it immediately escapes.*[31] "Holding down a gourd" means to press it down with your hands. When you plunge a hollow gourd into a stream and then hold it down, it immediately slips away to the side. Whatever you do, it won't stay in one place. The mind of someone who's attained realization doesn't attach to things for even a moment. It's just like the gourd in the stream, [which always escapes the hand] pressing it down.

*Without attaching anywhere, let the mind manifest itself.*[32] These characters are read *ōmushojūji jōgoshin.* What is meant is that in performing any action, when you deliberately *try* to do [it], the mind attaches to the action you are performing. Instead, without attaching anywhere, you should let the mind manifest *itself.*

Unless the mind manifests itself where it belongs, your hand won't even move. When [your hand] moves, the mind that is abiding there manifests itself; and while that happens, [if] you don't attach to it, that's what it means to be master of all the various Ways. It is from this attaching mind that the mind of clinging arises, and transmigration arises from there as well. This attaching mind constitutes the fetters of birth and death.

What this phrase ["Without attaching anywhere . . ."] conveys is that when you gaze at the cherry blossoms or the crimson autumn leaves, even while admiring the leaves or the blossoms you don't attach to them. A poem of Jien[33] says:

> Even the cherry blossoms
> > whose fragrance fills my brushwood gate—
> Let them be!
> How regrettable it is
> That people have spent
> > their days in the world gazing upon them

That is to say, the cherry blossoms emit their fragrance without attachment; but we attach our mind to the blossoms as we gaze upon them and regrettably are stained by this sort of attachment. Not to attach the mind in any particular place, whatever you see or hear, constitutes ultimate mastery.[34]

A commentary on [the meaning of] reverence says, "One should concentrate [the mind] in one place and not let it stray."[35] That is, concentrate the mind in one spot, and do not let it go elsewhere. Even when you draw your sword and kill the enemy behind you, it's essential that you not let your mind be caught up by the killing of the enemy. Particularly when receiving the honor of a special mission from your lord, you must carry it out with the [same] spirit of reverence.

In Buddhism, too, there is the mind of reverence. What's called the "reverence bell"[36] means that one shows reverence by ringing a bell three times and joining one's palms. This mind of reverence that addresses itself to the buddhas signifies the same thing as "concentrating the mind in one place and not letting it stray" and "one mind, undisturbed."[37] However, in Buddhism the mind of reverence does not constitute the ultimate. It is the teaching of how to keep the mind from being captured or disturbed. As this practice matures over the months and years, whatever place you have your mind go, you will reach the state of [perfect] freedom.

The state of not being attached anywhere, referred to above, is the stage of ultimate attainment. The mind of reverence is the stage in which you rein in the mind, preventing it from straying, thinking if you let it go free it's out of control, so that you're careful always to keep the mind tightly restrained. This is a temporary measure, for the moment only, to keep the mind from being distracted. But if the mind is kept like that all the time, it becomes inflexible. An example of this stage of practice is when you catch a baby sparrow and then have to keep the cat always tied tightly to its leash, never letting it loose. When you keep your mind, like the cat, on a tight leash, making it unfree, it can't function spontaneously. [However,] once you have the cat well trained, you [can] untie it and let it go wherever it likes, so that even if it's right next to the sparrow, it won't grab it. To practice like this is what is meant by the phrase "Without being attached anywhere let the mind manifest itself." It means that in using your mind you let it go free, as if you were turning loose the cat, so that even though it goes wherever it pleases, the mind doesn't attach [anywhere].

Applied to Your Lordship's art of swordsmanship, this means that you don't attach the mind to the hand wielding the sword. Completely forgetting the hand wielding [the sword], strike and kill your opponent, [but] don't fix the mind *on* your opponent. Realize that your opponent is empty, that you are empty, that both the hand wielding the sword and the sword being wielded are empty. Don't even let your mind be captured by emptiness!

It is said that the Zen master Wuxue of Kamakura[38] was captured in the course of the disturbances in China and was [about] to be killed, when he recited the *gatha* "Cleaving the spring wind in a flash of lightning." Thereupon [the Mongol warrior] abandoned his sword and fled.[39] Wuxue's meaning [in the poem] is that the swift raising of the sword is like a flash of lightning, without any intention or thought. The sword that is striking is also without intention, as is the person who is doing the killing, and even the one who is being killed. The one who kills is empty, his sword is empty, and the one who is attacked is empty, too. Thus the one who attacks is not a person. And the sword that strikes is not a sword. For the one who is attacked, it is just like cleaving in a lightning flash the breeze blowing in the spring sky. This is the mind that is never attached. The sword itself certainly has no awareness of slashing through the breeze. To completely forget the mind this way in carrying out all your myriad activities constitutes the stage of mastery.

In performing dance movements, one holds a folding fan in one's hand and stamps one's feet.[40] [But] if you're thinking, "I'm going to move my hands and feet right! I'm going to dance well!" instead of [simply] forgetting about it, that's not what's meant by mastery. So long as your mind still attaches to your hands and feet, your movement can't be splendid in all respects. All movement that fails to completely and utterly relinquish the mind is bad.

*Recover the lost mind* is a saying of Mencius. It means, find the mind that has been lost and return it to yourself. For example, when you lose a cat, dog, or chicken that's run away, you go looking for it, find it, and bring it back to your house. So, when the mind, being master of the body, runs away, taking an evil path, how can you not find it and bring it back? It's only natural for you to do so.

In contrast, Shao Kangjie[41] says, "Let the mind go!" This is completely different. According to this kind of approach, keeping the mind tightly restrained only exhausts you, with the result that, like the cat [on the leash], the body isn't able to function. So, thoroughly train the mind not to attach to things or to be stained by them, just leaving it alone and freeing it to go anywhere at all.

Since the mind is stained by and attached to things, the beginner's stage of practice is to think, "Don't let it be stained, don't let it be attached; find it and bring it back to yourself." [Rather,] be like the lotus, unstained by the mud. Even if the lotus is in the mud, it's no problem. Just as a finely polished piece of crystal is unstained if it falls into the mud,[42] in using your mind, let it go where it wants. If you tightly restrain the mind, it becomes inflexible. Keeping the mind tightly reined in is strictly for beginners. If you spend your whole life in that state, you'll never assume the superior position[43] but end up in the inferior position and be killed. When you're still training, Mencius' approach of "recovering the lost mind" is fine. But when you arrive at ultimate mastery, that is Shao Kangjie's "Let the mind go!"

Master Zhongfeng[44] says, "Free the mind now!" This means exactly the same as Shao Kangjie's "Let the mind go!" It means recover the lost mind, [but] don't restrain it, don't keep it in any particular place. There is also the saying "Make yourself steadfast!" These, too, are Zhongfeng's words. They mean that one [should] maintain a steady mind, without backsliding. What this means is to hold fast to the sort of mind that doesn't backslide into the stage in which you just try once or twice but then get tired and invariably give up.

*A ball hurled onto a rushing torrent, never staying still from one instant to the next.*[45] This [expression] means that when you hurl a ball onto a raging torrent, it rides along, tossed on the waves, never stopping anywhere.

*Cutting off past and future.*[46] Not letting go of the past mind and holding on to the present mind after the fact are wrong. What is being said here is "Sever the boundary between past and present, remove it! Cut off both past and future, let them go!" That is, don't attach the mind [anywhere].

*Water, being heated, rises; fire, being moistened, makes clouds appear.*[47]

> The fields of Musashi
> Do not burn them today
> My lover is hiding in the spring grass
> And I, too, am hiding there[48]

Someone, expressing the essence of this poem, wrote:

> When white clouds gather
> It is ready to fade—
> The morning glory's flower

ADDENDUM

These thoughts I had kept to myself, but with Your Lordship's encouragement, I have set them down, fortunate in having the opportunity to submit to you this rough outline of my reflections, for whatever worth you may find in them.

In the art of swordsmanship Your Lordship is an accomplished master, unparalleled in the past or present, hence the current glory of your official appointments, your stipend, and reputation. Whether asleep or awake, one must never forget the enormous debt of gratitude one owes [one's lord]. One must think of nothing else, day or night, but endeavoring to repay that debt through loyal service.

What is meant by loyal service is above all to keep one's mind upright and to lead a virtuous life, to be without any trace of duplicity toward one's lord, not to resent others or slander them but each day without fail to serve [one's master]. Within one's family, it means conscientiously demonstrating

filiality toward one's father and mother and not allowing the slightest discord in relations between husband and wife. Observing decorum, one should
not became attached to concubines but avoid lecherous pursuits. With one's
parents, one should conduct oneself in a dignified manner in accordance
with the Way. In managing subordinates, one should avoid showing personal
favor, employing those who are virtuous and keeping them by one's side. One
should be ready to acknowledge one's own shortcomings. One should rectify
the governance of the nation.

When one distances oneself from those lacking in virtue, the virtuous
will daily advance so that the unvirtuous themselves will be naturally
transformed by their lord's love of virtue, forsaking evil and turning to
goodness. In this manner, both lord and retainer, high and low, will become virtuous. When selfish desires lessen and people put a stop to pride,
the realm will fill with wealth, the commonfolk will enjoy prosperity and,
like children devoted to their parents, will follow their lord's bidding as
faithfully as if they were his own hands and feet so that the land will naturally be at peace. This is the beginning of loyalty.

If you have at your command, in any situation, such resolute warriors,
free of all duplicity, then, even if you employ ten million men, they will all
follow your wishes to perfection. In other words, just as all the arms of the
Thousand-Armed Kannon function when its mind is correct, the one
mind's functioning will be free when Your Lordship's art of swordsmanship is correct, and it will be as if several thousand attackers are subdued
by a single sword. Is this not great loyalty? When that mind is correct,
there is nothing else one needs to know.

When a thought arises, the duality of good and bad appears. But when
by perceiving the source of that good/bad duality you do good and refrain
from doing bad, the mind will naturally become straight and true. [In contrast,] knowing something to be bad but not giving it up results in the re-
morse of [succumbing to] selfish desire.

Whether it is attachment to sensual pleasure or a readiness to indulge
your arrogance, whatever your desires, you have a tendency to follow them.
So even if virtuous persons are available, unless they seem congenial to you,
you fail to do the right thing; while even if people are ignorant, so long as you
decide you like them, you hire them and show them special favor. Even
though virtuous persons are available, then, since you don't hire them, it's
just as if they didn't exist. The result is that, even if you have several thousand
men, when the time comes that you really need help, there won't be even *one*
able to serve his master. This bunch of ignorant evildoers whom you made up

your mind you liked are people whose minds are unrighteous from the start so that when they confront a critical situation, there's no chance of them being ready to lay down their lives. From ancient times one has never heard of anyone with an unrighteous mind who was of any use to his lord.

It is disturbing to hear that when Your Lordship has promoted disciples such things have occurred. You fail to recognize that showing even the slightest favor to those whom you like leads you to succumb to this disease and fall into wickedness. You may imagine others do not know, but as it is said, "Nothing is plainer than what is concealed."[49] Since you know it in your heart, it is known as well to heaven and earth, to the gods, and to all the people of the land. For defending the realm, is this not a truly perilous state of affairs? That is why I consider it the very greatest disloyalty.

For example, however valiantly you yourself might strive to loyally serve your master [the shogun], if the entire clan is not harmoniously united, and if the people of the Yagyū Valley domain[50] oppose [your rule], then everything will be in discord.

If you would judge any person's character, you have only to look at the retainers on whom he relies and the friends with whom he is intimate. When the master is virtuous, his trusted vassals will all be virtuous. When the master lacks rectitude, his retainers and friends will all lack rectitude. And when the common people then despise you, the neighboring domains, too, will hold you in contempt. This is what's meant by "When the [lord and his retainers] are virtuous, the people will be devoted to them."

The state, it has been said, regards the virtuous as its treasure. You should take this completely to heart. In the public sphere, if you give urgent attention to ridding yourself of your own improprieties, to distancing yourself from those who are mean and cherishing those who are wise, the administration of your domain will be increasingly virtuous, and you yourself will become the model of a loyal retainer.

Particularly as regards the conduct of Your Lordship's son,[51] if the parent lacks rectitude, it makes no sense to blame the child for being bad. If, first of all, you rectify yourself, then, when you admonish your son, he will naturally rectify [his own behavior]. And since his younger brother, the court steward,[52] can model his behavior on his older brother's and rectify himself as well, both father and sons will become men of virtue. Surely this will be cause for rejoicing!

It has been said that hiring or dismissing should be according to one's duty [to one's lord]. At this time, to use your position as a favored retainer [of the shogun] in order to extract gifts from the various daimyo would be to forget righteousness by being caught up in greed. Such things must never be allowed to occur.

To indulge unreservedly in Nō dancing, priding yourself on your ability, forcing your performances on the various daimyo, and promoting your own talent seems to me simply to be an illness. (I heard that you referred to His Lordship's [the shogun's] Nō chanting as Sarugaku.)[53] Similarly, interceding with the shogun on behalf of those daimyo who flatter you is something on which you should carefully and repeatedly reflect. A poem says:

> Mind itself leads mind astray
> Do not let mind [mislead] the mind[54]

## On the Sword Taie (*Tai'a ki*)

*As it seems to me, the art of swordsmanship is not about struggling over victory or defeat; nor is it concerned with strength or weakness. One neither advances a single step nor retreats a single step. Your opponent does not see you; you do not see your opponent. Penetrating to the place where heaven and earth have not yet separated or yang and yin emerged, you can directly realize the power of this practice.*[55]

*As it seems to me* (*kedashi*) means "I don't know exactly, but . . ." Originally this ideogram represented the cover of a container (*futa*). For instance, when a cover is placed on a set of nested boxes, you don't know what's inside, but, by guessing, six or seven times out of ten you can figure it out. Here, too, it expresses, "I don't know for sure" or "Without actually checking, I can't be certain, but . . ." Even if you know something for certain, you will show humility and won't talk as if you know it—that's the convention in writing. *The art of swordsmanship* is just as the characters indicate. *[It] is not about struggling over victory or defeat; nor is it concerned with strength or weakness* means not contending over victory or defeat, or being concerned with whether your actions are strong or weak. *One neither advances a single step nor retreats a single step* means that you neither take one step forward nor one step back but secure victory remaining right where you are.

*Your opponent does not see you.* "You" refers to the true self.[56] It is not the self of self-and-other. The self of self-and-other is something people can easily see, but to see the self of true self is rare indeed. That's why we say, "Your opponent does not see you." *You do not see your opponent* means that since you harbor no attachment to notions of self and other, you see beyond the opponent's fighting strategy based on self and other. When we speak of not seeing the opponent, it doesn't mean not seeing the opponent who's right in front of your eyes! Seeing yet not seeing—this is subtle mastery. The self of true self is the self before heaven and earth were divided and father and mother were born. It is the self that exists in all things—in ourselves as well as in birds, beasts, grasses, and trees. In other words, it is what's known as Buddha nature. It is a self that has no shape, no form, that is neither born nor dies. It is not the self seen with the everyday physical eye. It can be seen only by one who has realized enlightenment. One who has glimpsed it has seen his own nature and realized buddhahood.

In the distant past, the World-Honored One entered the snowy mountains[57] and, after six years spent in painful [practice], realized enlightenment. This is the awakening to true self. The usual, unenlightened person, lacking the power of faith, will not understand in three or five years. One who studies the Way will continually rouse his great power of faith for ten or twenty years without flagging, studying with teachers, heedless of hardship and suffering, never yielding in his resolve, like a parent who has lost a child, pondering deeply, searching intently, till he comes to where he has exhausted all views of buddha and Dharma and is able to spontaneously realize enlightenment.

*Penetrating to the place where heaven and earth have not yet separated or yang and yin emerged, you can directly realize the power of this practice.* This means, focus your attention on the place before heaven and earth separated and yang and yin emerged, and then, without employing reason or understanding, see things directly. Then the time may come when you realize great power.

*One who has achieved mastery does not use his sword to kill people. He uses his sword to bring people to life.*[58] *When he wants to kill them, he kills them immediately. When he wants to bring them to life, he brings them to life immediately. This is the* samadhi *of killing and the* samadhi *of bringing to life. Without viewing things [as] right and wrong, he is able to see the right and wrong [of things]. Without making distinctions, he is able to distinguish between things. He walks on water as if walking on land, walks on land as if walking on water.*[59] *If he realizes this freedom, what can anyone on earth do to him? He is completely without equal.*

*One who has achieved mastery* indicates one who is master of the art of swordsmanship. *Does not use his sword to kill people* means that although he does not use his sword to kill people, when people encounter this principle, all instinctively cower before it and become dead men, so that there is no *need* to kill them. *He uses his sword to bring people to life* means that by using his sword he keeps the opponent under control, while he remains free just to watch, as he lets the opponent move any way he wants. *When he wants to kill them, he kills them immediately. When he wants to bring them to life, he brings them to life immediately. This is the* samadhi *of killing and the* samadhi *of bringing to life* means that he freely kills or brings to life.

*Without viewing things [as] right and wrong, he is able to see the right and wrong [of things]. Without making distinctions, he is able to distinguish between things* means that in the art of swordsmanship he has no [fixed] views of right and wrong yet is able to *see* the right and wrong of things. Without making distinctions, he is *able* to make distinctions. For instance, if you take out a mirror and set it up, whatever things come before it, each and every one of their forms is reflected, so that each and every one appears. But because the mirror is without intention, even though it precisely reflects each and every thing, it doesn't make any distinctions between one thing and the other—"that is this, this is that." So, too, with those who practice the art of swordsmanship, when the mirror of the one mind is revealed, there is no intention to distinguish between right and wrong; yet since the mind's mirror is bright, precisely because distinctions between right and wrong *don't* appear, they are fully apparent.

*He walks on water as if walking on land, walks on land as if walking on water.* The meaning of this cannot be understood unless a person has awakened to what is original to *all* persons. The foolish imagine that if you walk on water as if on land, then even when walking on land, you'll probably sink, and if you walk on land as if on water, then even when walking on water, you'll go right across. What is meant is that only when you become a person who has completely forgotten about either land or water can you arrive at this principle.

*If he realizes this freedom, what can anyone on earth do to him? He is completely without equal.* For a warrior who has attained this sort of freedom, even if everyone on earth conspired to attack him, there's nothing they could do to him. *He is completely without equal* means that in the whole world no one can match him. As it's said, "In heaven and on earth, I alone am to be revered."[60]

*If you wish to attain this, then whether walking or standing, sitting or lying down, in speech or in silence, [drinking] tea or [eating] rice, you should practice assiduously, urgently focusing your attention, and by penetrating through and through, see directly. With the passing of the months and years, it will seem as if you naturally possessed a lamp in the darkness. You will obtain the wisdom that has no teacher[61] and manifest the marvelous function of acting without intention. At that very moment, without departing from the ordinary, you will transcend the ordinary. This is what is called the sword Taie.*

*If you wish to attain this.* "This" is the words referred to above, so it means, If you wish to realize the principle referred to previously. *Walking or standing, sitting or lying down* are the four [activities] known as the four dignities.[62] This is something everyone has in common. *In speech or in silence* means both while speaking and not speaking. *[Drinking] tea or [eating] rice* means even while drinking tea or eating rice.[63] *You should practice assiduously, urgently focusing your attention, and by penetrating through and through, see directly.* Practicing conscientiously and assiduously, always come back to your own self, urgently focusing your attention to master this principle and, recognizing what is right and what is wrong, directly see this principle in every situation.

*With the passing of the months and years, it will seem as if you naturally possessed a lamp in the darkness.* As you earnestly practice like this and the months and years go by, you will make progress and come to realize this marvelous principle, just as if on a pitch dark night you suddenly came upon a lamp's radiance. *You will obtain the wisdom that has no teacher.* You will attain the fundamental wisdom that even a teacher cannot pass on. *And manifest the marvelous function of acting without intention.* All the activities of the unenlightened person proceed from consciousness, so they are all based on intention and hence are nothing but suffering—while this acting *without* intention proceeds from original wisdom, so it's completely spontaneous and easy. That's why it's called marvelous functioning. *At that very moment* means when that time comes; in other words, *when you obtain the wisdom that has no teacher and manifest the marvelous function of acting without intention.*

*Without departing from the ordinary, you will transcend the ordinary.* This marvelous function of acting without intention does not manifest itself in some special sphere; rather, all your ordinary activities, without exception, completely become acting without intention, so that you never depart from the ordinary. In this way there is a complete transformation from the common unenlightened person's usual activity [based on] intention, with the result that *without departing from the ordinary, you will transcend the ordinary.*

*This is what is called the sword Taie.* The sword Taie is the name of a famous sword without equal anywhere on earth. It freely cuts through [all] hard [substances], from gold and iron to gems and rocks. Nothing under heaven can resist its blade. For one who has attained the marvelous function of acting without intention, none can oppose him whether it's the general of a great army or a formidable force of a million, in the same way that nothing can withstand the blade of this famous sword. That's why we call the power of this marvelous function the sword Taie.

*This sharp sword, the sword Taie, is intrinsically possessed by everyone. In each of us it is completely realized. One who illumines it will be feared by heavenly demons.*[64] *One who obscures it will be deceived by heretics. When two skilled [warriors] cross swords and fight to a draw, [it is just as when] the World-Honored One held up the flower and Mahākāshyapa smiled.*[65] *It is also just as when one thing is spoken of, understanding three things, or with one glance detecting the slightest difference in weight.*[66] *These are manifestations of our ordinary marvelous acuity. If there is one who has completely realized this matter, then even* before *one thing is spoken of,* before *three things are understood, [his blade] has already cut his opponent into three.*[67] *How much more so when meeting face to face.*

*This sharp sword, the sword Taie, is intrinsically possessed by everyone. In each of us it is completely realized.* This means that in all the world there is nothing able to withstand its blade. The famous sword, the sword Taie, is not in anyone else's possession; everyone, whoever it is, intrinsically possesses it. No one is missing any part of it at all, because it's completely realized [in every person]. It is none other than mind. This mind isn't born at the moment of birth, nor does it die at the moment of death. That's why it's called one's original face. Even heaven can't cover it, even earth can't support it; fire can't burn it, water can't wet it, wind can't pass through it. That's why it's said that there's nothing in the world able to withstand its blade.

*One who illumines it will be feared by heavenly demons. One who obscures it will be deceived by heretics.* Nothing in the vast universe can impede one who has realized this original face. Even heavenly demons have no way to use their supernatural powers on him but instead, quite the reverse, are themselves seen through *by* him, exposing their innermost thoughts and intentions, so that they fear him and dare not go anywhere near him. In contrast, one who obscures the original face and so goes astray accumulates every sort of deluded thought and notion, and, taking advantage of those deluded thoughts and notions, heretics can easily fool and deceive him.

*When two skilled [warriors] cross swords and fight to a draw . . .* What happens when two warriors who have both realized their original face confront one another, simultaneously unsheathe their Taie swords, cross blades, and fight to a draw? It's just like the encounter between the World-Honored One and Mahākāshyapa. . . . *The World-Honored One held up the flower and Mahākāshyapa smiled.* It's like the moment at the assembly on Vulture Peak, when the Buddha was about to die and he held up a golden lotus and showed it to the great gathering of eighty thousand monks. All of them remained silent. Only Mahākāshyapa smiled.[68] At that moment, the World-Honored One knew that Mahākāshyapa had realized enlightenment, and he sanctioned his realization, declaring, "I confer upon you my true Dharma, the special transmission outside the scriptures that does not depend on words and letters." From [Mahākāshyapa] this true Dharma was transmitted in India across twenty-eight generations to Bodhidharma;[69] in China, it was transmitted from Bodhidharma across six generations to the Sixth Patriarch, the Zen master Dajian.[70] Since this Zen master was a bodhisattva in the flesh, thereafter the Buddhadharma flourished increasingly in China as well, so that its branches and leaves spread luxuriantly, and the Five Houses and Seven Schools[71] prospered, continuing up through Xutang[72] from whom [the teaching passed] to our land's [masters] Daiō and Daitō. From [that time] to the present, the bloodline has remained unbroken.

Thus, the Dharma of "holding up the flower and smiling" is only achieved with the greatest difficulty. It is not something to be readily grasped through thinking or imagining. The buddhas themselves fall silent and become speechless. So, although this principle can't be expressed in words, if one is forced to liken it to something, it resembles one container of water being poured into a second container of water, so that [the first] water and [the second] water are mingled together, with no distinction between them. This is the oneness of the eyes of the World-Honored One and Mahākāshyapa. There's absolutely no difference between them. Whatever sorts of masters of the art of swordsmanship there may be, you won't find even one in a hundred thousand who's realized the truth of holding up the flower and smiling. Nevertheless, if there's a man with the capacity to study the very highest vehicle and he wants to realize [this truth], he must practice for thirty years more.[73] Should he go wrong, however, he will not only fail to master the art of swordsmanship but will fall into hell swift as an arrow shot [from a bow]. Take care! Take care!

*When one thing is spoken of, understanding three things* means that when someone shows you one thing, you instantly understand three. . . . *With one glance detecting the slightest difference in weight (mokki shuryō)* . . . Detecting at a single glance (*mokki*), refers to the eye's inherent skill or measuring by eye. *Shu* indicates measuring weight by eye. A *shu* is a weight of ten *shi*. Ten *shu* equal one *bu*, and ten *bu* constitute a *ryō*.[74] So this means that, no matter how much gold and silver there is, you can judge the exact amount by eye and won't be off by even as much as one *shu* or one *ryō*. This [expression, *mokki shuryō*,] signifies a person of keen perception and marvelous acuity. *These are manifestations of our ordinary marvelous acuity* means that, for one who is endowed with such marvelous acuity, this sort of keenness of perception is an everyday matter; it's nothing at all extraordinary.

*If there is one who has completely realized this matter, then even* before *one thing is spoken of, before* three things are understood, *[his blade] has already cut his opponent into three.* For one who has completely realized the great matter of Buddhadharma, even before one thing is spoken of, even before three things are understood, without revealing any sign of his intentions he has already thrust and cut his opponent into three. So, should you encounter this man, whatever you do will be useless. *How much more so when meeting face to face.* When one who has achieved such swift mastery of the art meets an opponent face to face, he can slay him so easily that his opponent's head will be severed before he even knows what's happened. That's how skillful he is!

*The point of such a man's sword is never revealed. It is swifter than a streak of lightning, faster than a sudden storm. Lacking this sort of skill, the moment you attach anywhere or intentionally direct the mind toward anything, you ruin the point of your weapon and injure your hand and will never be fit to achieve mastery. Do not use your deluded mind to speculate about this. It is not something that can be transmitted in words. Nor is it to be taught through forms. It is the Dharma of the special transmission outside the scriptures.*

*The point of such a man's sword is never revealed.* Such a master never shows the point of his sword. *It is swifter than a streak of lightning, faster than a sudden storm.* Even a streak of lightning that's gone in a flash isn't fast enough to catch his hand; even a hurricane spewing sand and rocks can't match his speed.

*Lacking this sort of skill, the moment you attach anywhere or intentionally direct the mind toward anything . . .* If, without such ability, you attach even the slightest bit to raising your sword or attach even the slightest bit to what you have in your mind . . . *you ruin the point of your weapon and injure your hand and will never be fit to achieve mastery.* You're certain to mar the point of your weapon and cut your own hand, and so never be worthy to be deemed a master.

*Do not use your deluded mind to speculate about this.* Deluded mind is the discriminating consciousness within the human mind. Speculating about things is conjecture. What's meant is that, no matter how much you try to speculate [about this] using the deluded mind, it will be to no avail. So try to go *beyond* speculative discrimination. *It is not something that can be transmitted in words. Nor is it something to be taught through forms.* This true art of swordsmanship can't be passed on through speech. And it also can't be learned through forms, by teaching things like what stances to take or where to strike. *It is the Dharma of the special transmission outside the scriptures.* Since it's an art that can't be transmitted with words or taught through exercises, it's called the Dharma of the special transmission outside the scriptures. The special transmission outside the scriptures is the Dharma you have to realize and attain for yourself, apart from any teacher's instruction.

*The great function manifesting itself immediately before you has nothing to do with fixed rules.*[75] *Moving freely in all directions, even heavenly beings cannot fathom it.*[76] *What, then, is this principle? A man of old said, "My home has no picture of the Baize.*[77] *Goblins like that do not exist."*[78] *If one is able to discipline himself and arrives at this priciple, he will pacify the entire kingdom with a single sword. You who study this, do not take it lightly!*

*The great function manifesting itself immediately before you has nothing to do with fixed rules.* When the function of the specially transmitted Dharma is manifesting here before you, it's completely free, so it doesn't depend on fixed rules. We call this "great function" because it pervades everywhere throughout the worlds in the ten directions, not missing so much as the tip of a rabbit's hair. Fixed rules, here, refers to laws and regulations. Laws and regulations that are like molds have nothing whatever to do with the great function immediately manifesting before you. *Moving freely in all directions, even heavenly beings cannot fathom it.* One for whom this great function is immediately manifesting is free and without obstruction whether he goes this way or that. Even heavenly beings can't figure it out! *What, then, is this principle?* "What sort of principle is this?" the text asks.

*A man of old said, "My home has no picture of the Baize. Goblins like that do not exist."* This is the answer to the preceding question. The Baize is a mythical creature said to have a body like an ox and a head like a man. It devours dreams and calamities, so that in China pictures of it are made and affixed to gates or stuck onto the pillars of homes. So putting up images of the Baize is a means of warding off domestic calamities. But someone who's never had any goblins in his house has no interest in putting up the Baize's pictures. What this [saying] means is that even heavenly beings can't plumb the mind of someone who's able to function freely wherever he goes, so [such a person] leaps clear of every sort of pain and joy; he has no calamities either in himself or in his home, and as a result has no interest in images of the Baize—his world is something utterly wonderful!

*If one is able to discipline himself and arrives at this principle, he will conquer the entire realm with a single sword.* If you are a free man, having practiced in this way, disciplining yourself [like] gold that's repeatedly and exhaustively tempered and refined, so that you're able to attain the highest mastery of the sword, you will surely resemble the eminent founder of the Han, who with a single blade subjugated the whole land.[79] *You who study this, do not take it lightly!* Those of you who are learning the marvelous principle of this sword should not carelessly give rise to vulgar thoughts, but polish your virtue and never be negligent, not for even an instant!

# 3 Happenings in a Dream

*Takuan's Story*

Takuan's life, like the difficult times in which he came of age, was marked by periods of considerable turbulence and uncertainty, and, though a dedicated Zen monk with a penchant for seclusion and rural retreat, the master encountered the sorts of extreme shifts in fortune common to many of the leading secular figures of the day. This experience surely shaped his view of the transitory, unreal nature of things and of the folly of attachment. "So long as those of us in this world consider that we have come as guests," Takuan reflects in his miscellany *Knotted Cords,* "we will be untroubled."

> When presented with food that's to our liking, we think we are being well treated. But even when the food is not to our taste, since we are guests, we've got to praise it and eat it all up. Whether it's the heat of summer or winter's chill, since we are guests we must bear it. . . .
>
> > Brought into this world by our parents
> > We came as temporary guests
> > So we can, without attachment
> > Return to our original home[1]

Takuan was born in 1573 in Izushi,[2] a castle town in the old province of Tajima (now Hyōgo Prefecture), on Japan's main island, Honshu. His family, the Akibas, were hereditary samurai retainers of the province's rulers, the Yamana clan. Takuan's Akiba forebears[3] had originally come from the east[4] to serve under Yamana Sōzen (1404–1473), a leading commander in the Ōnin War (1467–1477), a decadelong civil disturbance in which contending warlords had devastated the ancient capital of Kyoto. The conflict signaled the decline of the Muromachi shogunate (1333–1573), the military dynasty of the Ashikaga clan, which had ruled Japan since the early four-teenth century, and it inaugurated an era of violence and unrest in which various armies vied over Japan's cities and provinces.

The year of Takuan's birth witnessed the final collapse of Muromachi rule, with the last shogun, Yoshiaki, deposed by Oda Nobunaga (1534–1582), the first of a new generation of warlords who emerged as would-be unifiers of the country. When Nobunaga was murdered by one of his generals, he was succeeded by his former lieutenant Toyotomi Hideyoshi (1536–1598), after whose death power passed to Tokugawa Ieyasu (1542–1616), another of Nobunaga's commanders and Hideyoshi's onetime vassal. Only with Ieyasu's victory over his rivals at the Battle of Sekigahara in 1600 and at Osaka castle in 1615 were the long years of bloody conflict and internecine warfare brought to a close by the establishment of a new mili-tary dynasty, the Tokugawa shogunate, that would rule Japan in relative peace for the next two and a half centuries (1600–1867). This tumultuous period between the end of Muromachi rule and the founding of the Tokugawa state, a time of chronic insecurity, shifting allegiances, and dra-matic power struggles, framed Takuan's formative years.

Two stories surrounding Takuan's birth assert a miraculous connection with Buddhism. The first records a soothsayer's prophesy that the newborn baby would grow up to become an enlightened monk. The second relates that when Takuan's father, Akiba Tsunanori (1539–1606), was traveling on busi-ness for his lord, his wife took the family's prized miniature bronze buddha to bed with her at night for safekeeping, and when Tsunanori returned to find his wife pregnant, she offered this explanation in her defense.[5] There is, how-ever, no other recorded evidence for this story, which the early-nineteenth-century chronicler hastens to denounce as a fabrication.

Fanciful though they may be, both tales seek to account for why Takuan's father brought him at age six to a local Rinzai Zen temple, Sukyōji,[6] and asked a Kyoto priest in residence, Shūgaku Seidō (n.d.), to accept the child as his disciple when Takuan turned nine. Takuan was Tsunanori's eldest son[7] and as such would normally have been expected to succeed his father as family head. It is impossible to know if Tsunanori's decision to destine Takuan for the priesthood was the result of some supernatural revelation, doubts about Takuan's paternity, or merely a wish to shelter his child from the insecurity of a samurai's life in a period of almost constant warfare. Only exceptional circumstances, one imagines, could have im-pelled a Japanese warrior of Tsunanori's day to commit his eldest son to a Buddhist temple.

Also unexplained in the traditional accounts is why Takuan's father should have chosen to place him in a Zen establishment. The Akiba were connected with Nyoraiji, an Izushi temple of the Jōdo, or Pure Land, school, which emphasizes sincere repetition of the invocation to Amida Buddha (*nenbutsu*) leading to rebirth in the Pure Land, a Buddhist paradise in the western heavens. Possibly Tsunanori, like other samurai, patronized temples and priests of various Buddhist schools. Sukyōji was also the Yamana clan funerary temple (*bodaiji*), and placing Takuan there may simply have been a gesture of loyalty to Tsunanori's lord, who in turn might be counted on to help in advancing Takuan's career.

Sukyōji was a branch establishment of the great Kyoto temple Tōfukuji, and the Yamana daimyo, pleased to learn of Tsunanori's plans for his eldest son, announced that Tōfukuji's 218th-generation abbot would himself administer the precepts to Takuan on a forthcoming visit to the domain. Takuan would then formally become a novice, and the Tōfukuji abbot, Ikyō Eitetsu (n.d.), his precepts teacher. In 1580, however, Nobunaga's forces under Hideyoshi attacked Tajima. Izushi castle was taken and the Yamanas forced to flee westward to neighboring Inaba Province (Tottori Prefecture). Because of its position as the Yamana clan temple, Sukyōji's fortunes suffered temporary eclipse, and Takuan's precepts ceremony was canceled.

In 1582 Takuan entered Shōnenji, a temple of the Pure Land school in Izushi. Here he is said to have devoted himself to studying the principal Pure Land scriptures, spending each day copying them out by hand, then reciting them aloud, often staying up till dawn if he fell behind. In the end, the young novice became so adept that he was able to join in the regular temple chanting and had no trouble keeping up with the older monks, much to their amazement. Takuan's precociousness did not escape the notice of Shōnenji's abbot, who asked Tsunanori's permission to make the boy his disciple. By this time, however, Takuan's interests had reportedly begun to shift to Zen: "In his twelfth year, the Master considered, 'Even if I perform Pure Land practice and realize the path of calling the Buddha's name, unless I knock at the gate of Zen and encounter a Zen master, I'll be unable to realize the essentials of mind.' His longing to study Rinzai Zen became greater by the day."[8] In 1586, therefore, Takuan returned to Sukyōji, becoming the disciple of the Zen master Kisen Shūsen (d. 1591).

As a branch establishment of Tōfukuji, Sukyōji belonged to the Gozan, or "Five Mountains," system, a network of official Zen temples centered on six Kyoto temples heavily patronized by the Muromachi shoguns.[9] Sometimes referred to as the *sōrin* to distinguish them from the *rinka,* those Zen temples outside the official system, the Gozan were themselves divided along the lines of their principal subtemples, or *tatchū*, which might have only the most tenuous connections with the main temple.[10] In the Tokugawa period, as in our own day, all of the Gozan temples were classified as belonging to the Rinzai school, in contrast to the other leading Japanese Zen organization, the Sōtō school, which traces its lineage from Dōgen Kigen (1200–1253). In Muromachi Japan, however, (and well into the early Tokugawa period) such notions of sectarian identity were relatively weak, hence the classifications of *sōrin* and *rinka*, championed by the twentieth-century historian of Zen Tamamura Takeji.[11]

Zen (Ch. Chan) had been imported from China in the late twelfth and thirteenth centuries, and Japanese Zen monks and masters were commonly well versed in the Song dynasty (960–1279) literary idioms, especially poetry, in which the koan-centered Zen of the period was often conveyed. While *zazen* (seated meditation) and koan practice were central to the curriculum of all the early Japanese Zen temples, in the Gozan by the fifteenth century they had been gradually superseded by an emphasis on cultural specialties, particularly the study and composition of poetry in classical Chinese.

By contrast, two Kyoto Rinzai temples outside the Gozan system, Daitokuji, founded by Daitō Kokushi, and Myōshinji, founded by Daitō's disciple Kanzan Egen (1277–1360), prided themselves on a continued adherence to strict Zen practice and became a magnet for those Gozan priests impatient with the "literary Zen" of the official temples. Throughout the fifteenth and sixteenth centuries, young Zen priests continued to abandon the *sōrin* to swell the ranks of the *rinka* temples Daitokuji and Myōshinji; many among these were to become the temples' leading figures. Outsiders, much of whose early support had come from the emperor and court rather than the shogunate, Daitokuji and Myōshinji increasingly looked to patrons among the new warlords challenging the power of the Muromachi government. As the central authority of the shogunate declined and with it the prestige of the official Gozan temples, Daitokuji and Myōshinji found their fortunes rising in tandem with the success of their warrior patrons. By the late Muromachi period, the two former outsider temples had replaced the Gozan in importance, and along with their counterparts in the Sōtō lineage, another *rinka* group with strong provincial support, they dominated Japanese Zen. Not surprisingly, a certain rivalry and antipathy existed at times between the Gozan and the Kyoto Zen temples outside the official system. Tōfukuji, however, was something of an exception, a Gozan temple that was relatively open and maintained close connections with Daitokuji and Myōshinji. Takuan's new teacher, Kisen, for example, though a Tōfukuji priest, had studied under and succeeded a Zen master in the Myōshinji line.[12]

As was typical in Gozan temples, Takuan's course of study at Sukyōji focused on reading and writing in classical Chinese and, judging from Takuan's subsequent familiarity with Chinese literary culture, probably included not only Buddhist scriptures but the Confucian classics and secular Chinese poetry. As to Takuan's Zen training at Sukyōji, however, the records are unfortunately silent.

In 1591 Kisen died, and Takuan, inspired by the sermon of a visiting Myōshinji master, prepared to set off on pilgrimage, or *angya* ("going on foot"), the period during which a Zen monk leaves his home temple and travels to sound out and study under various teachers. In the meanwhile, however, a Daitokuji Zen master, Tōho Sōchū (1549–1601), arrived for an extended stay at Sukyōji at the invitation of the temple and the new Izushi daimyo, Maeno Nagayasu. Takuan resumed his Zen study under Tōho, and, when the master returned to Kyoto in 1594 to assume Daitokuji's abbacy, Takuan accompanied him to the capital, taking up residence at a Daitokuji subtemple, Sangen'in.[13]

Sangen'in had been established eight years before by Tōho's own master, Shun'oku (also Shunkaku) Sōen (d. 1611), a leading Daitokuji teacher who had attracted the support of many of the preeminent warlords of the day. He was also the teacher of the two priests who would be Takuan's colleagues and "codefendants" during the Purple Robe Affair, Gyokushitsu Sōhaku (1572–1641) and Kogetsu Sōgan (1574–1643). Before long, Takuan himself had begun Zen study under Shun'oku, receiving from the master the Buddhist name Sōhō. The first character, *sō*, signifies origin, teaching, or school—here, the Zen school. Normally pronounced *shū*, it is used commonly as the first character in the names of priests in the Daitokuji and Myōshinji lines, where it is read *sō*. The second character, *hō*, means vigor, or dynamism—thus the characters together translate roughly "Vigor of the Teaching." Those entering the priesthood in premodern Japan would be given Buddhist names (*hōki*) to replace their lay names,[14] and it was usual for priests to be given new Buddhist names when they changed schools or lineages. Thus Sōhō replaced the earlier Buddhist names Takuan had received, first as a novice at the Pure Land temple Shōnenji, where he was given the name Shun'ō, and then at the Tōfukuji branch temple Sukyōji, where Kisen had assigned him the name Shūki.

Though staying at Sangen'in, Takuan did not study exclusively under Shun'oku and during this time performed a kind of "internal" pilgrimage, making the rounds of the various Daitokuji masters. Little is known of the actual content and character of Zen study in the Daitokuji line at this period, and it is unclear what sort of training Takuan experienced under his various teachers. Meditation practice was certainly integral to the curriculum, particularly the two intensive ninety-day retreats (*kessei* or *ango*) observed in Zen temples, the first (*geango*) held during the spring and summer months, the second (*tōango*) extending from fall to midwinter and concluding on the sixteenth day of the new year. (Takuan, for example, is recorded teaching at such a retreat from spring to summer of 1629 at Kōtokuji, a Daitokuji branch temple in Edo.)[15] Also essential to a Daitokuji monk's education were koan study and conversance with associated Zen texts. This included the ability to wield the often cryptic phrases found in the records of earlier Zen teachers and in the medieval Chinese koan collections such as *Blue Cliff Record* (*Biyan lu*, J. *Hekigan roku*, 1128) and *Gateless Gate* (*Wumen guan*, J. *Mumonkan*, 1229).[16] Known as *agyo* (offered words),[17] such phrases, which drew on Buddhist sutras, Zen texts, and Chinese classical and popular culture, were employed to express individual understanding or appreciation of koans: "A snowflake on the burning furnace"; "When killing a man, be sure you see the blood"; "He doesn't know the smell of his own shit."[18]

While the koans themselves were, as their Chinese name, *gongan*, literally implies, "public cases," Zen teaching lines in late medieval Japan maintained their own closely guarded transmissions of which *agyo* "answered" particular koans, transmissions sometimes recorded in secret memoranda together with explanations and interpretations in vernacular Japanese. Such procedures formed the basis for koan study in many temples, so that receiving a Zen teacher's sanction came to signify transmission of his line's "secret" tradition of *agyo* and glosses for sets of koans. This practice of closed transmission for the *agyo* is sometimes referred to as *missan*, "secret study," and by the time of Takuan's novitiate the practice was common in all the major schools of Japanese Zen, both Rinzai and Sōtō, Gozan and non-Gozan.[19] In certain extreme instances, the koan interpretations presented in *missan* texts show the influence of Tantric sexual theories and yin-yang thought, although such bizarre transmissions, evident in Takuan's day, seem to have been confined to Sōtō and Gozan temples and do not appear in either the Daitokuji or Myōshinji line.[20]

At Daitokuji itself, the *missan* system appears to have been popular at least from the time of the iconoclastic Zen master and poet Ikkyū Sōjun. Writing in 1455, Ikkyū, who became Daitokuji's forty-seventh abbot, bitterly

lampoons *missan* Zen's rote character and its consequent abuse by ignorant teachers and laymen at the temple:

> One tradesman declares, "I did it in ten days!"
>
> Another announces, "I got transmission in an embarrassingly short
> time!..."[21]
>
> One nun grieved, thinking she'd lost the written explanation of
> "Zhaozhou's 'Cypress Tree in the Garden,'"[22] having actually placed it inside a
> handbox.
>
> Another nun wept, thinking she'd lost the memo she'd written with the an-
> swer to the koan "Who is it that doesn't accompany the ten thousand things?"[23]

The *missan* system continued in use at Daitokuji throughout Takuan's
period.[24] But whether its influence remained as pervasive as it had been
earlier is unclear, as is Takuan's own involvement with the system, as a student and a teacher.[25] In any event, Takuan's description of the traditional
curriculum at Daitokuji, part of his 1629 letter of protest to the government, discussed below, gives at least some sense of the importance of koan
study and the mastery of *agyo* in his own training at the temple:

> From the time of our temple's founder, through that of his second- and third-
> generation successors, [a course of study] was established for future generations
> of students [based on] the koans that [these three teachers] had taken up, com-
> prising the one hundred cases of *Blue Cliff Record* and the various koans con-
> tained in its associated poems and comments, as well as the koans of the records
> of Linji and Yunmen,[26] along with the capping phrases [*agyo*] for 120 koans that
> [Daitō] had selected for study[27] and essential poems and phrases drawn from
> various sutras and records. One studies these all intensively, so that the course
> of study in our temple can be completed in about twenty years.[28]

It must have been stimulating for a young priest fresh from Tajima to
reside in the capital at the heart of a great institution like Daitokuji, where
he was disciple of one of the temple's most prominent teachers. But whatever patronage Shun'oku as an individual or Sangen'in as an institution
may have enjoyed, Takuan lived in grinding poverty. He only survived by
hiring out as a copyist in whatever time he could spare from his studies,
barely able to feed himself or to buy enough oil for his lamp.

In early fall 1599, Tōho and Takuan accompanied Shun'oku to Sawayama,
a castle town in Ōmi (Shiga Prefecture) where Shun'oku had been invited by

the powerful lord of the province, Ishida Mitsunari (1560–1600), to inaugurate a new temple. With the ceremonies complete, Shun'oku returned to Daitokuji, leaving Tōho as abbot of the temple, Zuigakuji, and Takuan as his
assistant. No doubt Shun'oku hoped that under Mitsunari's patronage
Zuigakuji might provide a suitable situation for his two disciples. A favored
retainer of Hideyoshi, Mitsunari was a supporter of Hideyoshi's heir, Hideyori, and leader of the opposition to Tokugawa Ieyasu's efforts to unify Japan
under his own control. With Mitsunari's defeat at Sekigahara the following
autumn, Sawayama quickly fell to the Tokugawa forces, and Takuan, probably in company with Tōho, returned to Kyoto and Sangen'in. Poorer than
ever, he was reduced to selling even his few precious books for food.

In 1601 Tōho died. Takuan's precise movements during this interval are
unclear. What is known is that he briefly attended lectures by a scholar monk
in Nara, Japan's ancient capital and center of Buddhism, before traveling
later that year to Sakai to study with Bunsei Dōjin, a Zen teacher noted for
his calligraphy. Bunsei was a member of the Wanshi-ha,[29] a minor Sōtō lineage introduced by Chinese monks in the fourteenth century and affiliated
with the Gozan. Known for its literary and artistic expertise, the line eventually found a home in Echizen (Fukui Prefecture) under the patronage of the
Asakura clan, but with the Asakuras' destruction by Nobunaga in 1573, Bunsei and many of his Wanshi brethren had fled south to Kyoto and Sakai. The
principal city of Izumo Province, today included in the Osaka Municipal
District, Sakai had been Japan's chief port since the late Middle Ages. As
such, it was home to a prosperous merchant class whose leaders, like many of
the warlords of the day, often patronized Zen temples and teachers along
with associated arts, particularly the tea ceremony, itself to some extent a
product of the city's distinctive cultural milieu.

Bunsei had taken up residence at Daianji, a Tōfukuji branch temple,
where he attracted many lay followers. Takuan studied with Bunsei till the
latter's death in 1603 and must have impressed the calligrapher–Zen master, who bequeathed to Takuan all his books and personal effects. Takuan's
talents had begun to attract the notice of others as well. In 1602 Hosokawa
Fujitaka (1534–1610), a former ally of Nobunaga and Hideyoshi and a noted
authority on poetry, praised a collection of *waka* that Takuan had composed and submitted for his comments; and in the same year, two Daitokuji Zen masters[30] each sought Takuan as a disciple, though he declined
their repeated invitations. Takuan's economic situation, nevertheless, remained dismal, as a story from the summer of 1602 attests. Invited to attend a memorial service and vegetarian feast to be held the next morning

at Kaianji, a Tōfukuji branch temple in Sakai, Takuan realized he had only the one soiled and sweat-stained robe he was wearing. That evening he washed the robe in well water and left it to dry in the moonlight, but at dawn it remained soaking wet. Takuan was still hiding naked indoors waiting for the robe to dry when his brother monks arrived to collect him. In his embarrassment, he simply shut his door, leaving the others to proceed to the meal.

After Bunsei's death, Takuan resumed his Zen study under another Sakai master, Ittō Jōteki (also Shōteki, 1539–1606), first at Yōshun'an, Ittō's small, historic temple, and later at the grander Nanshūji (or Nansōji). The largest of the Sakai Zen temples, Nanshūji had been founded in 1556 by the Daitokuji master Dairin Sōtō (n.d.) and erected by the warlord Miyoshi Chōkei (1528–1564) in memory of his late father, Nagamoto (d. 1532). Nagamoto had perished in Sakai in 1532, committing *seppuku,* or ritual suicide, along with seventy of his retainers following defeat by a former ally, the daimyo Hosokawa Harumoto (1519–1563). Ittō had trained under Dairin and then under Dairin's successor Shōrei Sōkin (d. 1583), the teacher of Takuan's earlier instructor Shun'oku. According to Ittō's biography,[31] the master had endured terrible sufferings in his quest for enlightenment, meditating night and day, forgetting to eat or sleep, vowing to realize "the truth of his own being" even if he died in the attempt. In 1582, at age forty-three, Ittō suddenly experienced awakening. Shōrei acknowledged his attainment and the following day conferred on Ittō his *inka,* literally "seal of approval," the Zen master's written sanction of a student's realization. By 1594 Ittō had risen to become Daitokuji's 126th abbot.

Perhaps as a result of his own hard-won understanding, Ittō had a reputation as a fearsome and difficult master, and his temples contained few students. He appears to have initially rebuffed Takuan, but the earnest young monk persisted in his efforts to become Ittō's disciple. After repeated entreaties Ittō engaged Takuan in a Zen dialogue, or *mondō* (literally "question and answer"), and, satisfied with the results, admitted him to the temple.

In late summer 1604, less than a year after joining Ittō's assembly, Takuan received his new master's *inka.* Curiously, there is no mention in the traditional biographies of an actual enlightenment experience leading up to this event. The accounts of Takuan's biographer and personal Zen student Munetomo are silent on this score, and Takuan says nothing in his own writings of an enlightenment experience under Ittō or under any of his previous teachers. Mention of a "satori" culminating in a teacher's acknowledgment and sanction is a common though not universal feature of the recorded biographies of Rinzai-line priests in Takuan's period, as seen in Munetomo's own biography of Ittō, referred to above. It is possible Takuan was simply reticent about such inherently personal matters. But the aged Ittō, whose only other Dharma heir had predeceased him, clearly viewed Takuan as a promising successor, and his *inka* represented recognition both of Takuan's potential to carry on the teaching and of his prior spiritual attainments, the understanding Takuan had gleaned in his eighteen years of intensive Zen study under a variety of masters. A poem Ittō composed for the occasion affirms that Takuan had realized enlightenment (*goryō*) and expresses the fullest confidence in his Zen achievement:

> Training in the monks' hall and realizing enlightenment
> You've attained serenity and peace
> Others, you've recognized, slumber away in the sunlight
> An autumn stream, abundant, broad, flowing lazily on
> Night swallows the full moon and day conceals the hills[32]

Above this poem, in large, inky characters, Ittō brushed the name "Takuan" (marsh hermitage). This constituted Takuan's formal Buddhist name (*dōgō*), the new name conferred on a Zen monk in connection with his teacher's sanction of enlightenment. The formal name was placed before a priest's earlier, "Dharma," name (*hōki*) and was the name by which Zen masters in Takuan's day generally referred to themselves and were referred to by others. Thus, in Takuan's letters, he may refer to himself as "Takuan," while signing the letters "Sōhō," the more personal name he had received on first entering the Daitokuji line.[33]

Further confirmation of Takuan's attainment came in the first month of 1606 in a meeting with his old teacher Shun'oku. The occasion was a memorial service at which Shun'oku had been asked to officiate by the Sakai tea master Yamaoka Sōmu (n.d.) to honor Sōmu's late father, Matsunaga Hisahide (1510–1577). The daimyo of Yamato (Nara Prefecture), Hisahide was a notorious warlord who had been responsible for the death of the thirteenth Muromachi shogun, Yoshiteru (1535–1565), and had even ruled Kyoto for a time. Hisahide died by his own hand in a failed revolt against Nobunaga, but not before destroying a precious tea bowl coveted by his adversary, an incident celebrated in many accounts of the period. Yamaoka had invited Takuan to the service and a vegetarian meal that followed, and Shun'oku used the opportunity to interview Takuan privately in order to test his understanding in the direct give-and-take of a Zen dialogue. Shun'oku rigorously examined

Takuan, posing questions about various koans and related phrases to probe his erstwhile student's Zen. Takuan's responses are said to have been unerringly swift and penetrating, and, at the conclusion of the encounter, Shun'oku expressed his wholehearted approval. At Yoshun'an, Ittō, ill and in failing health, was delighted to learn of his Dharma brother's praise for Takuan, whom Ittō proudly pronounced "a son who has indeed surpassed his father."[34] Traditionally in Rinzai Zen the regular student-teacher koan interview (often referred to as *sanzen*) places a premium on directness, forcefulness, and spontaneity, and Takuan's experience in koan study, his "Dharma combat" with masters like Ittō and Shun'oku, may well have informed the emphasis on naturalness and instantaneity of response that marks his instruction on Zen and swordsmanship.

Takuan was generally cavalier about biographical records, honors, and the like, and the fact that his dialogue with Shun'oku survives probably indicates its importance to him. Along with Ittō's *inka*, the meeting with Shun'oku must have represented an important milestone in Takuan's completion of his Zen training. The dialogue, or at least salient portions of it, are included in Munetomo's 1648 *Account of the Life of Master Takuan* and offers not only an intimate picture of Takuan's relations with Shun'oku but a rare glimpse into the interactions between Japanese Zen teachers and students in the early years of the Tokugawa period.

| | |
|---|---|
| SHUN'OKU: | Who is it that does not accompany the ten thousand things?[35] |
| TAKUAN: | Piercing! |
| SHUN'OKU: | Meaning what? |
| TAKUAN: | In the eye it's called seeing; in the ear it's called hearing.[36] |
| SHUN'OKU: | Ultimately, what is it? |
| TAKUAN: | Totally manifesting.[37] |
| SHUN'OKU: | "Swallow the waters of the Western Lake in one gulp and I'll tell you."[38] What does this mean? |
| TAKUAN: | Mazu is like the springtime. True indeed are these words! |
| SHUN'OKU: | Meaning what? |
| TAKUAN: | The fine spring rain nurtures the flowers. |
| SHUN'OKU: | A fluent fellow![39] |

Three months later, in spring 1606, Ittō passed away, leaving Takuan his only surviving Dharma heir. That winter Takuan learned that his father, Tsunanori, was gravely ill, and he hastened home to Tajima. Tsunanori loved music and during his final illness would pass the time clapping and singing to himself. "Singing like this distracts me from my gloomy thoughts," he reassured his eldest son. "Don't take this for the delirious ravings of my dying hours."[40] Shortly thereafter Tsunanori died, and Takuan was able to conduct the funeral service before returning to Sakai, bidding farewell to his sixty-year-old mother, who within five months would follow her husband.

It was now twenty-eight years since Takuan's arrival at Sukyōji, twenty years since he had begun formal Zen study under Kisen. He had gained a wide experience of temples and teachers, risen to become his own teacher's heir, and as such could now expect to assume advanced standing within the Daitokuji line. Rinzai Zen's stated ideal may have been its founder Linji's "true man of no rank,"[41] but premodern Japanese society placed great emphasis on one's title and corresponding status within the group, and the Rinzai priesthood was no exception. Advancement in the temple hierarchy was a normal part of the successful priest's "career path," all the more so at an aristocratic establishment like Daitokuji with long-standing connections to the rank-obsessed imperial court.

In 1607 Takuan received appointment as head monk (*dai-ichi za*) of Daitokuji, along with abbacy of Tokuzenji, an important Daitokuji subtemple. These appointments advanced Takuan to the rank of *zendō*, signaling that he had received his master's sanction and was now a Zen teacher in his own right, able to take charge of disciples and temples. Indeed that summer Takuan was made abbot of Nanshūji, the Sakai temple where he had trained under Ittō.

His new rank also qualified Takuan to receive the purple robe by imperial command (*shie chokkyō*), the honor of imperial abbacy reserved to only a handful of Japanese Buddhist temples. At most imperial temples appointment of abbots was a complex process, and the emperor could not act until candidates had first been scrutinized and approved by the government. Daitokuji, however, owing to its special history of close connections with certain medieval Japanese emperors, enjoyed the rare honor of a direct imperial appointment, which altogether bypassed the authorities. The reigning emperor, on receiving the temple's letter of recommendation, issued a decree; the candidate selected for recognition then received the imperial messenger at the temple and, after performing the ceremony of investiture, assumed the imperially bestowed purple robe.[42] Thus, in early spring 1609, by command of the Emperor Go-Yōzei (r. 1586–1611), Takuan became the 153rd abbot of Daitokuji. A climax of Zen abbacy ceremonies is the offering of incense in public recognition of one's principal teacher, and Takuan took the occasion to formally express his indebtedness to Ittō.

Abbacies in Tokugawa Zen temples were largely honorary affairs and involved no actual administrative duties. At Daitokuji, the usual term was a mere three days, and a new abbot might be inaugurated every month.[43] As one Japanese scholar has observed, *becoming* abbot seems to have been more important than *being* abbot.[44] Nevertheless, the practice of having representatives of Daitokuji's various far-flung branches serve, even briefly, as abbot of the headquarters temple strengthened organizational cohesion and identity while augmenting the temple's coffers through the substantial donations required of each new abbot, a mainstay of Zen headquarters temples' economies. For his own installation, Takuan, however humble his personal finances, presumably managed to marshal sufficient support from wealthy merchant and samurai patrons to make a solid contribution of cash, goods, or services such as temple repairs.

Before departing for Nanshūji after the customary three days, Takuan appeared before the assembly of monks and recited a short poem of leave-taking:

> Mine has always been a life of drifting like a cloud,
> > flowing like a stream
> Office in a great temple, spring in the capital—
> > they're not for me
> I'm returning tomorrow to Nanshūji
> The white seagull does not fly amid red dust[45]

In the period following his abbacy, Takuan seems to have divided his time between Nanshūji and Daisen'in, a Daitokuji subtemple that was headquarters of the so-called Northern branch, the Daitokuji line to which Takuan belonged.[46] Takuan's fame had evidently begun to spread, and he was sought out by leading daimyo of the day, though the records, like many priest biographies, emphasize Takuan's determined efforts to avoid contact with many of the powerful and important persons who pursued him. Among Takuan's would-be patrons was Hideyoshi's heir, Hideyori, who in 1611 invited Takuan to Osaka castle, the Toyotomi stronghold whose fall four years later would mark the final collapse of resistance to Tokugawa rule. Takuan refused Hideyori's approaches, as he did those of Asano Yukinaga (1573–1613), lord of Kii (Wakayama Prefecture), a former lieutenant of Hideyoshi whom Takuan deliberately evaded when the daimyo arrived in person at Nanshūji to interview him. Takuan also resisted the repeated requests of another prominent warrior, Hosokawa Tadaoki (1564–1645), daimyo of Buzen (Fukuoka Prefecture), to found a temple in honor of his recently deceased father, Fujitaka (1534–1610). The Hosokawa were an ancient military clan, perhaps best known for their pivotal role in the Ōnin War, during which much of Kyoto had been destroyed in fighting between the Hosokawa and their rivals. Allies of Nobunaga, Hideyoshi, and later Ieyasu, the Hosokawa in Takuan's day had a reputation for political astuteness and cultural refinement. Tadaoki, who would play a key role in the capture of Osaka castle, was also known as a poet, a painter, and a devotee of tea, disciple of the famous tea master Sen no Rikyū (1521–1591). Ultimately he became one of Takuan's faithful backers, along with his son Tadatoshi (1586–1641), and the Hosokawa clan record contains intriguing details of Takuan's later years.

Takuan did not refuse all daimyo patronage at this time, and when his supporter Koide Yoshimasa (1565–1613) of Izumi died, Takuan accepted Yoshimasa's sons' request to perform the funeral service at the Koide's castle town of Kishiwada. With the large donation he received, Takuan created a new tower for the temple gong at Nanshūji, and he used the donation for performing the memorial service the following year to construct a library at Daisen'in. Takuan is portrayed in the traditional biographies as someone who, though courted by those in power, remains steadfastly plain and unassuming, giving away any sizable donations. In 1614 a series of floods devastated large areas of Japan, washing away bridges and dikes and drowning many people. Among the bridges destroyed was one in the village of Yase (now within the city of Kyoto), where Takuan found himself stranded by the flooding. Witnessing firsthand the suffering that resulted from the bridge's collapse, Takuan promptly contributed whatever funds he had toward reconstruction, to the joy of all the villagers.

Takuan's fund-raising skills were further taxed by the destruction that accompanied the anti-Toyotomi campaigns of 1614–1615, culminating in the suicide of Hideyori and the fall of Osaka castle after a grueling siege. Hideyori's cause had become a magnet for those disaffected with or displaced by Tokugawa rule, including thousands of *rōnin*, masterless samurai who found themselves stripped of both status and income in the new feudal structure, and the Osaka campaign involved the largest armies fielded in Japan to that time.[47] By spring 1615 the fighting had spread to Sakai, some twenty miles south of Osaka castle. Much of the city was reduced to ashes, including Nanshūji, reportedly destroyed on the anniversary of its founder, Dairin's, death.[48] Takuan had had the foresight to personally remove Dairin's robe, Ittō's *inka*, and other precious items to Daitokuji for safekeeping. But he was now confronted with the enormous task of rebuilding Nanshūji and restoring it to some semblance of its former grandeur.

In the interim, Takuan put up at Nikkōji, a Tendai temple in Kishiwada, the castle town of his patrons the Koide brothers Yoshichika (1590–1668) and Yoshihide (1586–1668), who jointly governed the Izumi domain.[49] Continually pestered by visits from the daimyo and their retainers, Takuan complained that he was unable to meditate and removed himself to a Jōdo temple, Gokurakuji, in the nearby village of Amarga.

Takuan had now found an important ally in Kitami Katsushige (d. 1627), the Sakai *bugyō*, or shogunal administrator, who in 1617 authorized Nanshūji's move to its current site in the southern part of the city. Construction could now legally proceed, and, with the assistance and support of Kitami, Yoshihide, and others, was completed over the following years, with Takuan named founder of the restored temple.

Throughout Takuan's life, there appears a constant tension between the demands of his public, institutional activities and his longing for quiet and seclusion. The next years found him often far from Sakai, sequestered in a series of small temples where he could meditate undisturbed. He spent one or two years in Kyoto at a former retreat of Ikkyū's, Shūon'an,[50] before returning in 1620 to his native Izushi. The previous year Koide Yoshihide had been transferred to the domain as the new Izushi daimyo, and Takuan had prevailed upon him to restore Sukyōji, which had suffered periods of neglect. Here, as at Nanshūji, Takuan was made the revived establishment's "second founder" but chose instead to occupy a modest hermitage that he erected behind the temple and dubbed Tōenken (Plunging into the Depths Pavilion).[51] Here Takuan lived peacefully and frugally, with one flax robe and a single small pot in which he cooked the roots of vegetables and boiled his own rice for gruel. He also posted a notice on the wall urging his students to live likewise and forswear all but minimal food, clothing, and shelter.[52] Austerity and frugality were frequently celebrated virtues in Takuan's period, not only for high-ranking Buddhist priests, too often regarded as tainted with worldliness, but for samurai and merchants, two groups whom the Confucian-influenced authorities regularly cautioned against the evils of conspicuous consumption.

During the winter of 1620, Takuan is said to have retired to the mountains to recuperate from a bout of what is enigmatically described as "melancholy" (*atsubyō*).[53] The statement appears only in the nineteenth-century *Record of the Founder of the Myriad Pines [Temple] (Manshōsoroku)*, which offers no further details (or supporting evidence). Funaoka Makoto discounts the notion that Takuan was experiencing anything similar to modern clinical depression, suggesting instead a mild sort of "Zen sickness," the result of the master's inability to escape the incessant demands of patrons, temple reconstruction, and the like in order to cultivate his enlightenment in an atmosphere free from noise and distraction.[54]

Back at Tōenken, Takuan's attempts to establish a quiet retreat were thwarted once again, this time by the arrival of groups of students anxious to seek his guidance.[55] Before long Takuan found himself surrounded by attendants, and it was apparently with these young followers in mind that in 1621 he composed *On the Distinction between Principle and Activity* (*Riki sabetsuron*), his earliest datable written instruction.[56] Rudimentary in character and strongly syncretic, much of the text consists of simple explanations of basic concepts drawn from Chinese religious traditions, especially yin-yang thought and Song Neo-Confucianism. The latter, a highly metaphysical variant of Confucianism that had been influenced by Zen, was imported to Japan by Zen monks in the late Middle Ages and served under the Tokugawa as a kind of official orthodoxy used to justify the country's feudal social structure.

Takuan takes up various terms, among them the title's principle (*ri*) and activity (*ki*), the former the unconditioned, unvarying absolute, the latter its dynamic manifestation in things; nature (*shō*), the essential, unchanging character of mind; and the ten thousand things (*banbutsu*), the phenomenal world in its multiplicity, including not only concrete, objective existence but the subjective realm of thoughts, emotions, and impulses, all regarded as "outside" original mind.[57] These concepts are discussed in terms of Neo-Confucianism, yin-yang thought, Buddhism, even Shinto and the worship of *kami*—the indigenous "gods" manifested within awesome natural forces and forms and powerful or eminent personalities. The Tokugawa had attempted to coopt aspects of Shinto, as well, and in 1617, a year after Ieyasu's death, an elaborate shrine-temple, Tōshōgu, was erected at Nikkō (Tochigi Prefecture), where the shogunate's founder was worshiped as a new *kami*. The worship of gods and buddhas had been closely intertwined in Japan since the early Middle Ages, and at the insistence of the Tendai priest Tenkai (1536–1643), one of Ieyasu's chief spiritual advisors, the *kami* at Nikkō was simultaneously revered as an avatar of the Healing Buddha Bhaisajyaguru (J. Yakushi) with the imperially bestowed title Tōshō Dai Gongen (Great Avatar Who Illuminates the East).

In his essay Takuan graphically equates "buddha" and *kami*, joining two circles containing the Chinese characters for each to the statement "Same substance, different name."⁵⁸ This is followed, in turn, by an analysis of *shin*, mind or heart, which, while employing overtly Shinto-related concepts that draw on popular religious beliefs, echoes many of the Buddhist themes to be found in Takuan's writings on Zen and the sword:

> Within each person, *kami* exists. The ignorant obscure this with delusion, obscuring principle within things, attaching to things. . . . When the mind attaches to things, it creates darkness, and then when you die, you'll remain in darkness. This is what's called demon [*oni*]. . . . *Kami* means expanding, never being attached in any particular place, just as water circulates unobstructed throughout the ocean. Demon means contracting. The spirit of ignorance contracts, attaching to things, so that unless we return to intrinsic *kami* [*honshin*], we get caught up with things. This is the Way of demons.⁵⁹

Beyond identifying *kami* with Buddha mind and demon with delusion, Takuan puts forward here several of his trademark ideas on Zen and Zen practice. In particular, he cites attachment to things (*mono ni todomaru*) as the basis of delusion, the mind that is artificial, rigid, and constricted. The cure for delusion is to reclaim the original mind, which, being free from attachment anywhere (*issho ni todomarazu*) is fluid and natural in its response. Takuan's treatment of mind is both descriptive and prescriptive. The immediate effect of attachment is to distort and constrain, to blot out the intrinsic clarity of the mind. But this insidious process is shortcircuited the moment we return to being direct, natural, and spontaneous, or, as Takuan says here, "honest," "straightforward" (*shōjiki*):

> The mind of man is twisted and turbid. Not being straightforward, *kami*, though present, is concealed and obscured. When you're straightforward, the water of mind becomes clear. . . . *Kami* dwells in a straightforward mind; *kami* doesn't dwell or manifest anywhere else. This means that, when your mind is straightforward and clear, your mind itself is *kami*. Whether it's *kami* or buddha, when you're enlightened, it's you, yourself. Those in whom the Way is illuminating are living buddhas.⁶⁰

Takuan concludes his essay by asserting that when the mind is straightforward and direct, when it doesn't lean one way or another, that is itself the essence of *kami*. Accomplish this, he promises his readers, and you'll "become a *kami* while you're alive, and when you die be worshiped like Ieyasu!"⁶¹

In alluding to popular veneration of Ieyasu, Takuan reflects the reverence for the ruling dynasty's founder that was standard in his day. However, relations between Takuan and the Tokugawa military government, or bakufu, were soon to become severely strained. Ieyasu, during his final years, had issued regulations for Daitokuji that many of its priests, including Takuan, opposed as incompatible with both Zen and the temple's traditions. Within a decade of Ieyasu's death, the resulting tensions would provoke perhaps the most serious crisis in Daitokuji's history, a crisis in which Takuan was to play a leading role.

The series of government decrees, or *hatto*, that form the background to the dispute were integral to Ieyasu's consolidation of power. Issued for the great samurai houses, the emperor and court, and the major Buddhist temples, the decrees sought to regulate and control the three groups that had been the principal power brokers during the age of civil wars, groups that might conceivably challenge the authority of the fledgling Tokugawa shogunate.

By the seventeenth century, the influence of the emperor and court was largely ceremonial, a source of honors and symbolic legitimacy, but whatever independence they retained was regarded by Ieyasu as a threat to the bakufu's monopoly of power.

Unlike the emperor and court, many of the large Buddhist establishments had a recent history of armed conflict, fielding forces that had often rivaled those of the contending warlords of the day. The monastic armies of the great Shingon and Tendai temples on Mounts Koya and Hiei and the troops commanded by the Ikkō (True Pure Land) and Nichiren sects had been key players in the volatile politics of sixteenth-century Japan, presenting serious obstacles to would-be unifiers of the country like Nobunaga and Hideyoshi. Nichiren forces occupied and governed the capital, Kyoto, from 1532 to 1536, when they were dislodged in turn by troops led by the Tendai warrior monks of Mount Hiei and financed by the Ikkō school.[62] Nobunaga's principal nemesis in his efforts to bring Japan under his sway had been the Ikkō armies of lay adherents, and it was not until Hideyoshi's victories in the mid-1580s that the last of the Buddhist military organizations were disbanded and all arms removed from the temples.

Although no longer a military threat, the great temples in the early years of the Tokugawa shogunate remained well endowed, well connected, and potentially troublesome institutions. Unlike most of the other major schools of Buddhism during the Middle Ages, the Zen schools had never participated in armed conflict or trained warrior monks. This was not because of any inherent pacifism on the part of Zen and may simply have been a function of the school's close connections with Japan's ruling military elite, resulting in greater scrutiny of the monasteries' activities. In any case, the fact that Zen temples themselves never garrisoned armies did not mean that individual Zen teachers and abbots were not directly involved in military affairs. When, following his defeat by Ieyasu at Sekigahara, Ishida Mitsunari was beheaded in Kyoto, beheaded alongside him was a Tōfukuji-line abbot, Ekei of Ankokuji, who had been one of Mitsunari's principal generals in the battle.[63] Ieyasu himself, in prosecuting the Osaka winter and summer campaigns that cemented his rule, was advised on strategy by a Gozan master, Isshin Sūden (1569–1633).

Because the Zen priesthood was highly educated and conversant with Chinese language and culture, it had served the Muromachi shoguns in a variety of diplomatic and administrative capacities. As Muromachi power faltered, it was not uncommon for Zen monks to be similarly employed as advisors by the new class of provincial warlords, and such monks, sometimes referred to as "black-robed ministers" (*kokue no saishō*), were a fixture of Takuan's period. Sūden, the most famous of the monk-advisors, was a former Nanzenji abbot who had been enlisted by Ieyasu from about 1608 to assist in consolidating Tokugawa rule. In tandem with the Kyoto shogunal administrator, or *shoshidai,* Sūden oversaw bakufu religious policy from his Edo temple, Konchi-in. But he is perhaps best known as a principal architect of the early Tokugawa decrees (*hatto*) regulating the samurai houses, the emperor and court, and the Buddhist temples.

An area of particular concern evident in the decrees to the temples is the special connection between the emperor and certain imperial Zen establishments such as Daitokuji and Myōshinji, specifically, the emperor's direct appointment of abbots, referred to earlier, a process allowing the emperor and the temples to bypass the government in installing imperial abbots and awarding the purple robe. Even such symbolic, traditional prerogatives were regarded by the bakufu as intolerable expressions of autonomy that challenged its control, and in 1613 an "Imperial Purple Robe Decree"[64] was promulgated, declaring that henceforth all imperial abbacies must first be submitted to the government for approval.

Perhaps because of Daitokuji's and Myōshinji's failure to honor the terms of the 1613 decree, the requirement for prior reporting of imperial abbacies was reiterated two years later in the Daitokuji and Myōshinji *hatto,* identical documents that were part of a series of individual codes issued in 1615 for the principal Zen headquarters temples and organizations. Beyond

their renewed insistence on government review of imperial abbacies, however, the 1615 decrees, sometimes referred to as the Genna decrees for the
reign year in which they appeared, present a veiled indictment of Daitokuji
and Myōshinji Zen themselves, alleging serious shortcomings in the actual
training and qualifications of the temples' abbots:

> In the practice and study of Zen, one consumes thirty years of diligent train-
> ing under a qualified teacher and, upon completing seventeen hundred koans,
> travels throughout the land, studying with different masters, everywhere
> pursuing the [Zen] teaching. . . .
>    Lately there have been indiscriminate imperial authorizations confer-
> ring abbacy upon persons who, at times, have not been priests for very long or
> are inexperienced in religious discipline. Such appointments not only sully
> the imperial temples but grossly violate the Buddha's precepts. Hereafter,
> those who scheme in such a manner are to be permanently expelled.[65]

The basis for the decrees' curious assertion that abbots must have completed thirty years' study of Zen and mastered seventeen hundred koans is
unclear. Neither requirement corresponds to any established system of study
at Daitokuji or Myōshinji, and neither appears in the code issued for the
Gozan,[66] to which Sūden, the 1615 code's principal architect, belonged. "Thirty
years" is a figure sometimes used to indicate the minimum time necessary for
Zen practice,[67] and the phrase "thirty more years of study" (*sara ni sanzeyo
sanjūnen*) appears frequently in *Blue Cliff Record*[68] and in case 19 of *Gateless
Gate*, "Ordinary Mind Is the Way" ("Even if Zhaozhou has experienced realization, only after thirty more years of study will he truly understand.").[69]

The expression "seventeen hundred koans" refers to the celebrated Song
collection of Zen biographies *Record of the Transmission of the Lamp of the
Jingde Era*. The work, published in 1011, contains most of the pre–Song dynasty koans, but the "seventeen hundred" figure derives not from the number of cases included in the text but merely from the number of Zen teachers
mentioned—1,701, of which only 963 receive actual biographies.[70] While the
phrase "seventeen hundred koans" was in use in medieval China,[71] one can
presume that its meaning, like that of other similar rounded figures employed in classical Chinese, was not so much literal as metaphorical, a general, poetic way of indicating a lot of something—"many" koans, just as
"thirty years" indicated "extensive" study and training.

The it has been suggested[72] that the 1615 codes' interpretation of these Zen
expressions simply reflects ignorance on the part of their drafters and the

bakufu. Sūden, though technically a Gozan abbot, was not primarily a Zen teacher or scholar but a government official, preoccupied with secular as much as religious affairs, and, in formulating the temple codes, he may have relied on incomplete or faulty information, or even misconstrued facts he received regarding traditional requirements for abbacy at non-Gozan temples like Daitokuji and Myōshinji.[73] Still, it is hard to believe that the Tokugawa government, whom Sūden represented, was seriously disturbed over a reported slippage in standards for the training of Zen masters at the two Kyoto temples, and the complaints about ill-prepared candidates receiving certification may have been largely a pretext for the bakufu to reaffirm its control over the appointment procedure for abbots. Ultimately, however, what the codes mean when they refer to thirty years of Zen study and mastery of seventeen hundred koans remains rather murky, as does the bakufu's rationale for including these statements.

The 1615 decrees, not surprisingly, provoked considerable indignation within Daitokuji and Myōshinji, suggesting as they did that standards for Zen study at the two temples had grown lax and that the selection process for Zen masters and abbots had become degenerate and possibly corrupt. On the issue of direct appointment of imperial abbots, it is not clear precisely why Daitokuji, Myōshinji, and the reigning emperor, Gomizuno'o (1596–1680), failed to observe the bakufu's prior-reporting requirement. One can only speculate that such old dignities and privileges were as precious to their holders as they were obnoxious to the Tokugawa. In the end, the temples' assemblies seem by and large to have dealt with the decrees by simply ignoring them, as did the emperor, both parties continuing unchanged the practice of direct appointment of abbots, in disregard of the bakufu's requirement for official approval. The priest Sūden confided to his diary his pique at this defiance of the shogunate's orders,[74] but for over a decade no decisive action was taken by the government to enforce the decrees or to punish the temples.

Finally, however, official patience seems to have run out, and in 1626, the tenth anniversary of Ieyasu's death, his successor, Tokugawa Hidetada (1579–1632), issued an oral command suspending abbacies at Daitokuji and Myōshinji owing to their continuing violations of the decrees. Daitokuji apparently chose to ignore this new decree as well, and in early 1627 Takuan returned to Kyoto from Tajima and recommended his Dharma brother Gyokushitsu's heir Shōin Sōchi (d. 1629) as the temple's next abbot. Gomizuno'o duly issued his imperial order, and Shōin was installed, receiving his appointment and purple robe.

Bakufu reaction this time was swift and came in the form of yet another decree, issued three months later at Hidetada's order. Titled "Addressed to the Various Buddhist Sects" (*Shoshū hatto*), the new decree, promulgated by Sūden and the Kyoto shogunal administrator, Itakura Shigemune (1587–1656), canceled all imperial abbacies awarded in violation of the 1615 codes and confiscated the abbots' purple robes pending review by the bakufu. At Daitokuji this meant that some fifteen senior Zen masters faced having their abbacies retroactively revoked.

The temple's leadership was thrown into turmoil, uncertain how to respond now that the government had finally called the Daitokuji line to account for over a decade's willful disregard of official pronouncements. Opinion was divided, with the temple's Northern line, led by Takuan and his colleagues Gyokushitsu and Kogetsu, urging Daitokuji to stand its ground and uphold its ancient traditions, while the Southern line advocated an immediate apology and accommodation of the bakufu's demands. The deliberations concluded without agreement, and Takuan departed Kyoto, retiring to Daifukuji, a temple in Izumi Province, in what is now the Osaka Municipal District.

In 1628 Shigemune followed up his last decree with a second, firm rebuke, censuring Daitokuji for allowing Shōin's abbacy and demanding an explanation. The temple now found itself on a collision course with the shogunal government, a confrontation referred to by Japanese historians as the "Purple Robe Affair" (*shie jiken*).[75] At the assembly's urging, Takuan returned to Daitokuji and assumed a leading role in formulating the temple's response to the government's charges. The result was a letter of protest, addressed to the bakufu and consisting of a point-by-point refutation of the articles of the 1615 decree.[76]

Handwritten in a mixture of Chinese characters and *kana*,[77] Takuan's letter of 1628, still preserved at the Sakai temple Kōunji, is unflinchingly straightforward, even blunt at times in refuting the assertions of the Genna code. Though nowhere does he specifically broach the vexed question of direct imperial appointment of abbots, Takuan vigorously rejects the code's imputations that unqualified priests have been elevated to high office at Daitokuji and awarded the purple robe. Appointments as abbot are never made rashly or casually, Takuan declares, but are carried out in strict accordance with the temple's ancient traditions. No appointment can proceed until the assembly of monks has met three times, the senior masters have jointly imprinted their seals, and the decision has been reported to the imperial court. Takuan also denies that priests proposed for Daitokuji abbot have ever been unprepared, lacking the requisite years of experience and training. While their ages may vary, candidates having entered the temple life at different times, their actual years of monastic residence are identical, he says, and are openly recorded in the temple register.

Takuan's keenest invective is reserved for the provisions of the decree pertaining to Zen study, namely, the insistence that candidates for Daitokuji abbot must have completed thirty years of training and passed seventeen hundred koans.[78] As should be obvious, Takuan writes, "thirty years" and "seventeen hundred koans" are merely set Zen expressions, enjoining diligent and thoroughgoing practice. To take them literally, as the code appears to do, can only result from ignorance on the part of the drafter, as it reveals a basic misunderstanding of the character of Zen realization, which alone qualifies a priest to be certified a Zen master or abbot. By its very nature, Takuan contends, the enlightenment experience varies with the individual and cannot be arbitrarily quantified in terms of number of years of study or number of koans passed.

The issue of thirty years' training for abbots may have been a sensitive one for Takuan, who, it will be recalled, had received Daitokuji's abbacy only twenty-seven years after entering the Pure Land temple Shōnenji and only twenty-three years after beginning his actual practice of Zen at Sukyōji. In any case, he finds the whole notion to be without basis in either history or common sense. In neither China nor Japan, he points out, has there ever been a rule requiring thirty years of Zen training, and as proof he adduces the careers of numerous venerated medieval teachers who would have failed to meet the decree's artificially rigid standard. Myōan Eisai (1141–1215), often credited with being the first to transmit Zen to Japan, spent only five years with his Chinese teacher, Takuan observes, before receiving *inka* and returning to found the Kyoto temple Kenninji; Tōfukuji's founder, Enni Ben'en (Shōichi Kokushi, 1202–1280), received his Chinese teacher's *inka* after seven years' study, as did Nanpo Jōmyō (Daiō Kokushi), progenitor of the Daitokuji line; Daitō, Nanpo's heir and the founder of Daitokuji, was awarded sanction after only five years with his master; while Musō Sōseki (1275–1351), patriarch of the principal Gozan lineage, from which Sūden himself traced his descent, received *inka* a mere two years after meeting his teacher, the Rinzai Zen master and former imperial prince Kōhō Kennichi (1241–1316). Even on purely practical grounds, Takuan maintains, the thirty-year standard is untenable, as old monks alone could qualify as teachers and would lack the time needed to produce suitable heirs, imperiling the Zen transmission. The human life span, after all, is limited, and some gifted masters, like Daitō, die young.

Equally unreasonable, Takuan protests, is the code's call for mastery of seventeen hundred koans, another requirement without precedent in Chinese or Japanese Zen, seventeen hundred merely alluding to the number of teachers cited in *Transmission of the Lamp*. Daitō himself, Takuan says, completed only one hundred eighty koans under Nanpo, while Daitō's principal heir, Tettō Gikō (1295–1369), received Daitō's *inka* after passing a total of eighty-eight cases.[79] Takuan details the current Daitokuji koan curriculum,[80] which includes study of Daitō's capping phrases and of cases drawn from a variety of Chinese Zen classics, probably amounting to no more than two or three hundred koans altogether. "To declare that anyone has completed seventeen hundred koans nowadays," Takuan fumes, "is just trying to flatter them by spouting falsehoods."[81] Just as Zen enlightenment cannot be reduced to a fixed period of study, Takuan explains, it is not dependent on passing a certain number of koans or even on the koan method itself:

The Zen school has its own special transmission—it doesn't necessarily depend on koans. Precisely because of this, there have been many in the past who, even after mastering koans, failed to obtain *inka*.

During the Song dynasty, there were many Confucian officials who studied Zen. But because they were widely learned, greatly imbued with the teachings of all the various schools of thought, they were unable to concentrate their practice. They were therefore given one koan, and by centering their practice on this basic koan, they received an aid in their practice and readily penetrated the truth of Zen.[82] Studying koans, therefore, is for the purpose of bringing forth enlightenment. Once enlightenment has been realized, it is senseless to go on studying koans; so at that time, one is considered to have finished his training. All the words of the buddhas and patriarchs constitute koans, and one could not hope to finish with them even after five or seven *lifetimes* of study! Hence, finishing one's training does not mean that one has studied [all the koans].

In the past, attaining enlightenment was considered to mark the end of one's training, just as one needs a raft to cross a stream but, once having reached the other shore, the boat can be forgotten.[83] Enlightenment is not necessarily dependent on koans or on the number of years one spends in practice—it's [sudden] as a spark struck from flint or a flash of lightning. Once having finished his koan study, an accomplished teacher can, whether he's [finished] fifty or one hundred koans, thoroughly realize the teachings of the buddhas and patriarchs, using the wisdom that realizing one thing illumines ten thousand. . . .

... The fact that [monks nowadays] are studying more koans than the accomplished teachers of the past and declare themselves to have studied a large number of them in no way means that they are *superior* to the worthies of long ago! When out of ten [koans], a person can, by realizing two or three, realize the remaining seven as well, that constitutes widely pervading wisdom. However, if he cannot gain realization unless he goes through ten out of ten, that means he is *inferior* to his wise predecessors. As I have noted above, the number of years of study completed by the accomplished teachers of the past might be merely five, six, or seven. If they'd had to complete seventeen hundred koans, it would have been impossible in five or six years, even for an accomplished teacher. I don't know about the practice in other establishments, but here in our temple, the course of study is twenty years. There's nothing either now or in the past about needing thirty years of study.[84]

In protesting the terms of the code, Takuan insists that Daitokuji is not willfully defying the bakufu, but merely seeking to uphold its own time-honored traditions, among them its standards for the appointment of teachers and abbots. "In all things, including Zen study and practice, our temple has remained faithful to its ancient ways," he sums up. "To say it has done otherwise is a lie."[85] The document closes with the plea that Daitokuji be allowed to continue installing its imperial abbots as it has done for over three hundred years.

Takuan's letter was cosigned by Gyokushitsu and Kogetsu and addressed to the Kyoto administrator, Itakura Shigemune, who duly forwarded it to the capital. The document's vehemence and lack of contrition could hardly have been expected to mollify the bakufu, and early in 1629 the three Zen masters were summoned together to Edo. Here, in an attempt to defuse the increasingly volatile situation, they submitted a joint apology of sorts to the shogun's principal counselor, Doi Toshikatsu (1573–1644).[86] Regretting any lapses in courtesy, the new statement, once again handwritten by Takuan, apologizes for Daitokuji's failure to obtain prior approval of imperial abbacies and pledges in future to observe the government's directives on notification. The letter, that is, recognized, albeit belatedly, the terms of the Purple Robe Decree of 1613. It said nothing, however, of the additional issues raised in the subsequent (1615) Daitokuji code and as such was unlikely to satisfy the bakufu's representatives, particularly those like Sūden who had been personally instrumental in the code's drafting and promulgation.

In Edo the three masters put up at a Daitokuji branch temple, Kōtokuji, in the city's Kanda district, while their case was considered by a committee consisting of the priests Sūden, Tenkai, and the daimyo Tōdō Takatora. Takatora (1556–1630), a onetime Shingon priest who had returned to lay life, served under both Nobunaga and Hideyoshi and was currently daimyo of Ise Province (Mie Prefecture). Tenkai, a high-ranking Tendai abbot mentioned earlier as a formulator of Ieyasu's Nikkō cult, was, like Sūden and Takatora, the product of a warrior family, and he had served the early shoguns in a primarily religious capacity, performing rites that invoked the power of various buddhas and bodhisattvas to assure the welfare of the state and its rulers.

Called before the committee and examined, Takuan and Gyokushitsu reportedly refused to back down, reaffirming their criticisms of the Genna decree, though Kogetsu appears to have been more accommodating.[87] Provoked by Takuan's and Gyokushitsu's intransigence, Sūden demanded they be punished harshly. Both had knowingly and repeatedly rejected the terms of the shogunate's decrees, he declared, and had displayed disrespect for the authorities. Tenkai and Takatora, while acknowledging the masters' guilt, argued instead for milder measures, according to the account in the clan record of Takuan's patrons the Hosokawas, which details aspects of the committee's deliberations.[88] In particular, Tenkai is said to have been impressed that Takuan had taken full responsibility for the letter of protest to the bakufu and had asked that Gyokushitsu and Kogetsu be pardoned.

Even as powerful forces were being arrayed against Takuan and his colleagues, there emerged allies from within the shogunate's senior ranks. Chief among these, Takuan tells us, were Hori Naoyori and Yagyū Munenori. Naoyori, the lord of Echigo Province (Niigata Prefecture), fought under Hideyoshi and later Ieyasu, distinguishing himself during the Osaka campaign, in which he is said to have taken eighty-seven heads.[89] Munenori, as discussed earlier, was leader of the New Shadow school of swordsmanship (Shinkageryū) and sword instructor to both the shogun Hidetada and Hidetada's son and heir, Iemitsu. Munenori's father, Munetoshi, from whom he received headship of the New Shadow school, had ruled a modest domain in Yamato Province, in what is now Nara Prefecture. Confiscated by Hideyoshi, the Yagyū lands were restored to the clan by Ieyasu in recognition of Munenori's services at the Battle of Sekigahara. Also commended for his activities in the Osaka campaign, Munenori was, by the time of the Purple Robe Affair, a rising star in the capital and a member of the shogun's inner circle. Munenori apparently studied Zen, including koans, with Takuan, and in his 1632 *Art of the Sword* refers to Takuan as "my Dharma teacher."[90] It is unclear from the surviving accounts when he or Naoyori, both devoted patrons of Takuan, first met the master and under what circumstances.[91] But whether their association with Takuan was of long standing or largely a product of the master's 1629 sojourn in Edo, it is evident that both these samurai, with close ties to the shogunal administration, rallied to Takuan's support on personal rather than political grounds. "During this crisis over Daitokuji," Takuan recalled several years later, "no one else but these two lords, Yagyū and Hori, showed such sympathy, recognizing what a perilous situation I faced."[92] Takuan describes how the two samurai, placing their own palanquins at the disposal of himself and Gyokushitsu, personally escorted them to see Tenkai at the latter's temple in Ueno as well as meeting repeatedly with the shogun's senior advisors in attempts to intercede on the beleagured priests' behalf.[93]

During the spring of 1629, as Takuan awaited the bakufu's judgment, he participated in Kōtokuji's ninety-day *kessei*, or Zen retreat, in which he seems to have assumed a teaching role. For every day of the retreat,[94] he assigned to the temple's monks a Buddhist poem (*ge* or *geju*) he composed in classical Chinese, one for each of the eighty-seven characters of the Zen master Yuanwu Keqin's (1063–1135) introduction to *Blue Cliff Record* plus four additional poems. The resulting work, *Ninety Verses on Blue Cliff Record* (*Hekigan kyūjūge*),[95] testifies to the enduring popularity of this Zen classic in the Daitokuji line and to the fact that Takuan during this time was not wholly preoccupied by his imbroglio with the bakufu.

Barely a week after the retreat at Kōtokuji concluded, the shogunate rendered judgment in the Purple Robe Affair. Of the fifteen Daitokuji priests who had received imperial abbacy in defiance of the bakufu decrees, those still surviving, six masters altogether, had their titles revoked and their purple robes confiscated. Future imperial abbacies at Daitokuji remained suspended, and the temple's senior leadership was placed under house arrest. Similar punishments were imposed at Myōshinji, elements of which had joined in opposing the terms of the decrees. Emperor Gomizuno'o, who had issued the orders for the contested abbacies and had been at loggerheads with the bakufu for some time, registered his protest against the government's actions by abdicating at age thirty-three in favor of his six-year-old daughter, Empress Meishō (r. 1629–1643)—one of the rare instances of a woman assuming the Japanese throne.

As for the three signers of Daitokuji's letter of vindication, Takuan and Gyokushitsu were sentenced to exile in Japan's north, Takuan in lower Dewa (Yamagata Prefecture) and Gyokushitsu in Mutsu (Aomori Prefecture), then the country's northernmost province. Kogetsu, having apologized, was pardoned, spared punishment, according to the *Hosokawa Clan*

*Record,* because his guilt in the matter was deemed lighter than Takuan's or Gyokushitsu's and because the shogun wished to assure continuity of the Daitokuji Northern line's teaching. In return, however, Kogetsu had to pledge henceforth to strictly uphold the provisions of the bakufu's decrees.[96] There is no indication that Kogetsu's apology and pardon were regarded by either Takuan or Gyokushitsu as a betrayal. Relations among the three seem to have remained friendly, and during the years his companions passed in exile, Kogetsu is said to have busied himself in the capital actively campaigning for their release.[97]

No sooner had his sentence of exile been handed down than Takuan's daimyo patron Koide Yoshihide and his brother Yoshichika wrote asking to call on him, though Takuan, in his reply the next day, demurs, pointing out that he should not be meeting with anyone during this period.[98] These and other high-ranking samurai supporters, despite their fealty to the regime, seem to have stood loyally by Takuan in what can only have been a highly delicate situation for them.

Popular opinion, too, sided squarely with Takuan and Gyokushitsu, seen by members of all classes as principled victims of bullying by Sūden, who in turn was pilloried as the "evil national teacher of the temple of audacity on the mountain of greed."[99] Kogetsu, unfairly or not, was excoriated as craven for evading punishment and leaving his colleagues to face the government's wrath. "Painted scrolls by Kogetsu are being torn up and destroyed," Hosokawa Tadatoshi wrote from Edo to his father, Tadaoki, "and lampoons are scribbled on the city's major bridges: 'old bamboo blind,' 'beat-up umbrella,' 'scrawny nag,' 'old shop curtain' are some of the remarks."[100] In a similar vein, a satiric poem current in Edo played on the literal meanings of the names of the three Daitokuji Zen masters:

> When it rained
> The hut in the marsh [Takuan] and the jeweled chamber
> 		[Gyokushitsu] were washed away
> Leaving only the moon in the muddy river [Kogetsu].[101]

Many of the issues behind the Purple Robe Affair remain obscure to us today. Tsuji Zennosuke, in his extensive account of the episode, considers the entire standoff between Sūden and the Daitokuji faction led by Takuan to be at heart a struggle between the Tokugawa shogunate, of which Sūden was merely the representative, and the emperor. That is, he sees the temples and priests involved primarily as surrogates in a political tug of war between the bakufu and Gomizuno'o, the latter resisting the further erosion of his already much-diminished powers and privileges.[102] But in the end, we can only speculate as to the underlying causes, the actual rivalries and tensions that may have precipitated the crisis. What stands forth with considerable clarity, however, is the courageousness of Takuan's stand. In Tokugawa Japan, open questioning of the writ of the feudal authorities by any individual, even a high-ranking priest, was a serious undertaking that placed not only one's position but one's life in immediate jeopardy. The decrees regarding both the purple robe abbacies and Daitokuji had been issued during Ieyasu's lifetime, under his seal, and objections to them were bound to be construed as an affront to the shogunate's founder himself. The Tokugawa shoguns were notoriously touchy when it came to their dignity or that of their house, and even minor infractions or perceived evidence of disrespect could meet with swift and severe punishment.[103]

Within a week of the bakufu's sentence being handed down, Takuan and Gyokushitsu left Edo on their way into exile. Escorted to the city limits by friends and well-wishers who pressed on them gifts of incense, the two traveled together for the first three days of their journey north, parting at what is now the town of Odawara (Tochigi Prefecture), where they exchanged farewell verses.

On the fifteenth day of the eighth month of 1629, after more than two weeks on the road, Takuan arrived at his remote, northern place of exile, Kaminoyama, the castle town of the domain's young daimyo, Toki Yoriyuki. Though Takuan's warder as much as his host, Yoriyuki was certainly aware that his charge, while currently under an official cloud, was a person of distinction who retained prominent and influential friends in the shogunal administration. In any event, Yorikyuki, who himself had arrived in the domain only the previous year, seems to have taken immediately to the exiled Zen master. In the nearby village of Matsuyama, the daimyo erected for Takuan a retreat that included an antechamber, storeroom, bath and latrine, as well as servants' quarters and a verandah provided with double-paneled sliding doors as protection against the harsh northern winter. A deerskin was placed under Takuan's sleeping area to keep out the cold from below and prevent the master from catching a chill.[104] Takuan dubbed his new home "Spring Rain Hermitage" (Harusame-an), carving the characters "spring rain" into a wooden tablet that he hung over the entrance.[105]

Writing to his brother Hanbei, Takuan describes the extreme solicitousness of Yorikyuki and his family and followers, who appear to have done whatever they could to make the master's exile in the remote domain as comfortable as possible. He is a frequent visitor at the castle, Takuan reports, and at the hermitage all his needs are conscientiously anticipated and supplied. Rice, miso, salt, kindling, cooking oil, and vegetables arrive in a constant stream from the Toki larder itself. Every year Yoriyuki sends a robe from the capital, and the daimyo's wife has had made up for Takuan an underrobe of silk wadding.[106] "From time to time for my diversion, there arrive from the castle or the senior retainers lunch boxes [bentō] and such. To protest would be useless. Occasionally tea cakes are delivered, and even rice cakes ... which I ate every single day last winter and, needless to say, at New Year's. And this New Year's, too, I'm assured of an abundant supply."[107]

Even when Yoriyuki leaves the domain with his retinue to travel to Edo, Takuan says, he will stop after only two or three miles and order his senior retainers to see that in his absence the master lacks for nothing. "His Lordship," Takuan marvels to another correspondent, "treats me with a degree of cordiality that I would not have received in my native province. Even his samurai retainers display a rare level of hospitality, as if I were His Lordship's own grandfather."[108] Nor did Takuan's old friends neglect him. Letters and gifts arrived regularly from various benefactors, among them daimyo and senior government officials. One sends a robe, Takuan writes Hanbei, another tea. "If these people were afraid of His Highness [i.e., the shogun], they would never be able to send things. Yet look what's happening, how thoughtful they are!"[109]

Takuan's spirits could not but be buoyed by these expressions of support. He seems to have gathered from his correspondents, moreover, that sympathy for his and his colleagues' stand in the Purple Robe Affair remained strong, even among the population at large. "In all of Japan," he exults to Hanbei, "no one, it seems, speaks badly of us."[110] Musing on his personal situation, Takuan could reflect that whatever trials he had had to endure, his honor at least remained intact. Writing to Naoyori within days of his arrival at Kaminoyama, Takuan was philosophical. "Having spoken out harshly regarding the affairs of my sect," he tells his daimyo patron, "I displeased the authorities and was sent in exile to Dewa, something of which people will surely continue to speak for two or three generations. In this degenerate age, that one has a reputation to be preserved is satisfying in itself. So long as one's mind is free from dust and defilement, the body's sufferings mean nothing at all."[111]

To another acquaintance concerned for his welfare, Takuan observes that a monk, while subject in the same way as a layman to the vagaries of existence, must not be unduly troubled by them, aware of their ultimate

ephemerality. Having sacrificed everything to defend the true teaching of
Zen, Takuan writes, it would be unseemly for him now to betray the twin
principles of impermanence and nonattachment by giving way to self-pity
or even by encouraging others' concern:

> That one who leaves home [i.e., a monk] takes the three worlds[112] as his dwell-
> ing is to be expected, so there is nothing at all unhappy in his change of cir-
> cumstances. My current situation is not different from that of a samurai
> being transferred to another domain. So there is no cause for you to feel dis-
> turbed. To bewail things in the world or lament one's situation is for lay people.
> And even a lay person who has attained some understanding will not do this.
> How, then, can I, who have come to this pass for the sake of the Dharma and
> my late teacher, indulge in grief? There is no reason to distress yourself. It
> may be I'll be pardoned in the end, having been punished in the first place,
> and, if destiny allows, we two shall succeed in meeting again.[113]

At Kaminoyama, Takuan was visited by a former student, the young Zen
monk Isshi Monju.[114] Born into a court family, the Iwakura, Isshi began his
training at fourteen at the Kyoto Gozan headquarters temple Shōkokuji but
later traveled to Sakai, intending to study koans under Takuan. The young
priest had been elated to hear that by understanding one koan you could simultaneously understand ten thousand. But when he presented his understanding of Zen, Takuan, it is said, only laughed and told him, "I don't tie up
students by burdening them with a lot of useless talk. With one pill I cure all
their illnesses!"[115] Discouraged, Isshi left Sakai and received ordination from
a priest of the Precepts (Ritsu) school, but he subsequently returned to
Takuan. Always something of a loner, Isshi throughout his life would retain
his enthusiasm for koan practice and his devotion to the Buddhist precepts.
He is the only monk follower of Takuan's known to have joined the master in
Dewa, where he arrived sometime in late 1629 and remained for as much as a
year, serving as Takuan's attendant.[116]

There is scant record of Takuan's religious activities at this period. The
chronicles do not reveal, for example, whether Isshi, during his stay, continued koan study with Takuan or whether, during the course of the master's exile, any other monks came to seek his formal instruction, either
from local temples or from farther afield. Takuan's host, the daimyo Toki
Yoriyuki, however, reportedly received Takuan's teaching of Zen as it related to the martial arts, specifically to combat with the Japanese lance
(*yari*), of which Yoriyuki was an adept, a disciple of a noted master of the

day, Matsumoto Sadayoshi.[117] "Master [Takuan]," *Record of the Founder of the Myriad Pines [Temple]* records, "had a valorous spirit, and always in teaching [Yoriyuki] the meaning of Zen spoke about the military arts, truly exhausting their ineffable principles. Therefore, Lord Yoriyuki, in discussing the lance with the master, was able to attain the inner spirit of its art, founding his own school of the lance, which he called the Self-Attainment school. The master even composed a transmission document [*densho*] of several *kan* and presented it to His Lordship."[118] Yoriyuki's teacher, Sadayoshi, also is said to have been deeply struck by Takuan's teaching of Zen and the lance, visiting the master in Kaminoyama on several occasions and, like Yoriyuki, receiving a transmission document composed by Takuan.[119] Sadly, neither of these documents survives.

In his letters from Kaminoyama, Takuan refuses to lament the injustice of his punishment by the authorities or to voice any feelings of discouragement he may have harbored regarding his situation. Physically, however, the years had begun to take their toll, and Takuan had no compunction about mourning the unmistakable signs of advancing age. "This year I will be fifty-eight," he writes in 1630 to a young samurai acquaintance. "My sight is growing dim, and I have difficulty even in deciphering correspondence. For Your Lordship, at fifteen or sixteen, yesterday is much like today. But before one realizes, one has become an old man."[120]

In 1632 Tokugawa Hidetada died at age fifty-three, leaving his son and heir Iemitsu to assume full authority as shogun. Hidetada had formally retired in 1623, but, following a common precedent for Japanese emperors and shoguns, continued to rule from behind the scenes, effectively directing all the government's actions, including management of the Purple Robe Affair. That is, Iemitsu, though nominally the reigning shogun during the period of Daitokuji's confrontation with the bakufu, had no personal involvement in the events that led to Takuan's letter of protest and eventual punishment.

As was customary upon the death of a ruler, a general amnesty was declared following Hidetada's demise. The religious merit accruing from such clemency, it was believed, could be transferred to the spirit of the deceased, but amnesty was also considered an auspicious way to inaugurate a new and hopefully virtuous reign. The result was that, in late summer 1632, Takuan and Gyokushitsu found themselves pardoned and on their way back to Edo from their places of exile. Both priests were shortly reunited in the capital, settling in once more at Kōtokuji to await further developments in their case.[121]

While in Edo, Takuan was frequently able to visit Lord Yoriyuki, who had been in the city when Takuan's pardon was announced. On Yoriyuki's return to Dewa that fall, Takuan wrote expressing his gratitude for the young daimyo's kindness,[122] and the following year he painted a portrait of Yoriyuki, adding a dedicatory verse. Takuan seems to have remained in close contact with Yoriyuki, and *Record of the Founder of the Myriad Pines [Temple]* claims that the domainal library preserved no fewer than ninety letters from the master to the daimyo.[123]

During the winter of 1632, Takuan had left Kōtokuji for the Edo residence of Hori Naoyori. Tokugawa daimyo typically maintained comfortable, well-appointed villas in the capital, and Naoyori must have been pleased to host Takuan after the master's nearly three years in exile. Although able to make an excursion to nearby Kamakura, Takuan was still forbidden to travel to Kyoto, and the Daitokuji leadership itself remained under house arrest. It was not until summer 1634 that Takuan and Gyokushitsu were permitted at last to return to Daitokuji, and the temple's leadership together with that of Myōshinji were released from their sentence of confinement.

Arriving in Kyoto after five years' absence, the masters first paid their respects to the shogunate's representative, Itakura Shigemune, at his headquarters before proceeding to Daitokuji, where Takuan informed the assembled monks of the bakufu's decision. In a letter to Yoshihide, Takuan proclaims his satisfaction at the latest turn of events, which had only been made possible, he says, through the intercession of Naoyori and Tenkai.[124] The two had been untiring in their campaign on Takuan's behalf since the inception of his difficulties with the government and had continued their efforts throughout the master's years in exile in Dewa. Now, with both Hidetada and Sūden having passed on and a new, younger shogun installed in full command, Takuan's allies must have seen an opportunity to engineer the master's full rehabilitation.

Several days after his return to Daitokuji, Takuan left Kyoto for Sakai and his home temple, Nanshūji. From there he hoped to travel to his native Tajima, but his plans were delayed by the arrival of a messenger from Naoyori, Tenkai, and Munenori advising that the shogun was on his way to Kyoto and urging Takuan to use the occasion to thank Iemitsu and the senior bakufu advisors for his pardon. Initially, Takuan says, he tried to beg off, insisting that he was too insignificant a person to meet the shogun,[125] but his friends were persistent, and after two more messengers were dispatched, Takuan relented.

Iemitsu arrived in Kyoto early in the seventh month of 1634 at the head of a retinue of thirty thousand warriors and inaugurated his stay by distributing five thousand pieces of silver to the townspeople. Kyoto was not only Japan's former capital, headquarters of the Muromachi bakufu, but remained after eight hundred years the seat of the emperor and the court, making the shogun's progress to the ancient city very much a state event. It has been suggested that a primary purpose of Iemitsu's visit was to patch up relations with the throne, severely strained under the policies of Iemitsu's father and grandfather.[126] Indeed Iemitsu took the opportunity to meet with the empress and the retired emperor, Gomizuno'o, and to considerably increase the latter's stipend. Gomizuno'o had been directly involved in the Purple Robe Affair, complicit with Takuan in the temples' resistance to the government; and the lifting of restrictions against the Daitokuji and Myōshinji leaders, the remission of Takuan's and Gyokushitsu's exile, even Iemitsu's willingness to receive Takuan in audience may all have been part of a larger effort to smooth over bakufu-imperial tensions.

Accompanied by Naoyori and Munenori, Takuan was received by Iemitsu at Nijō Palace, the shogun's official residence in Kyoto, erected by Ieyasu in 1603.[127] Nothing is known of the content of Takuan's audience with the shogun, which may have been more formal than substantive, and the following day the master paid his respects to the shogun's senior advisors before preparing to return to Sakai. A messenger, however, arrived from Iemitsu, asking Takuan to prolong his stay, an overture hinting that the master already had captured the shogun's interest.

Takuan seems to have been quite ill during this period, and his original reluctance to leave Sakai to meet Iemitsu may have been attributable as much to poor physical health as to modesty. "I feel half dead and half alive," he confided to Yoshihide from Kyoto. "From here on I have lost my strength."[128] Even Iemitsu, who himself suffered debilitating bouts of illness, expressed his concern when he met the master.

While in Kyoto that summer, Takuan was also summoned on two occasions by Gomizuno'o, with whom he discussed Zen. The retired emperor, twenty-three years Takuan's junior, cultivated a sincere interest in the school and over the course of his lifetime patronized and associated with many of the eminent Rinzai priests of his day, not only Takuan and Takuan's student Isshi Monju but the Myōshinji teacher Gudō Tōshoku (1579–1661) and even the immigrant Ming master Yinyuan Longqi (1592–1673).

By autumn Takuan was able to resume his itinerary, returning to Sakai, where he officiated as founder of a newly completed temple, Shōunji, erected

for him by a wealthy merchant follower.[129] He then continued on to his
final destination, Izushi, and his beloved retreat, Tōenken. Soon, however,
there arrived a summons commanding Takuan to appear before the shogun in Edo together with Gyokushitsu and Kogetsu. Even poor health
could not excuse Takuan from complying with this order, which bore the
joint signatures of the shogun's senior advisors, including Itakura Shigemune and Doi Toshikatsu. Reluctantly, therefore, Takuan had to abandon
the serenity of Tōenken and set off once more for Edo, where he arrived in
the winter of 1636.

On this occasion, Takuan stayed at the Azabu[130] mansion of his patron
Yagyū Munenori, who in the period since Takuan's exile had continued his
ascent in the shogunal administration. As Iemitsu's sword instructor,
Munenori was an intimate of the young shogun, who in 1632 appointed
him to the office of *sōmetsuke,* or inspector general. The position involved
monitoring those daimyo and their retainers who held bakufu office and
reporting any suspicious activity among their ranks.[131] The appointment
lasted until 1636, when as a sign of the shogun's increasing favor, Munenori
himself was awarded the rank of daimyo and his stipend increased to ten
thousand *koku,* or bushels of rice.[132]

It is Munenori who is traditionally credited with first bringing Takuan
to Iemitsu's notice. Iemitsu, the stories have it, had mastered the art of the
sword through unremitting practice yet could never best his teacher,
Munenori. Asked why this was so, Munenori told the shogun that he had
taught him everything he knew that could be imparted verbally but that to
go beyond that Iemitsu would have to master the art within his own mind,
as Munenori himself had done by studying with a certain Zen monk. "Who
is he?" Iemitsu then demanded. "Send him here now!" Munenori replied
that the priest was Takuan of Daitokuji, a distant Dharma descendant of
the temple's founder, Daitō. When Munenori was still inexperienced, he
explained to the shogun, he had asked Takuan about Zen and been told the
principle of Kannon's whole body being arms and eyes.[133] From that moment, whether asleep or awake, he worked on understanding this and finally attained the realm of freedom, he said, so that now no swordsman
could touch him, and he remained at all times in harmony with this one
constant principle. Munenori's mastery of the sword, he confided to Iemitsu, was entirely the result of his Zen study with Takuan.[134]

It was not until that summer (1636) that Takuan, Gyokushitsu, and Kogetsu were called to Edo castle for their audience with Iemitsu. The shogun
questioned them in turn about various topics involving Buddhism and Zen,

and also reportedly pressed the three regarding their previous opposition to the bakufu's temple codes. In the possibly overblown account of the audience recorded in the Hosokawa clan record, the shogun gently chides Gyokushitsu, telling him, "From here on, I presume, you will accept the divine ancestor's [i.e., Ieyasu's] decree that one becomes a Zen master only after thirty years' hard practice and reaching the age of fifty."[135] To which Gyokushitsu bluntly replies, "If one has not attained enlightenment, then whether he is fifty or a hundred, he will not be able to become a Zen master. Becoming a Zen master has nothing to do with one's age—only with whether one has realized the Way." Acknowledging Gyokushitsu's explanation, Iemitsu declares, "I now realize that Sūden's statements were outrageous!"[136]

Takuan's own responses at the audience are said to have particularly impressed Iemitsu,[137] and, while Gyokushitsu and Kogetsu were permitted to return to Kyoto, Takuan was detained in the capital. Early that fall, he was summoned one evening to attend the shogun along with Munenori, who was ordered to present his views on the art of swordsmanship. Iemitsu invited his senior advisor Hotta Masamori to join the discussion. Masamori, a devoted retainer who fifteen years later would commit ritual suicide to follow Iemitsu in death,[138] proceeded to draw out Takuan on different subjects. The shogun took such pleasure in the exchange that he requested Takuan to make a record of what had been said; he was so occupied with affairs of state, Iemitsu complained, he sometimes tended to forget things. Over the next three days, Takuan duly compiled an account of what transpired at this and subsequent meetings, which he submitted, to the delight of the shogun.[139]

Finally allowed to leave Edo, Takuan traveled to Kyoto, then journeyed north to Tajima, returning to Kyoto and Daitokuji in time for the three hundredth anniversary of the death of Daitō. Takuan remarked on the crowds attending the elaborate commemorative service, not only monks of the Daitokuji line but representatives of the Gozan temples and the imperial court as well as high-ranking samurai and commoners.[140]

The new year found Takuan back at the Sakai Nanshūji, the temple he had inherited from his teacher and painstakingly restored after its destruction in the Osaka campaign. Although the assembly of monks beseeched him to retain personal charge of the temple, Takuan was anxious to turn over custody of Nanshūji to the Daitokuji Northern branch. The master was in poor health and yearned to spend whatever years remained to him in some quiet, rural retreat, unburdened by the administrative responsibilities entailed by abbacy of a large Zen temple and relieved of the increasingly frequent demands to attend the young Tokugawa shogun, demands that threatened to trap Takuan in the capital for much of the year. "If only I can hand over Nanshūji," Takuan writes Yoshihide, "... I'll have nothing more weighing on my mind and can live in retreat in the mountains, spending at least a year in some dwelling remote from human contact, freed from care. I'd like nothing better than to live out the remainder of my days like that, but being called to Edo means endless trouble and annoyance.... Even if I manage to hang on till I'm seventy, that's only another five years—a brief time. I have no interest in fame or fortune. How relieved I'd feel if only I could spend what's left of my life in the mountains of Your Lordship's domain,[141] even if it were for just one year or half a year."[142]

Part of Takuan's urgency in transferring responsibility for Nanshūji had been his very real fear that, when he departed in three months for Edo to join Iemitsu, he might die en route, leaving no one suitable to inherit the temple.[143] And in fact the master did fall seriously ill on his journey back to the capital in spring 1637, delaying his return.

Sixteen thirty-seven was a disquieting year for the Tokugawa shogunate, which confronted a rebellion centered in Shimabara (Nagasaki Prefecture), a peninsula on Japan's southern island of Kyushu. Protesting the oppressive rule of the local daimyo—the lords of Shimabara and the nearby Amakusa islands[144]—a coalition of aggrieved samurai, peasants, and Christian adherents had entrenched themselves behind the walls of a deserted castle, where they were besieged by the bakufu's forces under Itakura Shigemune's younger brother, Shigemasa (1588–1638). Takuan mentions the rebellion in his correspondence, noting that the rebels numbered 24,300 men and women, including apostate Christians and townspeople.[145] The bakufu was hard put to quell the uprising, and Shigemasa was felled by an arrow as he led one of the many failed assaults on the redoubt. Takuan remarks on Shigemasa's death as well as the fall of the castle in spring 1638 to a massive force under the shogun's retainer Matsudaira Nobutsuna (1596–1662), an event accompanied by the massacre of all the stronghold's surviving defenders.[146] The two daimyo whose misrule had ignited the rebellion were stripped of their domains and died by their own hands in disgrace. The protracted campaign, while a reminder that the age of armed conflict was not wholly past, proved to be the last serious military challenge the regime would face for over two hundred years.

In Edo, Takuan put up once again at Munenori's Azabu mansion. He was summoned more and more frequently to attend the shogun, visiting regularly at the castle and joining Iemitsu in his tea hut and at private Nō performances. (Tea and Nō were art forms popular with the period's warrior elite, who were themselves often amateur practitioners. Iemitsu was an avid tea ceremony devotee and Munenori a Nō enthusiast who delighted in performing.) In a letter to his hometown acquaintances,[147] Takuan breathlessly recounts his growing intimacy with Iemitsu. "I was invited to join [the shogun] at his charcoal brazier [*kotatsu*] on the dais," Takuan writes, "where for two hours we sat and conversed, our knees only two *shaku* [approximately two feet] apart. No one else remains for so long so close to His Majesty."[148]

Iemitsu at this time was convalescing from a serious illness and, as Takuan notes to his friends, refused to admit even the leading daimyo to his presence, whether at the palace proper or at his tea hut, where meetings with the senior counselors were often convened. Even other Buddhist priests, with the exception of Tenkai, were barred from the shogun's quarters during his recovery. Yet Iemitsu not only summoned Takuan regularly, the master reports, but had even visited him at the Yagyū mansion, where, joined by Munenori, they talked from noon till dusk. The very next day, called by Iemitsu to the palace, the three talked well into the night.

Takuan continues his accounting of Iemitsu's special acts of favor with a description of how, one evening several days afterward, he and Munenori were commanded to join the shogun at his tea hut. Takuan, like many Daitokuji masters of the period, was a tea aficionado, and Iemitsu had expressed a wish to see Takuan's personal collection of tea utensils. Escorted along the lantern-lit path by the shogun's retainer Matsudaira Nobutsuna, who the following year would lead the bakufu forces to victory at Shimabara, Takuan and Munenori arrived at the shogun's tea hut. As he crouched to enter, Takuan saw that the scroll Iemitsu had chosen for the occasion[149] displayed calligraphy by Xutang Zhiyu, Nanpo's Chinese teacher and the progenitor of Takuan's Daitokuji teaching line. Iemitsu himself then appeared and, calling for a candle to be lit, had Takuan set out for him the various tea items he had brought—a tea kettle, tea bowls, a vase for flowers, a water dipper, and so forth.[150] On another occasion, Iemitsu's senior retainers were greatly surprised when the shogun showed Takuan several of his own tea things, items he had never before displayed. Takuan seems at times overwhelmed by the shogun's extraordinary attentions, marks of favor that he is sure, he tells his Tajima friends, will gratify Lord Yoshihide, to whom they will presumably pass on the information in the letter.[151]

Takuan's closeness with Iemitsu was also noted by Hosokawa Tadatoshi. In a report to his domain, Tadatoshi records his own growing admiration for the master and cites an episode involving Takuan's advice to a grieving parent:

Master Takuan is well and daily increases in the shogun's favor. I often have the opportunity to speak with [Takuan], and the better I get to know him, the more impressed with him I become. A fascinating phenomenon!

Some time ago there was a parent grieving the loss of his child, who had been killed. I heard something interesting in this connection. A person came and told the parent, "Do not grieve for what is gone forever." To which the Master declared, "Grieve as much as you want! In happiness, be happy; in sadness, be sad. This is the supreme truth of Buddhism."

Taking the Master's words as they are, it seems as if he is no different from ordinary people. It made me understand that by being happy or sad, sharing the same feelings as ordinary people, one enters the place that is lofty as the mountains, deep as the ocean.[152]

Takuan affirms here the importance of one's natural, authentic response, offering a very human example of the spontaneity and directness of mind that he espoused in his early essay on principle and function and that he sets at the heart of his instructions on Zen and the sword. Tadatoshi's account, included in the Hosokawa clan record, suggests the combination of honesty, charm, and compassion that must have made Takuan so appealing to Iemitsu and the members of his entourage.

As Tokugawa shogun, Iemitsu faced few limits on his power or his whims, and in both personal and political matters he was generally accustomed to having his way. We know from Takuan's correspondence that Iemitsu delighted in the master's company, valued his counsel, and chafed at constantly having to recall Takuan to the capital when he wished him in attendance. Even before Takuan's return to Edo in spring 1637, Iemitsu had set afoot plans to find him permanent lodgings in the city, ordering his senior retainer Hotta Masamori to erect a mansion for the master in Edo. On his return, however, Takuan declined to settle in the newly constructed home, and Iemitsu had to order it destroyed. Takuan feared that a regular residence in the capital would leave him a virtual prisoner to Iemitsu's constant demands for his society, which, flattering as they were, already constrained the master from freely visiting Kyoto and Sakai or enjoying for long the quiet and solitude of his Tajima retreat. Consequently, Takuan elected to continue living as a guest in Munenori's Edo compound, where he occupied a detached dwelling he sardonically dubbed "Detention Hermitage" (Kensoku-an).

Undeterred, Iemitsu continued to press Takuan to establish appropriate quarters of his own in Edo and simply visit Kyoto as needed, for therapeutic baths and such. But Takuan remained adamant in his refusal, telling

Iemitsu, "For thirty years now I have abandoned the world to make my home in the mountains and forests. One or two years is all I have left, so I beg Your Highness to excuse me."[153] The shogun, however, urged Takuan to reconsider, for the sake of both Daitokuji and Buddhism.

In 1638 Iemitsu abandoned the notion of establishing Takuan in a mansion and proposed instead erecting a temple in Edo exclusively for the master's use.[154] Takuan, by his own account, remained a frequent and conspicuous visitor at the palace, consulted by Iemitsu on a variety of questions, and Iemitsu complained that it was unseemly for some monk living in a corner of Munenori's home to be constantly summoned by the shogun in private like a spy or secret agent. Moreover, Iemitsu told Takuan, he expected to have the master advise him on issues regarding the Buddhist sects, much as Iemitsu's father and grandfather had been advised by Sūden. For all these reasons, he concluded, it would be more suitable for Takuan to occupy his own temple in the capital. But this idea, too, the master rejected, prompting the exasperated Iemitsu to exclaim, "From the foot of Kyushu to the tip of Mutsu [then the southernmost and northernmost areas of Japan], what other monk or layman but you would dare to decline my request!"[155] And he again pointedly reminded Takuan that such a shogunally endowed branch temple in the capital would surely redound to the glory of Daitokuji.

Iemitsu also discussed the proposed temple with Munenori, Takuan's host, stating that he envisioned an establishment at least equal in grandeur to Konchi-in, Sūden's Edo headquarters. Munenori, however, knowing Takuan as he did, warned that the master was likely to resist such a plan, to which Iemitsu peevishly protested that all he ever heard was that Takuan would be bothered by this or that, while his, Iemitsu's, own concerns were never taken into account.

Munenori's advice to Takuan, however, stressed the futility of further provoking Iemitsu. Even if Takuan refused to accept the shogun's offer, Munenori pointed out, he would inevitably find himself detained in Edo by Iemitsu on one pretext or another. Whether Takuan made his home in Edo and spent time in Kyoto, or made his home in Kyoto (and presumably Sakai) only to have Iemitsu repeatedly call him to the capital, the problem would remain essentially the same.[156]

In spring 1638 Iemitsu summoned Takuan to Edo castle and demanded the master's final answer to his proposal. Takuan declared that he was prepared to accede to the shogun's wishes but begged to be excused from serving in any official, government capacity and fulfilling the sort of role performed by his late tormentor, the priest-administrator Sūden.[157]

Several days later Iemitsu formally announced the plans for Takuan's temple at a meeting of his five senior counselors, the leading figures in the shogunal government,[158] specially assembled for the purpose along with Takuan at Iemitsu's new tea hut in the town of Shinagawa. It was here in Shinagawa, Iemitsu told his retainers, that he intended to erect the new temple, on a site that he found both aesthetically pleasing and convenient to visit. Everyone congratulated Takuan on his good fortune, and the meeting broke up, with the counselors returning to the capital. Takuan wished to join them but was detained till nightfall by Iemitsu, talking and exchanging poems. It was the first day of the fourth month of the lunar calendar (approximately May 5), the day of the seasonal "change of clothes" (*koromogamae*) that heralded the approach of summer, and the shogun offered a *waka* that seemed to hint gently at the coming change in Takuan's own situation:

> From today we shed our old robes
> > that had cloaked us like spring mist
> The mind grows clear
> Along with the mountains and the sea[159]

Now a part of Tokyo's central business district, Shinagawa in Takuan's day was a rural village, the southern gateway to Edo and the fifty-second station on the Tōkaidō, or "Eastern-Sea Road," the great fifty-three-station highway that linked Kyoto and the shogunal capital.[160] Iemitsu is said to have personally escorted Takuan to the temple's proposed site, which, as suggested by the shogun's poem, was surrounded by hills on several sides and commanded a view of the sea to the east. Rice fields stood nearby, along with a forest of bamboo and a Shinto shrine set amid a grove of pine trees, the likely inspiration for the temple's formal name, Manshōzan, "mountain of myriad pines." Its actual temple name, Tōkaiji, "temple of the eastern sea," may have referred in part to its prospect of what is now Tokyo Bay and its situation on the Tōkaidō; but it referred primarily to the last line of a famous poem given to Nanpo Jōmyō on his departure from Song China by his transmission teacher, Xutang: "My heirs in the eastern sea [i.e., Japan] will increase day by day."[161] The verse expresses confidence not only in Nanpo's realization but in his ability to spread Xutang's Zen in Japan and as such foretells the founding of Daitokuji's teaching line by Nanpo's successor Daitō.

Doubtless the name Tōkaiji had been chosen by Takuan himself to honor Daitokuji and its patriarchs. But neither the temple's auspicious name nor its scenic surroundings managed to dispel the master's overriding sense of entrapment. Forced to relinquish his hopes of retiring to the serenity of an isolated mountain hermitage, Takuan foresaw that with the erection of Tōkaiji he would find himself largely confined to the capital, living out his final years at the shogun's beck and call. To Yoshihide, the master lamented that he felt like a monkey that, because it could imitate human beings, was tied to a leash and pulled about—a clear result, Takuan concedes, of his own karma.[162]

Construction of Tōkaiji began immediately. A memorial service for Takuan's teacher Ittō was to be held later that month at Daitokuji, an event Takuan was no doubt anxious to attend. But he was prevailed upon by Tenkai and Tadakatsu to delay his departure while arrangements regarding Tōkaiji were being finalized and did not leave for Kyoto till midsummer 1638.[163] After paying his respects at Daitokuji, Takuan traveled south through the provinces of Yamato and Kii (present-day Nara, Mie, and Nakayama Prefectures), stopping at Nanshūji in Sakai before returning to Kyoto in the fall. Here he was summoned by Gomizuno'o, his old ally in the Purple Robe Affair, who urged Takuan to remain for a time in the city. Over several days Takuan lectured for the retired emperor on various Buddhist texts, including *On the Original Nature of Man* (*Yuan ren lun*), a celebrated work by the Tang dynasty Zen and Huayan master Zongmi (780–841).

Later that fall, Gomizuno'o announced his intention to award Takuan the title of National Teacher (*kokushi*). This was the highest honor a Japanese Zen master could receive and one that was often bestowed posthumously. Takuan, however, declined, asking instead that the title be given to Daitokuji's first-generation abbot, Daitō's successor Tettō Gikō. Six weeks later, Gomizuno'o complied, personally inscribing the imperial proclamation, which Takuan read out to the assembled monks in the Daitokuji Dharma hall. Isshi Monju, Takuan's former student and a favorite of the retired emperor, was so moved by Takuan's actions that he added a verse and preface to the imperial rescript, praising the master's selflessness and his simple and austere way of life.[164]

Another laudatory comment was appended by Takuan's colleague the Daitokuji abbot Tenyū Jōkō (d. 1666). In his remarks Tenyū briefly surveys Takuan's recent history: the master's letter to the bakufu upholding Daitokuji's ancient traditions; his exile, eventual pardon, and return to Daitokuji; his patronage by Iemitsu; and the founding of Tōkaiji at the shogun's insistence. He particularly notes Takuan's utter lack of self-seeking, evidenced by the master's declining the proffered National Teacher title in favor of Tettō and by his trying to decline Iemitsu's offer of a temple—all proof, Tenyū insists, of a rare and outstanding humility.[165] The close of Tenyū's tribute includes an oblique reference to another aspect of Takuan's story widely remarked by his contemporaries: the master's unwillingness to designate a Zen successor, or Dharma heir. "The transmission that is not transmitted," Tenyū tersely observes in acclaiming Takuan, "transcends the transmission that is transmitted."[166]

Following the ceremony bestowing Tettō's posthumous title, Takuan proceeded to Tajima, where he seems to have passed the winter, returning to Edo only in spring of 1639. The master may have availed himself of this opportunity to make an extended stay in his home province before the erection of Tōkaiji effectively clipped his wings, compelling his regular presence in the capital. Within a week of his arrival in Edo, Takuan was summoned to an audience with Iemitsu, and three days later he undertook the move to Shinagawa and the newly completed Tōkaiji. The next month Iemitsu paid what would be the first of the shogun's many visits to the temple, some seventy-five altogether over Takuan's seven-year residence.[167]

Great care had been taken to ensure that Tōkaiji had all the resources required to function smoothly and sustain itself as a suitable headquarters for Takuan, a place where he could comfortably receive the shogun and other distinguished guests. The temple was assigned a staff of five cleaning monks and eight servants to tend to the buildings and the extensive grounds, where Takuan notes that tall grasses grew wild.[168] As a shogunally conferred temple (*shuinji*), moreover, Tōkaiji was endowed by Iemitsu with an annual stipend of five hundred *koku,* supplemented by a further twenty *hyo* (sacks of rice) for the support of the monks and lay servants. Takuan balked at the stipend, which he regarded as excessive, protesting to the shogun that such luxury was unnecessary. To have enough to eat every day of the year, he informed Iemitsu, seven *tō* and two *shō,* less than a single *koku* of rice, was more than sufficient.[169] Iemitsu, however, ignored Takuan's qualms on this score and for good measure had the surrounding rice fields made over to the temple in perpetuity.[170] Even a night watch was provided at the shogun's insistence, recruited from the local peasants, who would patrol the precincts nine men at a time.[171]

More than any other single event, the founding of Tōkaiji bore witness to the dramatic change that had occurred in Takuan's circumstances, his transformation from exiled agitator to shogunal confidant. Over a decade had passed since the Purple Robe Affair and Takuan's sentence of exile. But, while the master's own situation had altered drastically, Daitokuji itself continued to labor under the punitive restrictions on new abbacies imposed by

Sūden and the bakufu. This remained a matter of intense concern to Takuan, who used every opportunity to raise the issue with Iemitsu and his advisors. Takuan reports that he explained the actual circumstances of the Purple Robe Affair to Sakai Tadakatsu, who confessed, "I hadn't any idea at all about these things!" declaring himself surprised to learn the facts of the dispute, which Takuan insisted never should have gone as far as an official proceeding.[172] Takuan's comments imply that the blame for what he regards as the exorbitant punishment meted out to the temples lay squarely with Sūden for misleading the government and senior samurai officials like Tadakatsu. Although, following his pardon, Takuan disavowed any lingering grudge against Sūden,[173] he would later angrily denounce the priest as "an evil spirit and heretic."[174]

By 1640 Iemitsu's health had greatly improved, making him a frequent visitor at Tōkaiji and doubtless allowing Takuan to redouble his efforts to have the shogun lift the ban on Daitokuji abbacies. Writing to Yoshihide, Takuan described his elation on learning that Kogetsu and Tenyū had been summoned from Kyoto by the authorities to consult on resolving the outstanding problems arising from the Purple Robe Affair. To see Daitokuji's imperial abbacy reinstated and have the temple assume its full former dignity, Takuan confides to Yoshihide, would be the crowning joy of his life.[175]

In early spring 1641 Takuan was summoned to appear before the shogun's privy council. There he was informed by Tadakatsu, the council's spokesman, that in the interest of seeing the Dharma flourish, Iemitsu had forgiven Daitokuji and Myōshinji, and revoked the suspension of new abbacies at the temples. The document setting forth the government's decision, while affirming the "excellence of the divine ancestor's decrees," states that henceforth the temples are to resume their time-honored traditions of imperial abbacy, with the stipulation that all appointments must first be reported to the Kyoto shogunal representative before being brought to the attention of the emperor.[176] Takuan conveyed the bakufu's decision to Daitokuji's elders, who transmitted it to the joyous assembly of monks.

After a fourteen-year hiatus, imperial abbacies at Daitokuji quickly resumed, and, perhaps in a bid to make up for lost time, the period 1641–1642 saw a great many abbots installed at the temple.[177] To Kōkō Shuso, a colleague at Nanshūji, Takuan confided something of his own delight and sense of relief at the long struggle's successful outcome:

> I hope all is well at Nanshūji. I received your letter of some time back but was
> unable to answer it. Since last winter I've had the two senior priests [Kogetsu

and Tenyū] here at the temple and have been constantly beset by visitors and official matters so that, as you can imagine, I haven't had a moment to myself. However, the fact that Daitokuji's affairs have now been resolved, the fruit of years of hard work, gives me great satisfaction. . . . This is the happiest moment of my life. Now I can simply wait for death.[178]

Through his intimate connection with Iemitsu, Takuan had played a central role in engineering restoration of Daitokuji's imperial abbacy, a fact Iemitsu himself seemed to acknowledge when in spring of 1641 he summoned the master to his tea hut. This time as Takuan knelt to enter, he noted that the calligraphy displayed in the alcove belonged to Kogaku Sōkō (1465–1548), a previous Daitokuji abbot. The shogun announced that he had chosen the piece deliberately because Kogaku was a Zen master in Takuan's line and added that now that he, Iemitsu, had dealt with Daitokuji's situation in accord with Takuan's long-standing wishes, he imagined that the master was not dissatisfied.[179]

The resumption of imperial abbacies also represented a kind of personal vindication for Takuan. "The assemblies of both temples," the *Account of the Life of Master Takuan* observes, "were overjoyed to see their traditions restored. Previously all the monks had impugned the Master for associating with the powerful and important, seeking after fame and fortune. Now, however, they reversed their earlier opinion, declaring, 'But for the Master, things would never have been put to rights!'"[180]

As the *Account* suggests, Takuan's proximity to Iemitsu and his ties to prominent Tokugawa daimyo apparently troubled many of his contemporaries at Daitokuji and Myōshinji, who regarded such connections as incompatible with Takuan's position as a Zen teacher and abbot. If the traditional biographies are to be believed, however, Takuan over the course of his career declined as many contacts with the powerful and eminent as he accepted. As noted earlier, Hideyoshi's heir, Hideyori, and the warlords Kuroda Nagamasa and Ishida Mitsunari all found their overtures to Takuan rebuffed. Yet the master seems to have been genuinely close to some of his daimyo patrons such as Munenori and Yoshihide, the latter the recipient of the bulk of Takuan's surviving correspondence. As for Iemitsu, one must bear in mind that the Tokugawa shogun wielded virtually absolute power, and his commands were not to be ignored, even by a distinguished Zen master with a reputation for stubborn integrity.

To some extent, Takuan did manage to impose his own terms on the relationship with Iemitsu. In particular, he elicited the shogun's agreement to spare him the sort of bureaucratic tasks formerly undertaken by Sūden, such as drafting official codes and refereeing disputes within and between the various Japanese schools of Buddhism. Takuan's attitude toward the other Japanese Buddhist sects as well as Shinto was generally open and receptive, and, whatever the master's qualms, from Iemitsu's standpoint Takuan's ecumenism must have made him ideally qualified to arbitrate sectarian disagreements.

In 1642 Takuan was drafted to judge a debate between Iden (n.d.), abbot of the Edo Pure Land temple Sōjōji, and Nichikei (n.d.), abbot of Honkōji, a Shinagawa Nichiren temple. The debate, held at Honkōji, was attended by Iemitsu himself, accompanied by several members of the privy council, among them Masamori and Tadakatsu. Debates between the two schools, founded respectively by the medieval priests Hōnen (1133–1212) and Nichiren (1222–1282), were common in Japan during the sixteenth and early seventeenth centuries.[181] Both teachings claimed to offer paths to salvation uniquely suited to the degenerate age of the Dharma: the Pure Land school advocating reliance on the saving grace of Amitābha Buddha, expressed through repetition of the *nenbutsu;* the Nichiren school invoking the power of the *Lotus Sutra* (expressed through the mantra "Hail to the sutra of the Lotus of the Marvelous Law!" [J. *Namu myōhō rengekyō*]) and emphasizing the messianic role of the sect's founder, Nichiren.

The Tokugawa clan, while patronizing priests from a variety of Buddhist schools, had since the time of Ieyasu been closely identified with the Pure Land sect, which may explain Iemitsu's interest in the debate. While the contest's outcome is not recorded, Takuan is reported to have told Iemitsu, whether on this or some similar occasion, that both Hōnen and Nichiren had realized the inner truths of Buddhism. However, unlike the other, older Buddhist schools, which articulated their teachings on the deepest, absolute level, Hōnen and Nichiren, Takuan maintains, had both conceived their teachings for a later, degenerate age when Buddhism and people's spiritual capacities were in decline, so that the particular, temporary expedients they proposed often appeared to be in conflict.[182] Takuan compares this to climbing Mount Fuji. The older Buddhist teachings, he tells Iemitsu, whatever their superficial differences, were all established on the summit. Hōnen, too, reached the mountain's peak but in order to save the sentient beings of his age was then forced to descend partway; Nichiren, coming later, had to descend further yet, although he also had attained the summit. Iemitsu declared himself in complete agreement with Takuan's analysis, which attempts to remove the apparent conflicts between the teachings of the Buddhist sects by pointing to

the common ground from which they spring.[183] A *waka* by Takuan, "No Conflict between the Temporary and the Real," is included with the account of the
debate and offers a lyrical statement of the master's catholic point of view:

> Can anything be said to exist
>     outside the Dharma—
> Even the wild cherry blossoms
> Or the color and aroma of the plum
>     flowering beneath the eaves?[184]

Despite his reluctance to involve himself in the internal affairs of the
various Buddhist schools, Takuan does seem to have consulted on a dispute
involving the monks of Mount Koya, the celebrated Shingon monastic center
northeast of Kyoto. Two groups at Koya, the scholar monks (*gakuryō*) and
the worker monks (*gyōnin*), were at loggerheads over a scholar monk's promise to give the initiation for Dharma transmission (*denbō kanjō*) to a worker-
monk colleague. The other scholar monks protested that this contravened
the temple's ancient traditions, which reserved the transmission exclusively
to their brethren, and the ceremony was consequently canceled, inflaming
the worker monks. Various complex issues underlay the dispute, which was
resolved by the bakufu only several years later. Takuan's actual role in the
matter is unclear, and it is not known whether he merely advised the government or personally mediated between the opposing factions. Iemitsu had
dispatched Koide Yoshihide to Mount Koya as the bakufu's representative,
and Takuan, writing to him in 1640, appears to side on principle with the
monastery's scholar monks. Initiation for Dharma transmission in Shingon,
Takuan argues in his letter, is essentially the same as *inka* in Zen. It is, therefore, something the master in question must decide whether and when to
bestow, and never something the student can demand.[185]

In commenting to Yoshihide on the troubles at Mount Koya, Takuan
had thus defended a Buddhist teacher's absolute right to grant or withhold
Dharma transmission. Significantly, Takuan himself, though now well on
in years, had continued to refuse to give anyone transmission and to designate a successor. Training and sanction of a suitable Dharma heir was and
continues to be regarded in Japan as a Rinzai Zen master's most solemn
duty, ensuring continuity of not merely his own legacy but that of his temple and teaching line. Yet Takuan held firm, resisting mounting pressure to
select from among the monks of his Daitokuji lineage some candidate to
carry on his and his teacher's Zen.

Takuan speaks openly of this in a 1642 letter to his daimyo patron Hosokawa Mitsunao (1619–1649) regarding the mortuary temples for Mitsunao's father, Tadatoshi. Tadatoshi, who had died the previous year, had
been among Takuan's leading supporters. His father, Tadaoki, a prominent
warlord of the late sixteenth century, had fought under Ieyasu at Sekigahara, and Tadatoshi himself had participated in Iemitsu's suppression of
the Shimabara rebellion. Having a Christian mother, Tadatoshi had been
baptized as a child but subsequently apostatized. He is said to have studied
Zen under Takuan, who officiated at his funeral service and bestowed on
him the Buddhist name Myōge (Marvelous Understanding). With Takuan's
permission, Mitsunao erected a mortuary temple, Myōge-in, in his father's
honor at Tōkaiji. (The temple was the first of five such temples established
at Tōkaiji by Takuan's various daimyo patrons.)[186] A second namesake temple was planned at the family seat in Kumamoto, capital of the wealthy
Higo domain, which the Hosokawa had received from the shogunate ten
years earlier, and Mitsunao asked Takuan to suggest a distinguished monk
to serve as the proposed temple's abbot.

In his letter of reply, Takuan proposes a Daitokuji priest of his acquaintance, Keishitsu Sōei (n.d.). But he takes pains to remind Mitsunao that
there is no one in the Daitokuji lineage whom he considers his disciple. "In
regard to the construction of [the Kumamoto] Myōge-in," Takuan writes,
"you have asked me to recommend someone to serve as the temple's abbot.
As Your Lordship knows, I have no disciples. And I find no suitable person
anywhere in the [Daitokuji] Northern line. The Zen priest Keishitsu holds
advanced standing and, though not a scholar or man of letters, has completed his religious training in the Daitokuji line and obtained *inka*. In the
next several years he is likely to receive appointment to the abbacy of Daitokuji and has trained at the temple from childhood."[187]

Despite Keishitsu's impressive attainments, his *inka*, advanced rank, and
good prospects, Takuan offers what is in essence a qualified endorsement,
pointedly coupled with critical remarks about the dearth of promising students at Daitokuji. The passage is the only place where Takuan addresses, albeit obliquely, his reason for not having an heir, namely, what he contends is
the poor quality of contemporary monks, whether or not they hold temple
office, possess the requisite years of training, or have their teacher's Zen
sanction. The problem, as Takuan suggests elsewhere, is that the integrity of
Dharma transmission in the temples has been compromised. Students lack
the self-motivation and independence necessary in the quest for enlightenment, while teachers shamelessly cosset and promote their favorites. Takuan

contrasts this to his own youth in the temples, when a Zen monk would spend years without a designated master, practicing alone and traveling on pilgrimage from one teacher and temple to the next till at last he was able to attain realization by dint of his own strenuous efforts. Only then did he receive acknowledgment from a qualified master, who by testifying to the student's experience became his teacher. Nowadays, Takuan laments, Zen monks no longer travel on pilgrimage or leave their home temples, in effect having become laymen with their heads shaved. Their teachers dote on them, arbitrarily declare their studies complete, and write out certificates of *inka*, making Dharma transmission a kind of charade and an increasingly incestuous transaction. Originally, Takuan observes, all Daitokuji's celebrated teachers came from other Zen temples, beginning with the first-generation abbot, Tettō,[188] and continuing through Takuan's former teacher Shun'oku. Many of these figures, and Takuan himself, it is implied, might easily have been excluded from Daitokuji's ranks under the present parochial system.[189] "Murasakino's Buddhism is useless in the present day," Takuan concludes in a letter to Yoshihide,[190] referring to Daitokuji by its common epithet, Murasakino, literally "violet field," the name of the northern Kyoto district in which the temple is situated.

As he found standards so distorted and talent in such short supply, it is hardly surprising that Takuan—as much in protest as in despair—largely withdrew from the Zen master's normal business of training and grooming Dharma heirs. "I do not think at all about what will be after my death," Takuan confesses in a 1641 letter to the shogun's retainer Hata Chūan. "For thirty years now I have given up on the Buddhism of this degenerate age. So I don't give any thought to the succession or even to what will become of the temple [i.e., Tōkaiji]."[191] Takuan was, in fact, chided by his former pupil Isshi Monju for failing to train monks at Tōkaiji, a lapse that Isshi attributes to Takuan's excessively high expectations, an insistence that students meet his own exacting standards. Isshi's criticisms are outlined in a letter, "Reply to Master Takuan," in which he gently takes his old teacher to task:

> The teacher [Takuan], pressed by the patron [Iemitsu], took charge of a temple [Tōkaiji]. The temple is abundantly provided with religious accouterments and funds. Why, then, is it poorly endowed when it comes to monks training in Zen? Is this not perhaps attributable to the teacher's selecting only those of suitable wisdom and ability? To obtain superior students while not casting aside the indifferent is a Zen master's characteristic noble generosity. It is my wish that the teacher would accept students without concern for whether

they are wise or foolish. If he did so and personally gave them the benefit of his intimate instruction, how difficult would it be to speedily transform even those who are dull into precious vehicles of the teaching?[192]

In a statement included in the posthumous collection *Record of Myriad Pines [Temple]*, Takuan in essence pleads guilty to the particulars of Isshi's charges. At the same time, he insists that, however mortifying to him personally, his predicament—that of a Zen master without students—has been forced upon him by circumstances. "After becoming a priest," Takuan reflects, "I made a determined effort to study Zen and pursue the way, and received my teacher's sanction. I was awarded imperial abbacy at Daitokuji and assumed the purple robe. Seeing this, people probably mistake me for a fine teacher of men and *devas*,[193] but I'm nothing more than a poor apology for an arhat![194] In the forty years since I received my teacher's sanction, I've taught others using a single koan,[195] but there hasn't been a single person who has realized true understanding. If the past is any indication, even if I were to linger on fifty years more, it's doubtful I could manage to save anyone. And without saving others, [being a Zen teacher] becomes nothing more than just another way to make a living. Shameful, isn't it! So I've abandoned the Buddha Dharma and don't teach anymore."[196]

Funaoka suggests that among the factors influencing Takuan's refusal to produce a successor was a corrosive self-hatred resulting from the master's closeness to Iemitsu and the bastions of secular power. This association, Funaoka believes, not only compromised Takuan's integrity in the eyes of many of his Zen peers, but monopolized much of the master's energy, presumably preventing Takuan from concentrating on Zen and the teaching of monks.[197] It is possible that the eventful fifteen-year period from Takuan's exile till his death and particularly Takuan's nine final years, when he was frequently in attendance on Iemitsu, left the master little opportunity or inclination for intensive training of disciples. But this fails to explain why Takuan also produced no disciples in the twenty years before this period, following his 1609 appointment as a Zen master in the Daitokuji line. Nor does it account for Takuan's 1641 statement to Chūan that thirty years before he had already given up on the degraded Zen of his day. Indeed, on the question of Dharma transmission, Takuan's stand remained remarkably consistent. He never at any point in his teaching career appears to have found a monk able to measure up, and he refused to defile the teaching by sanctioning an heir whose realization was in his estimation anything less than fully authentic. To do so, he implied, would only have compounded Japanese Zen's decline, further debasing the currency of *inka* by producing another generation of unenlightened teachers, men with nothing to offer their students but empty posturing. "In today's world there are a great many who claim to have realized the Dharma," Takuan caustically observes. "But if you compare them with [the great teachers of] the past, it's obvious most are just pretending. Pretending is pretending; it's not the real thing. And if you try to save others with a Dharma that's not the real thing, it isn't saving them but casting them into a dark pit."[198]

The aged and increasingly frail Takuan's lack of a Dharma heir was felt keenly by Iemitsu, who broached the subject directly to the master. The *Biographical Record* describes how, on an early autumn day in 1643, the shogun visited Takuan at Tōkaiji. Through the descending twilight, the moon appeared, and Takuan and Iemitsu retired to a small pavilion overlooking the temple's artificial pond. The shogun seized the moment to voice his concerns:

> "Although Your Reverence is already well on in years, I have not heard of your designating a Dharma successor. Is it perhaps that no one you find suitable has appeared among your followers? Even Mahākāshyapa, as I recall, pitifully inferior though he was to the Buddha, like a fly attaching itself to a horse's tail, received the World-Honored One's Dharma, which has been transmitted faithfully from generation to generation down to the present so that numerous living beings enjoy the benefits of salvation. This is the meaning of the secret transmission on Vulture Peak. If you find any among your students who has realized even some small measure of enlightenment, you too should sanction him as your successor and so transmit your Dharma to future generations. It is only to tell you this that I have come knocking at the door of your Zen hut tonight."
>
> The master thanked His Highness for his concern. He then went to his students and told them, "While His Highness' wishes are weighty indeed, I do not intend to have any descendants to continue my Dharma."[199]

Another prominent patron troubled by Takuan's lack of a successor was the retired emperor. Consequently, when Takuan found himself in Kyoto early the following year (1644) en route to Tajima and the hot springs, he was summoned to the imperial palace for an audience with the thirty-two-year-old Gomizuno'o. Like Iemitsu, the retired emperor remonstrated tactfully with Takuan. "I understand," Gomizuno'o is recorded as saying, "that Your Reverence has determined to cut off your line without

any heir, a source to me of constant regret. For the sake of the world's beings, you should choose from among your students one who has attained
realization and transmit to him the great Dharma."[200] Takuan thanked the
retired emperor for his concern and withdrew, but this appeal, as well,
failed to alter the master's conviction.[201]

Takuan's refusal to appoint a successor, while unusual in the Japanese
context, was hardly unique. Some 150 years earlier, Ikkyū Sōjun, after
Daitō perhaps the most illustrious of Daitokuji's medieval teachers, had
died without designating a Dharma heir, withholding his *inka* in protest
against the degeneration of transmission at the temple. In 1455 Ikkyū had
openly stated his position in *Jikaishū* (Take Warning!), his rambling jere-
miad against the corruption of Daitokuji Zen. At the work's conclusion,
Ikkyū announces, as if it were a matter of pride in view of the depreciation
of *inka* at Daitokuji, that he intends never to bestow his sanction:

> I have never given *inka* to anyone. . . . This is public knowledge. Yet here right
> under my nose there are plenty of people who claim to have it. . . . So if after
> I'm gone someone comes claiming to have my *inka*, you should report him to
> the authorities and prosecute for criminal misconduct. That's why I'm telling
> everyone the facts by ways of a written testament. . . . However much people
> may insist they hold my *inka*, even if they say they've studied with me for
> many years . . . do not believe them![202]

Takuan's contemporaries would not have failed to note the parallels
between Ikkyū's outspoken stand on the transmission and Takuan's own
decision to cut off his line. Indeed Takuan's last admonitions (*yuikai*) to
his monks open with bluntly worded instructions on the matter of succession that clearly invoke Ikkyū's language in *Jikaishū* and leave little doubt
that Takuan consciously saw himself as emulating his famous predeces-
sor's example. "I have no disciple who has succeeded to my Dharma,"
Takuan declares. "After I'm dead, if anyone says he's my heir, that person is
a Dharma thief. Report him to the authorities and see that he's punished
severely!"[203] And near the close of the document, Takuan adds: "Should
there be anyone who presents a special Dharma name given them by me,
or an inscribed portrait, and claims it to be his *inka*, that person should be
reported to the authorities for criminal misconduct!"[204]

Implicit in Takuan's forceful refusal to perpetuate his line is rejection of
the oft-stated belief that the torch of Zen can only continue to burn if handed
on in an unbroken transmission from master to disciple. Once allowed to go

out, the torch will be extinguished forever, condemning future generations to darkness and ignorance. Takuan, by contrast, insists that the Zen
teacher's role is limited, with *inka* no more than a recognition of the student's own unstinting efforts. "The special transmission outside the scriptures [i.e., Zen]," Takuan comments in *The Sword Taie*, "is the Dharma you
have to realize and attain for yourself, apart from any teacher's instruction." Zen mind exists any time a dedicated practitioner experiences realization, with or without a teacher's sanction and support. Because
enlightenment is one's own intrinsic being, it cannot truly be passed on,
Takuan asserts, but only experienced for oneself. In the same way, the
truth of Zen, of the Buddha's original Dharma, can never be destroyed but
is always present, ready to be rediscovered by the right person at the right
time. "That which is the Dharma cannot be passed on," Takuan muses in
*Night Talks at Tōkaiji*. "That which can be passed on is not the
Dharma. . . . When the Dharma obtains suitable men, it is revealed; when
it does not, it is concealed. When concealed, it is like the sun; when revealed, it is also like the sun."[205] The light of original nature, like the sun
amid passing clouds, cannot be blotted out, Takuan argues, but only tem-
porarily obscured. The real transmission does not depend on an unbroken
line of teachers and heirs but on the enlightenment experience itself,
which simultaneously replicates and renews the experience of Zen's patriarchs, whether in India, China, or Japan. "While it seems as if one is transmitting this [i.e., Zen], actually one does not transmit it," Takuan observes
in "Teacher," one of the verses he composed for the instruction of
Kōtokuji's monks in winter 1629 on the eve of his exile. "Since heaven's
truth[206] exists within you, you must know it for yourself."[207] And in another verse from the collection, titled "Zen," Takuan elaborates his views
on the independent character of enlightenment:

> The Zen style in this degenerate period of the Dharma is for people to seek to
> confer and receive the teaching. But Zen cannot be conferred. It was passed
> on from generation to generation among the twenty-eight Indian patri-
> archs;[208] but, even if it seems something was being passed on, it was not. The
> same for the six patriarchs in China—even if it seems something was being
> transmitted, it was not. When a student's mind awakens, if he has a teacher,
> the teacher can confirm his awakening. That's all there is to it. If there is no
> teacher to offer confirmation, just say, "I've grasped Zen. I've attained the
> Way." But if you rashly open your mouth without cause, you won't escape
> having your tongue torn out in hell![209]

While conditions vary from age to age, the real transmission, Takuan seems to say, does not depend on students having teachers or teachers having disciples. In Takuan's Zen, both teacher and student are ultimately on their own, not relying on one another or on any external support, but freely availing themselves of the power of nonself, of the original, ever-present, enlightened mind. "I do have a disciple," Takuan maintains ironically at the close of *Night Talks at Tōkaiji*. "His name is Attendant Emptiness. Nothing is known of his family or the circumstances of his birth, when he arrived or when he'll leave. I scold him, but he shows no sign of anger. Untroubled by illness, he doesn't resort to medicine. Fortunately, among my followers, there is this one whom I find truly suitable."[210]

Whatever Takuan's own travails, the years 1642 to 1643 had been exceptionally trying ones for the common people of Japan. The country was devastated by famine, and all attempts by the government to relieve the disaster proved unavailing. Thousands were reduced to begging, and Takuan's letters of this period note the sufferings he observed around him. In the provinces of Tango and Tanba, he writes Mitsunao, the number of beggars has continued to grow, and one can see the corpses of those who died of starvation lying by the roadside. In Edo itself, Takuan describes, every evening at Nihonbashi,[211] when the city gates are locked there gather some six hundred beggars, several of whom perish every day, "a truly pitiful sight." As the present year (1643) has been bad for crops, Takuan adds, the situation only seems to be worsening.[212] Apart from expressing his obvious distress, Takuan makes no further comment on the famine and the beggars' desperate situation. We know, however, that the master saw a direct connection between the people's plight and their rulers' patterns of consumption, a view reflecting prevailing Confucian "zero-sum" economic theory. Takuan articulates these beliefs in a 1634 letter to Munenori, urging the shogun's advisor, and by extension the ruling class as a whole, to avoid excess and embrace austerity for the good of the nation. "If Your Lordship only forbids extravagance," Takuan writes, "then even if the people do not offer you wealth, they will be at peace. It is because of extravagance that both the humble and the eminent fall into want. Put an end to the mining of silver. By allocating land for growing tobacco, you will create shortages of rice and millet. As large numbers of workers enter the silver mines, no one will work the fields, and once [existing supplies] of rice and millet are consumed, the people of the world will be in difficulty. When those who harvest the five grains[213] are few while those who consume them are many, gold and silver will be abundant but the world hard-pressed."[214]

Following his interview with Gomizuno'o in spring 1644, Takuan traveled to Sakai, and that autumn he proceeded to Izushi and his beloved retreat. In a letter to Yoshihide, Takuan described his pleasure in the hermitage's idyllic surroundings. The trees had grown luxuriant, the tatami had been freshly changed, and here Takuan could banish all thoughts of the capital.[215]

While in Izushi, the master was also able to renew various old friendships and to visit his eighty-one-year-old sister and his brother Hanbei. With the death of Tsunanori in 1606, headship of the Akiba family had passed to Takuan's brother. Hanbei, however, seems to have gotten into bad company and, at least for a time, earned a reputation for being free-spending and dissolute. Takuan had relinquished all standing within the Akiba clan when he left home and entered the Buddhist priesthood, but he must have been chagrined by reports he received regarding Hanbei and consequently felt compelled to take his younger brother to task. A surviving letter by Takuan chiding Hanbei for his misbehavior refers to an earlier exchange on the subject, in which Hanbei had protested that he was simply following "nature's way" (*tendō*), in a kind of unintended parody of Takuan's teachings on the spontaneity and naturalness of original mind. In reply, Takuan challenges his brother's argument as both self-serving and tendentious:

> In your last letter you spoke of leaving things to nature's way. While reasonable enough, this idea is something that ordinary people don't understand. From of old, pine needles have been thin, lotus flowers, round. In the same way, one should clearly recognize how nature's way is suited to one's particular position in life. One of modest position should not indulge in luxury, while one who is a daimyo should uphold his position accordingly. This is nature's way. Thus, if you have a stipend of one *koku* of rice and proceed to use it all up, with the idea that you're letting things follow nature's way, there won't be any more rice left. And when that happens, there's no way you're going to be able to borrow the money or rice from nature's way! To fail to recognize this and say you're following nature's way, just sleeping, waking, and imagining that nature will provide you with funds, is a gross error.
>
> No craftsman, whoever he is, can manage without a carpenter's square. If you take as your standard those who think like you, you're bound to go wrong. Instead, your standard should be those of your own social position who are of sound judgment and don't squander their income. If you're going to use a twisted measure, you'll never get a straight result. For a man with an income of one hundred *koku* to act like someone with two hundred goes against nature's way.

You've been parading around arrogantly, it seems, which also goes against nature's way. Look at the moon: for fifteen nights it's waxing, but part of the time it's waning. This is a warning to human beings.

> Simply reflect on how the moon,
> > once full, then wanes
> In the sky of the sixteenth night
> For such is life in the world of man

This poem makes an excellent point.

My letter has been long and probably annoying, but as your older brother I thought it in your best interest to set forth these matters. I urge you to change your profligate ways so that you will not have to borrow money. To distance oneself from one's family and bear ill will toward one's close friends is mostly the result of selfishness.

Yours,

Takuan[216]

While much of this letter is scolding in tone and expresses the sort of humorless, Confucian-inspired moralism standard in the period, Takuan uses the occasion to make a broader point about the meaning of naturalness and freedom. There is a crucial difference, he suggests to Hanbei, between being one's natural, authentic self and being merely self-indulgent. To be truly free, natural, and spontaneous, as Takuan argues in *Record of Immovable Wisdom,* is the very opposite of being impulsive, which renders one, like Hanbei, a perpetual slave to attachment, blind to the consequences of one's acts.

Takuan's letter is undated but was likely composed when Hanbei was a headstrong young adult in need of guidance. By the time of Takuan's 1644 visit, his younger brother, now himself an old man, had surely long since reformed, and, as the newsy report Takuan penned to him from exile shows, the two remained on friendly terms.

Always reluctant to part with Takuan for any extended period, Iemitsu had ordered the master to return to the capital by early May 1644, but Takuan, unwilling to abandon the serenity of Izushi, did not arrive back at Tōkaiji until some two months later. Presumably by this period Takuan's advanced age and increasingly precarious health had given him greater latitude in dealing with his demanding patron.

Despite Takuan's avowed distaste for life in the capital, Iemitsu seems to have had an almost insatiable desire for the master's company. Takuan was often at Edo castle late into the night, detained by Iemitsu watching the moon or composing poetry, at times till dawn. Unable to make the journey back to Shinagawa and Tōkaiji, Takuan would spend the night at Munenori's villa, situated near the castle, and eventually Munenori simply established special lodgings for the master's use on such occasions. Even when Iemitsu traveled to Nikkō in 1639 to pay his respects at Ieyasu's shrine, he insisted that the master accompany him.[217]

Takuan had long been sickly and in his letters frequently complained of various physical ailments. By 1645, however, his health was rapidly deteriorating. To Isshi Monju, now a Zen master in the Myōshinji line, Takuan wrote that from the end of the previous year (1644) he had experienced serious illness, which had only continued to worsen.[218] Realizing that little time remained and prodded by those around him, Takuan began to settle his affairs, though doing so with his usual marked disregard for convention. In a last letter to his Daitokuji colleague Tenyū, included in the *Account*, Takuan observes, "Everyone delivers a final verse. Lately this has become a standard procedure. But I do not intend to do any such thing. When the time comes to die, one should simply shut one's mouth and go." "Tenyū," the chronicler adds, "understanding the master's mind as he did, was not in the least surprised to read these words."[219]

Late that spring, Takuan took two blank scrolls and, summoning a painter, had him brush on each a single large circle, at the center of which the master himself placed a dot. Takuan's inscription states: "An unnamed person told me, 'I'm worried about obtaining a devotional portrait of Your Reverence.' So I had someone draw a circle and within it placed a dot. . . . This circle enfolds heaven and earth, with nothing left outside. Boundless, it pervades the myriad lands." Directly addressing his followers, Takuan concludes:

> Here, today, everything is already settled. The medicine and the illness cure each other.[220] Worthy monks, just don't attach to things, be without preferences; don't reject things, be without dislikes. If you're concerned whether circumstances are for or against you, the road to your native place is still far off!
>
> Seventh day of the fifth month, second year of Shōhō [1645]. Inscribed by the monk Takuan of Tōkaiji, former abbot of Daitokuji, in his seventy-third year.[221]

The circle, which appears frequently in the brushwork of Rinzai masters from Takuan's period on,[222] is a well-known Zen symbol of emptiness. As such it made an appropriate "portrait" for Takuan, whose teachings display a special affinity for the concept, from his lone disciple "Attendant

Emptiness" to his keen sense of the ephemerality of his own achievement and his stress on the dynamic function of emptiness at the heart of *Record of Immovable Wisdom*. Takuan had one scroll deposited at Tōkaiji, the other at Nanshūji, and cautioned the temples' monks that after his death they were not to hang portraits of him in a purple robe but to display the circle with the dot instead.[223]

In fall 1645 Iemitsu paid what would be his last visit to Tōkaiji. Hotta Masamori acted as host and served lunch, after which the shogun and his retinue went seine fishing on the beach and, to Iemitsu's delight, netted a large catch before returning to Edo castle at dusk.

Three months later, on the tenth day of the twelfth month, Takuan suddenly became ill and took to his bed. Iemitsu immediately dispatched a famous doctor and ordered attendants to care for Takuan, but the master's condition continued to deteriorate. Iemitsu now insisted on visiting Takuan's bedside in person, but it was feared that this would only weaken the master further, and the shogun had to content himself with sending in his stead two prominent retainers, Matsudaira Nobutsuna and Nakane Masamori (1588–1665).

"If Your Reverence wishes anything," Masamori told Takuan, "you have only to speak and I will inform His Highness."

In response, Takuan called to his attendant to fetch paper and brush, and wrote out a list of measures to be taken after his death to enhance and preserve Tōkaiji:

1. Erect the temple gate and Buddha hall.
2. Alter the mountain path behind the temple to forever put an end to foot traffic.
3. Move the lay dwellings that are just outside the temple gate to avert danger [to the temple] from fire.

Takuan then handed the list to Masamori, saying, "Please present this to His Highness."[224]

That afternoon Takuan felt well enough to receive Kōsetsu Sōryū (d. 1666), a fellow Daitokuji master who was an heir of Kogetsu and had formerly studied under Takuan. They talked, and Takuan composed a *waka* in appreciation of Kōsetsu's visit.

That night, however, at the hour of the tiger (about 4:00 a.m.), Takuan's illness abruptly worsened. Fearing that the master's last moments were at hand, Tōkaiji's monks begged him for a death verse. Takuan initially resisted their entreaties but finally gave way and, taking up his brush, inscribed in large, powerful strokes the single Chinese character "dream" (read *yūme* or *mu* in Japanese). To its left, in smaller, cursive characters, he wrote:

> A hundred years, thirty-six thousand days
> Miroku and Kannon—Right! Wrong! How many times?
> Right is a dream, and wrong is a dream
> Miroku, a dream; Kannon, a dream
> Buddha said, "This is how things should be viewed."

The old rustic Takuan scribbled this in a hurry.[225]

Takuan then put down his brush and passed away.

The meaning of Takuan's death verse remains obscure. A hundred years is a classical Chinese metaphor for the span of human life; Miroku (Skt. Maitreya) is the buddha of the future, a bodhisattva who meditates in the Tusita heaven waiting to be reborn in the world and realize buddhahood; while the bodhisattva Kannon, as noted earlier, symbolizes the enlightened mind's infinite compassion, freedom, and adaptability. The poem's final line is taken from a famous *gatha* at the close of the *Diamond Sutra*: "All created things / Are like a dream, a bubble / A dewdrop or a flash of lightning. / This is how things should be viewed."[226] The quotation together with the other references to dreams reinforce the poem's theme of evanescence and heighten the effect of the single bold character that fills the entire right half of the page.

The dreamlike nature of worldly existence is a fundamental Buddhist notion and one that seems to have been often on Takuan's mind. Earlier that year, noting the death of an acquaintance, Takuan had grieved in a letter, "Doctor Okamoto Genji has passed on. Nothing can be done—all is a dream."[227] And a passage in *Knotted Cords* expands on the familiar Buddhist metaphor:

> In a dream you may seem to be fighting, struggling, tussling with others, enraged, bellowing, lashing out. But when you awake there's no "you" or "them" to be seen. Your anger is gone; there are no sticks or swords. What you thought was screaming and clamor is only the sound of wind in the pines. Waking from your dream, you shake yourself. "Well, well," you realize, "all those things I saw while I was asleep—every trace of them is gone!" Just so, the good and bad things that happen while we are in this world, our

resentment of and complaints about others, all the various matters that concern us, are all just happenings in a dream.[228]

This same sense of the fleetingness and vanity of things is on display in the final testament (*yuikai*) Takuan bequeathed to Tōkaiji's monks, a document marked by a rejection of all tributes and memorials. "Bury me under the hill behind the temple," Takuan commands. "Just cover me with dirt and go away. Don't chant sutras. Don't offer a funeral meal. Don't accept any condolence presents from priests or laymen. As for you monks, put on your robes, eat your meals, behave just as you would normally. Don't erect any gravestones or install any portraits. Don't set up any memorial tablets. Don't try to obtain for me any posthumous titles. Don't install a wooden memorial tablet in the founder's hall of the headquarters temple [i.e., Daitokuji]. And don't write any biographies!"[229]

Following Takuan's instructions, Tōkaiji's monks buried him without ceremony on a slope northwest of the temple. A single pine tree was planted atop the unmarked grave, the only sign that this was the final resting place of the temple's founder. Iemitsu, on learning of Takuan's death, was disconsolate and sought to hold a lavish funeral service, but he yielded to the objections of Tōkaiji's monks, who conveyed to him Takuan's wishes in the matter. On the fifth day of the new year (1646), the shogun visited Takuan's grave, and the following day he ordered Hotta Masamori to build there a memorial stupa in the master's memory. Masamori accompanied a team of artisans to the site, but once again Tōkaiji's assembly intervened, urging respect for Takuan's admonitions, and construction never proceeded beyond clearing and leveling the area. Eventually, however, Iemitsu prevailed, and a simple yet elegant monument was erected, an oblong natural stone, without inscription, set atop a stone pedestal and surrounded by a low stone fence.[230]

## Takuan Tales

His refusal to sanction a Dharma successor meant that, formally speaking, Takuan's Zen came to an end upon his death. But Takuan's life and reputation continued to inspire many in Japan, both inside and outside the temples. This was, after all, a Zen master who had played a part in momentous events and displayed great daring and force of character in repeatedly confronting the nation's rulers. Having suffered punishment in defense of the principles of his school, Takuan had finally been vindicated and ended his life as an intimate of the third Tokugawa shogun, patronized by Iemitsu and the members of his inner circle. As such, Takuan's career combined two features much prized in traditional Japanese Zen hagiography: a close personal association with representatives of the ruling elite and a simultaneous readiness to speak plainly and directly to those of power and importance.

In the society at large, the impact of Takuan's story lay precisely in the tension between Takuan's own sense of integrity, his unflinching honesty and straightforwardness, and his proximity to eminences like Iemitsu and Munenori. It was above all this aspect of Takuan's life that imprinted itself on the popular imagination, inspiring the various tales that began to appear after Takuan's death, tales that, however fanciful, sought to capture and preserve some hint of the master's Zen. Such stories were first collected in the late eighteenth and early nineteenth centuries, with a number even included in the 1844 Takuan biography *Record of the Founder of the Myriad Pines [Temple]*. While some of the legends concern traditions at Tōkaiji, most present Takuan "in action," matching wits with the shogun and the shogun's master of swordsmanship, Munenori, or offering advice to various samurai retainers. Quite apart from their inherent charm, the stories, a selection of which follows, form a counterpoint of sorts to the conventional tone of Munetomo's two biographies and as such convey something of what might be called Takuan's informal Zen legacy.[231]

### TAKUAN AND THE ONENESS OF THINGS

Once when the shogun Iemitsu was sympathizing with Takuan's long and painful years of exile, the Master observed: "Man is of the same root as heaven, earth, and all things, so it makes no difference where one lives."

At that moment, Iemitsu raised his folding fan and struck the tatami, demanding, "Well, does it hurt?"

The Master, without a moment's hesitation replied, "Exactly like cutting one's nails or hair."

His Majesty's intention was, I understand, to ask Takuan, "If you are one with all things and I strike the tatami, does it hurt *you*?" He was greatly impressed by the ready wit of the Master's reply.[232]

### TAKUAN AND THE SHOGUN'S SPECIAL MEAL

The shogun Iemitsu complained to Takuan that none of the food he was served at the palace interested him any longer. Takuan then invited the shogun to a special meal at the temple. He assured Iemitsu that the meal would revive the shogun's jaded appetite but made him first promise that, whatever happened, he would not leave before the meal had concluded.

Iemitsu arrived at the temple prepared for a feast. But he waited and waited, and, despite repeated assurances that the meal was almost ready, an hour passed, then two, then three. Eventually, five hours had gone by, and the shogun's stomach was growling with hunger. Only then did Takuan finally appear, bearing a bowl of boiled rice, over which was ladled some hot water and a yellow substance, which turned out to be pickled Japanese radish [*daikon*].

So hungry was Iemitsu that he pronounced the food the most delicious he had ever tasted. Takuan then scolded the shogun for his self-indulgence, which kept him from realizing how delicious simple foods can be when one is hungry and one's tastes have not grown jaded. Iemitsu agreed and the next day demanded the recipe for Takuan's pickled radish, which thereafter became famous as "Takuan pickles" and were served even at Edo castle.[233]

### TAKUAN AND THE SHOGUN'S MONKEY

Iemitsu had a favorite pet monkey. When someone would try to hit it with a fan, the monkey would seize the fan before it could be hit. However they exerted their ingenuity, the shogun's samurai retainers all failed to hit the monkey.

Seeing this, Takuan took out his own fan and struck the monkey, which, only *after* being hit, grabbed the Master's fan. Takuan did this again and again. Amazed, everyone demanded to know how the Master had succeeded.

Takuan explained, "When each of you went to strike the monkey, you betrayed your intention before doing so. The monkey immediately sensed it and, expecting the blow, seized the fan. I hit the monkey without any intention in mind; hence it couldn't know what was in store. That is why my blow landed and only *after* could the monkey seize the fan."

This story was recounted by an elder in my domain.[234]

## TAKUAN'S QUICK MOVEMENT

The shogun Iemitsu was learning the art of quick movement from the sword master Yagyū Munenori. Munenori told the shogun that he couldn't claim to have achieved true agility until on rainy days he could leap from the verandah onto the stepping stones in the garden and back without getting wet. So Iemitsu, whenever he had free time, would practice assiduously to do this.

Visiting the castle one rainy day, Takuan saw the shogun repeatedly leaping back and forth like this from the verandah and asked, "Your Majesty, what are you doing?"

"Ah, Takuan!" Iemitsu greeted him. "Lately I've been practicing quick movement, and I'm really making good progress. I can jump out in the rain like this and back again without even getting wet. That's real agility, don't you think?"

"Most impressive," the aged master agreed. "Nevertheless, your movements are still nowhere near as fast as my own."

"Very interesting," Iemitsu said. "Why don't you show me how fast *you* can move."

"Certainly, Your Majesty," Takuan replied and, slipping on a pair of garden *geta* [traditional Japanese wooden platform sandals], stepped out into the rain.

As Iemitsu was wondering how the Master was going to demonstrate his agility wearing garden clogs, Takuan faced him and, soaking wet, announced, "This is my lightning movement!"

"How?" Iemitsu demanded. "You're soaking wet!"

Takuan brushed off the rain and rebuked the shogun, saying, "Of course if you don't use an umbrella when it rains, you're going to get wet like this. If one doesn't get wet, that's not yet true agility. Your Majesty requires more training!"

At these words, it is said, Iemitsu first understood the Master's meaning.[235]

## TAKUAN HELPS A SAMURAI FIGHT BOREDOM

Inaba Masamori, lord of Mino, had no time away from his duties at the shogun's castle. "Please," he asked Takuan, "instruct me how I may avoid boredom when I spend long days on my official duties."

Immediately seizing his brush, the Master wrote

> Today never comes again.
> Each instant is a foot of precious jade.

and added:

> How wretched when we reflect
> how day after day departs.
> Yesterday will never meet today.

Lord Inaba read what the Master had written and, reciting it with deep feeling, he never again, it is said, experienced tedium in the course of his long days and nights of official duties.[236]

## NO MAN, NO HORSE

Yagyū Munenori rode his horse to Mount Atago.[237] Recalling that the warrior Magaki Heiguro[238] had ridden his horse up and down the mountain's stone steps, Munenori thought he would try it himself but found the stairs too steep to manage. "Even if I were able to get to the top," he wondered, "how would I ever get back down?" He led his horse up the slope alongside the steps, but when he tried to take his horse back down the stairs found it impossible.

The following day Munenori went to Tōkaiji and sought Takuan's advice. "During the Kanei era [1624–1643]," he explained to Takuan, "Magaki rode his horse up and down the stone steps of Mount Atago at the request of Lord Hidetsugu.[239] But when I tried the same thing yesterday, I failed utterly."

Takuan replied, "Your Lordship couldn't do it? I can do it."

The Master then suggested they go there together so that he could show Munenori on the spot.

Skeptically, Munenori accompanied Takuan, who, mounting Munenori's horse, proceeded to race easily up and down the stone steps as if they had been level ground.

Astounded, Munenori begged the Master to tell him how he had done it.

"Your Lordship," Takuan replied, "there is no special technique: only that there must be no man on top of the saddle and no horse under the saddle."[240]

Munenori suddenly experienced awakening and, mounting the horse, he, too, rode the stairs as if riding on level ground.[241]

## TAKUAN AND THE SHOGUN'S WATERMELON

One summer day when Takuan visited Iemitsu, the shogun offered him watermelon that he had sprinkled with sugar to enhance the melon's sweetness. Takuan thanked him and proceeded to eat, but Iemitsu noticed that the Master only ate those parts of the melon without any sugar on them. When he questioned Takuan about this, Takuan, in turn, asked Iemitsu, "This is melon, isn't it?"

"Of course," the shogun replied.

"If you offer me melon," Takuan explained, "I'll eat melon. If you offer me sugar, I'll eat sugar."

When Iemitsu persisted, Takuan admonished him, saying, "Your Highness, all things have their own nature. The watermelon has its watermelon nature, and it is because I love watermelon that I eat the parts *without* sugar. To erase the heaven-sent nature of something you eat is the same as distorting the character of someone you employ."[242]

## TŌKAIJI'S "TAKUAN GUARDS"

At Tōkaiji in Shinagawa are what are known as "Takuan guards" [*Takuan ban*]. These are farmers who belong to the temple's fief and stand guard every night at the temple's gate. I understand that the origin of this is as follows:

Master Takuan being a priest of eminent virtue, His Lordship the shogun was greatly devoted to him, summoning Takuan to Edo castle and even visiting him at Tōkaiji on numerous occasions. The Master, however, did not wish to remain constantly at the temple and from time to time would try to leave. His Majesty the shogun was distraught over this and had the local people stand guard to prevent Takuan's departure.

Even after Takuan's death this remained a custom and was maintained as it had been in the past. Today if you ask the local farmers, "Why do you stand guard at Tōkaiji's gate every night?" they'll tell you, "Because otherwise Master Takuan will escape!"

A truly endearing example of the farmers' simple honesty and one that imparts something of the flavor of long ago.[243]

## Tōkaiji's Monks' Tombstones

At Tōkaiji near Takuan's grave, many round stones lie on the ground where they are left to roll onto the road, trampled underfoot by passersby. Yet all these stones were, I understand, the gravestones of the temple's monks. Because they bore no inscription, people outside Tōkaiji didn't realize this. In the temple itself, however, was kept a listing of their locations, charting in detail whose gravestone was number such-and-such to the north or south.[244]

# Notes

## Abbreviations

HK   Watanabe Ichirō, ed. *Heihō kadensho*. Tokyo, 1985.
T    Takakusu Junjirō et al., eds. *Taishō shinshū daizōkyō*. Tokyo, 1914–1922.
TZI  Zen Bunka Kenkyūjo. *Takuan zenji itsuwasen*. Kyoto, 2001.
TON  Ogisu Jundō, ed. *Takuan oshō nenpu*. Kyoto, 1983.
TOZ  Takuan Oshō Zenshū Kankōkai, ed. *Takuan oshō zenshū*. Tokyo, 1928–1930. 6 vols.

## Preface

1. De Bary, ed., *The Buddhist Tradition*, 376–380.
2. In Watanabe, ed., *Heihō kadensho*. The term *heihō* can be translated "art of combat," "martial arts," and so forth, but, because Munenori's work deals with swordsmanship specifically, I have rendered it as "art of the sword," a sense in which *heihō* was commonly used in Munenori's period. While the term is sometimes read *hyōhō*, a 1619 letter from Iemitsu to Munenori gives the word in *kana* as *heihō*, and I have therefore used this reading. See ibid., 172.
3. *TOZ*, 5: 1–27 and 1–13, respectively (page numbering of all works is internal).
4. Suzuki Daisetsu, *Zen and Japanese Culture*, 95–115, 166–168. Other English translations include *Fudōchi shinmyō roku*, translated by Akashi and Tohen; Wilson, *The Unfettered Mind*; Sato, *The Sword and the Mind* (partial translation), 111–125; Hirose, *Immovable Wisdom*, 21–48; and Cleary, *Soul of the Samurai*, 100–141, 142–154. Along with Yoshito Hakeda's translations from *Immovable Wisdom* referred to earlier, portions of the text are translated by William M. Bodiford in the second edtion of de Bary et al., *Sources of Japanese Tradition*, vol. 2, 528–531.
5. Both works are in Sino-Japanese (*kanbun*). The full title of the *Account* is *Manshōzan* [also romanized *Banshōzan*] *Tōkaizenji kaizan Takuan dai-o-shō gyōjō* (Account of the Life of the Great Master Takuan, Founder of the

Zen Temple Tōkaiji of the Myriad Pines). The versions of Munetomo's *Gyōjō* and *Kinenroku* cited here are those included in Ogisu, *Takuan oshō nenpu*, 147–174 and 35–146, respectively.

## Chapter 1: An Introduction to Takuan's Writings on Zen and Swordsmanship

1. Tsuji, *Nihon bukkyōshi*, 8:485.
2. All are undated and included in volume 5 of *TOZ*. (Works are internally numbered.) The title *Knotted Cords* alludes to an ancient Chinese mode of reckoning and recording by tying knots on a string or rope (*ketsujō*). Tsuji speculates that *Knotted Cords* was directed to Takuan's daimyo patron Hori Naoyori (1577–1639). At the opening of the work, Takuan speaks of "replying to matters you had asked me about in your letter from Echigo," Naoyori's domain in what is now Niigata Prefecture. Tsuji, *Nihon bukkyōshi*, 8:485.
3. The next earliest such material of which I am aware is the brief set of instructions on Zen and the art of combat composed by the Rinzai Zen master Bankei Yōtaku (1622–1693) for his patron Katō Yasuoki (1618–1677), daimyo of Ōzu and an expert in the Japanese lance, or *yari*. Bankei's instructions echo many of Takuan's themes in *Record of Immovable Wisdom* and *The Sword Taie*, stressing the importance of direct intuitive response, of moving naturally with "no-mind" and no fixed form, no "you" and no opponent. The piece can be dated to the third quarter of the seventeenth century, the period between 1655, when Bankei first met Yasuoki, and the daimyo's death in 1677, that is, probably at least a generation or two after Takuan composed his own works on Zen and the martial arts. Bankei's instruction to Yasuoki is translated in my *Bankei Zen*, 138–139. For the text, see Akao, *Bankei zenji zenshū*, 940. Sōtō school initiation-style koan transmissions from the late medieval and early modern periods also deal with swordsmanship and Zen mind. Bodiford translates such a document, dated 1664, which calls on the samurai confronting an opponent to remain in his original "baby" mind so that any spilled blood will be pure and free of pollution. The document, which also urges repetition of the *nenbutsu* in meditating on the koan "sword upraised," or "sword blades upward" (*kenjinjō* or *kenninjō*), is translated in full in Bodiford, "Zen and Japanese Swordsmanship Reconsidered," 88. Besides use in koan study, such documents, Bodiford points out, were offerings at funeral and memorial services, representing talismans of a sort. See ibid., 85–94, and Ishikawa, *Zenshū sōden shiryō no kenkyū*, vol. 2, 134. All, however, represent secret transmission-type documents as developed in late medieval Japan. Takuan's sword writings, in contrast, seem to fit more naturally within the context of the simplified, popular approaches to Zen mind of such early Tokugawa teachers as Bankei and Suzuki Shōsan (1579–1655).

4. "There exists a work on the art of the sword composed by the master," Yuki-hiro writes. "It bears such titles as *Record of Spiritual Light, Spark Struck from Flint, Immovable Wisdom,* and so forth." *Manshōsoroku, TOZ,* 6: 119. Satō Rentarō argues that the original title was simply *Immovable Wisdom (Fudōchi)* and that the current, extended title was probably added after the Meiji period (1867–1912). Satō, "Takuan sōhō 'Fudōchi shinmyōroku' ko sha-hon sanshu, 'Tai'a ki' ko shagon isshu," 24. The earliest surviving versions of *Record of Immovable Wisdom* are manuscript copies dated 1703 in the pos-session of Komazawa and Ōtani Universities. Various woodblock editions appeared later during the Tokugawa period, the earliest dated 1779 and 1791. See Satō, "Takuan Sōhō 'Fudōchi shinmyō roku' no shohon," 282.

5. *Ketsujōshū, TOZ,* 5:7–8.

6. Funaoka, *Takuan,* 150. Bodiford dissents from the notion that *Record of Im-movable Wisdom* articulates Zen and argues that basic Buddhism, with an admixture of Neo-Confucianism, is the principal element of Takuan's teach-ing in the work, which concerns "self-cultivation" generally. Bodiford, "Zen and Japanese Swordsmanship Reconsidered," 75–76, 95. Bodiford points out, for example, that the expression *shinmyō* (marvelous power) in the work's title is more closely associated with Neo-Confucianism than Zen (ibid., 76). However, the title of Takuan's work, as previously noted, may have been added posthumously, and the expression appears nowhere in the text itself. The term *shinmyō* appears in Hin'atsu Shigetaka's *Honchō bukke shōden* (Au-thentic Transmission of Martial Arts of Japan, 1714), chapter 6, where a tech-nique known as *shinmyōken* (sword of marvelous power) is said to be associated with the New Shadow school of swordsmanship. See translation and comments in Rogers, "Arts of War in Times of Peace: Swordsmanship in *Honchō bukke shōden*" (1991), 180. Hin'atsu's work, as Rogers concedes, is a colorful but not always accurate guide to the martial arts world of sixteenth- and seventeenth-century Japan. Ibid. (1990), 417.

7. Unless otherwise indicated, all quotations in this section are from the par-ticular essay under discussion (*Record of Immovable Wisdom* or *The Sword Taie*) and appear in the translation.

8. Takuan's argument here bears some resemblance to aspects of the swords-man Miyamoto Musashi's (1584–1645) discussion in the final chapter, "Emp-tiness" (Kū), of his *Book of Five Rings* (*Gorin no sho*), composed in 1640. The mind of the warrior, Musashi insists, must remain in a state of emptiness, never allowed to stop or to rely on predetermined stances (*kata*) but re-sponding immediately as circumstances require. See Uozumi, "Research of Miyamoto Musashi's 'Gorin no sho' from the Perspective of Japanese Intel-lectual History," 49–55.

9. Senju Kannon. Also known as *senju sengen Kanjizai,* "Kannon with a thou-sand arms and eyes." A popular form of the bodhisattva Avalokitesvara,

characterized by multiple arms. Each hand holds various ritual and symbolic objects—a bow, an arrow, a rope, and so forth—indicating the bodhisattva's infinite means of saving sentient beings. An eye on the palm of each hand symbolizes the bodhisattva's all-seeing compassionate activity. "One thousand" here is a general number, signifying "many," and actual images of this deity in Japan often have forty or so arms.

10. Apparently referring to the famous passage in the *Record of Linji* cited by Takuan in his 1606 interview with Shun'oku Sōen, cited below, p. 68.

11. *Tōkai yawa* (1), *TOZ*, 5:86–87.

12. The Four Books were the *Great Learning* (*Da xue*), the *Mean* (*Zhong yong*), the *Analects* (*Lun yu*), and the *Mencius* (*Mengzi*). The first two works form part of the *Book of Rites* (*Li ji*). The Four Books concept was formulated by Zhu Xi (1130–1200), regarded as the leading exponent of Song Neo-Confucianism.

13. Alan K. L. Chan, "A Matter of Taste: *Qi* (Vital Energy) and the Tending of the Heart (*Xin*) in Mencius 2A2," 42.

14. Nakamura Hajime, ed., *Bukkyō go daijiten* (Tokyo, 1975), 2:1170a–b. Nakamura's dictionary lists some dozen definitions for *fudō*, among them a description of the bodhisattva Manjusri, embodiment of intuitive wisdom.

15. See, for example, *On the Distinction between Principle and Activity* (*Riki sabetsuron*), discussed below, and many of the miscellaneous writings in *Night Talks at Tōkaiji*.

16. *Knotted Cords*, *TOZ*, 5:10–11.

17. *Night Talks at Tōkaiji* (1), *TOZ*, 5:84.

18. Ibid., 5:85–86.

19. See, for example, Friday and Seki, *Legacies of the Sword*, 158; and Friday, "Beyond Valor and Bloodshed," 8.

20. De Bary et al., *Sources of Chinese Tradition*, vol. 1, 475. See also Tucker, "Quiet-Sitting and Political Activism," 109–130.

21. Wing-tsit Chan, *A Source Book in Chinese Philosophy*, 606–607.

22. *Knotted Cords*, *TOZ*, 5:14–15.

23. *Ki* (Ch. *qi*), as Takuan discusses it here, is a kind of vital force, the dynamic physical manifestation of mind. The concept remains important in many Chinese and Japanese martial arts. Originally in China the term was particularly associated with Daoism, Han Confucianism, and Neo-Confucianism. It has been variously translated vital force, material force, spirit, energy, breath, vital breath, and so on. If *ki* is blocked at any point or prevented from circulating freely throughout the body, it becomes a source of illness (*yamai*), both physical and psychological. Conversely, freeing and nourishing *ki* is an important aspect of hygiene, crucial to ridding oneself of all illness. For Takuan's views on *ki* and illness, which generally follow traditional Chinese teachings on the subject, see Kasai Tetsu, "Takuan ni okeru ki no shisō ni tsuite," 733–735.

24. Sacred formulas recited in Hinduism and Buddhism, where they are incorporated in various sutras.
25. *Knotted Cords, TOZ*, 5:26–27.
26. Translation based on Milburn, *The Glory of Yue*, 284–287. The original text can be found at Donald Sturgeon's Chinese Text Project, http://dsturgeon.net, *Yue-jue shu, Waichuanji baojian*, sections 2 and 3. Famous swords often received names in premodern China and Japan. For the practice in ancient China, see Millburn's comments in *The Glory of Yue*, 287–293. John M. Rogers notes the popularity of ancient Chinese mythology, cosmology, magic, and ideas of statecraft in early Tokugawa Japan among both upper-ranking samurai and Confucian scholars. Rogers, "Development of the Military Profession in Tokugawa Japan," 66–72.
27. For the religious background of the sword in Japan, see Suzuki Masaya, *Katana to kubi tori: sengoku kassen isetsu*, 22–26, 37, 45.
28. Hori, *Zen Sand*, 686. See also Lishka, "Zen and the Creative Process," 141.
29. For the Chinese-character text, see Hori, *Zen Sand*, 480, 450, 591, and 343, respectively. (Translation of the third phrase is by Hori.) The index for *Zen Sand* lists fifty-eight phrases referring to swords.
30. Cited by Janine Anderson Sawada in "Religious Conflict in Bakumatsu Japan," 216. Sawada's paraphrase is from section 82 of Kōsen's *A Wave on the Sea of Zen* (*Zenkai ichiran*, 1862). The original passage reads: "When confronted with a koan one cannot understand, one makes it into a sharp sword and single-mindedly and utterly slays the robber-mind of ignorance to realize one's own bright virtue. . . . Thus, those who enter my room [for koan study] must make it their urgent task to slay the self." Morinaga Sōkō, *Zenkai ichiran*, 265-266.
31. Translation and text in R. F. Sasaki, *The Record of Linji*, 219. Sasaki states that the source of the verse Linji quotes is unknown but notes that the term "sword of wisdom" (*zhi jian*) appears in chapter 10 of the *Vimalakīrti Sūtra*, describing the activity of the bodhisattva, who "with the sword of wisdom [*zhihui jian*] destroys the thieves of evil passions" (*T* 14:554b). "Ordinary mind is the Way" is a celebrated saying of the Tang Zen master Mazu Daoyi (709–788): "The Way doesn't need to be practiced—just don't stain it. What do I mean by staining? Having the mind of samsara [birth and death] and proceeding along with artificial effort—all that is staining. If you want to know this Way directly, ordinary mind is the Way. And what is ordinary mind? No artificial effort, no right or wrong, no grasping or rejecting, no impermanence or permanence, no common or holy." *Jingde chuandeng lu* (Jingde Era Record of the Transmission of the Lamp, 1011), *T* 51:440a. (Passage cited in Sasaki, *Linji*, 219.)
32. Sokei-an's English-language commentary on the *Record of Linji* was delivered in New York City during the 1930s in the form of extemporaneous

lectures that were recorded by his American students. The collated notes of the commentary together with Sokei-an's English translation of the complete text (the first in a Western language) are in the archives of the First Zen Institute of America in New York City. Over the years, the institute has issued Sokei-an's *Linji* translation and commentary piecemeal in its periodical *Zen Notes*, and it expects shortly to publish the entire work in book form.

33. *Heizei no issai no shiwaza.*

34. Rogers, "Military Profession," 85–89, 136–139.

35. Literally, "Chinese writing" or "Chinese literature," the term *kanbun* also refers specifically to the mode evolved in medieval Japan for reading Chinese-character texts in classical Japanese—a language very different in syntax from classical Chinese, despite the Japanese adoption of Chinese characters. The process was performed chiefly through addition of markings to indicate the reordering of subjects, objects, verbs, dependent phrases, and so forth, to allow Chinese texts, such as Confucian and Buddhist scriptures, to be read in classical Japanese (*yomi kudashi*). Modern Japanese editions of Chinese Zen scriptures, for example, might include the original Chinese, with or without its *kanbun* markings, followed by the same text in its classical Japanese reading, and often a third reading in modern Japanese, along with notes and commentary.

36. Funaoka suggests the possibility that the work was prepared for Munenori. *Takuan*, 147. Kasai Akira speculates that the intended recipient may have been Munenori's son Mitsutoshi, whose ideas he sees echoing parts of *The Sword Taie*. "Takuan zen to bugei," 649.

37. Sato, *Sword and the Mind*, 12.

38. Takuan's exile and his transmissions to Yoriyuki and Sadayoshi are discussed below. For an overview of *densho* and secret transmissions for the martial arts in premodern Japan, see Bodiford, "Written Texts: Japan," 763–764.

39. For the letter and Takuan's description of the event, see the biographical section below.

40. Satō Rentarō, "Shohon," 273. Satō outlines here the theory of Imamura Yoshio, and quotes the undated letter from Imamura's *Shiryō Yagyû Shinkageryū* (Tokyo, 1962).

41. Satō, "Shohon," 276–288.

42. The three appear in photographic facsimile and corrected transcription in Satō Rentarō, "Shahon sanshu," 36–53, 73–89, and 91–139, respectively. A chart by Satō showing the hypothetical development of the different surviving versions of *Record of Immovable Wisdom*, both premodern and modern, appears in Satō, "Shohon," 287–288.

43. Satō, "Shahon sanshu," 73, 79–81.

44. Ibid., 89.

45. Ibid., 131–139.
46. Sato, *Sword and the Mind*, 100; *HK*, 101. While unarmed techniques were not unique to the Shinkage school, it was Munenori's father's—Munetoshi's—own elaboration of the technique (discussed below) that the New Shadow school regarded as far superior to those of all other sword traditions. Friday and Humitake find other examples of such techniques in Japan in the sixteenth century. Friday and Humitake, *The Kashima Shrine*, 143.
47. Satō, "Shohon," 284.
48. Both letters are discussed below. Yagyū had apparently complained for some time of chest pains, and in the 1634 letter Takuan admonishes him that if he fails to stop smoking tobacco, the pains are likely to continue. Letter to Munenori (1634), *TOZ*, 4:140. Introduced from the West in the sixteenth century, smoking, generally done with a long-stemmed, small-bowled pipe, became a popular leisure-time activity in premodern Japan. Technically speaking, smoking was forbidden to Tokugawa samurai, and the 1615 bakufu code for samurai conduct states, "Anyone caught smoking tobacco is to be punished on the spot." Jōmoku of Genna 1 (1615), no. 2219, quoted in Rogers, "Military Profession," 59, from Joshi Ryōsuke, ed., *Tokugawa kinrei-kō* (Tokyo, 1961), 4:226–227.
49. The English rendering of the title follows in part Hiroaki Sato's translation, "Family-Transmitted Book on Swordsmanship," in *The Sword and the Mind*.
50. A few examples are Kasai Akira, "Takuan zen to bugei," 647–648; Sato, *Sword and the Mind*, 16–17; Suzuki Daisetsu, *Zen and Japanese Culture*, 151; *HK*, 162; and Imamura, *Yagyū ichizoku*, 170–177.
51. *HK*, 63.
52. Mitsutoshi's statement, from his 1637 work *Hie*, is quoted in Watanabe's appended remarks in ibid., 162–163. I follow Watanabe in taking the word for "teacher" (*zenchishiki*) to be singular rather than plural and to refer specifically to Takuan. See ibid., 112; also Sato, *Sword and the Mind*, 78. Watanabe states that the term *chishiki* (teacher) is similarly used by Munenori in *Art of the Sword* to indicate Takuan (*HK*, 112, note). For "koan," Mitsutoshi here uses the term *kosoku watō*.
53. *HK, Kaisetsu*, 176.
54. Imamura, *Yagyū ichizoku*, 170–177. Imamura suggests dating *Record of Immovable Wisdom* and its addendum to 1629–1632, that is, the period spanning Takuan's arrival in Edo to appear before the authorities and his return to the capital following his remission of exile. Ibid., 177. Satō Rentarō, by contrast, argues that *Art of the Sword* predates *Record of Immovable Wisdom*, reflecting Takuan's direct Zen instruction to Munenori, as opposed to simply a rehash or appropriation of Takuan's written teachings. Takuan, Satō suggests, would have revised and rewritten portions of Munenori's text, some of which would presumably reappear in *Record of Immovable Wisdom*, whose addendum Takuan composed at a later period. Satō, "Shohon," 274. Part of the argument

for dating the text before *Art of the Sword* (1632) revolves around Takuan's use of Munenori's childhood name "Mataemon" (also Uemon) in section 4 of *Record of Immovable Wisdom* rather than the title Tajima no Kami, which Munenori received from Iemitsu in 1629. Given the context, however, this may have been merely an acceptable expression of familiarity on Takuan's part.

55. Hidetsuna's dates are uncertain. Hon'etsu Shigetaka's *Honchō Bugei shoden* gives 1573 (Rogers, "Arts of War" [1991], 79), but others place his death in the late 1570s or 1580s. Hon'etsu claims that Hidetsuna's New Shadow style spread even to China and Korea. See Rogers' translation in ibid., 100.

56. Hidetsuna's name was changed to Nobutsuna during his period of service with Takeda Shingen, "Nobu" being a Japanese reading for "Shin," the first of the two Chinese characters that make up Shingen, a Buddhist name the warlord had assumed in 1551. However, the swordsman is referred to by Munenori in *Art of the Sword* as Hidetsuna, the name generally employed by modern Japanese scholars and by the modern Yagyū school. Ise no Kami (literally, governor of Ise [Province]) was a court title bestowed on Hidetsuna.

57. An English translation of Munetoshi's *inka* from Hidetsuna is included in Sato, *Sword and the Mind*, 5. The term *mokuroku* (catalog) was used in premodern Japan for documents given to students on completion of martial arts training, certifying the particular skills in which they had qualified (*Kōjien*, 2187). Bodiford translates the term "curriculum." "Zen and Japanese Swordsmanship," 73. The term *inka*, used in both Zen and Esoteric Buddhism, was also adopted by certain schools of martial arts in premodern Japan. See Rogers, "Arts of War" (1991), 174.

58. Phrases appearing in *Blue Cliff Record* (*Piyan lu*), case 65 (*T* 48:196a) and case 77 (*T* 48:204c), respectively.

59. Katō Takao and Yagyū Nobuharu, "Tairon," 5. Sato describes *marobashi* as "the ability to shift the sword and the mind fluidly and at will." *Sword and the Mind*, 105, n. 1. The image of the gem rolling in a tray may well derive from Zen literature. A similar expression occurs in the second line of a "capping verse" included by Hori in *Zen Sand*: "Go east, go west—in the wide world / Roll left, roll right—like pearls round a tray" (558).

60. Quoted in Katō Takao, "Tairon," 6.

61. *T* 48:177b. "Baizhang said, 'Manifold appearances and myriad forms, and all spoken words each should be turned and returned to oneself and made to turn freely.'" Translated in Thomas Cleary and J. C. . Cleary, *The Blue Cliff Record*, 241. In Japanese, *ten* is the *on*, or Chinese-derived, reading of the character for *marobashi*. *Roku-roku* (Ch. *lulu*) is onomatopoetic and describes the sound of turning wheels. *Ji* is an adverbial suffix. The translation of *ten roku-roku* is from Hori, *Zen Sand*, 246: "Rolling, rolling along; turning, turning along" (*ten roku-roku; a roku-roku*). Baizhang is the noted Chinese Zen master Baizhang Huihai (720–814).

62. *Linji lu*, based on the translation in Sasaki, *Record of Linji*, 244. ("Shifts" follows the translation in Sato, *Sword and the Mind*, 104. The Chinese character for "shifting" is the character read *ten*, discussed above.) Manorhita is said to have been a disciple of the Buddhist teacher Vasubandhu. Two teachers bearing the name Vasubandhu lived in India, one in the fourth, the other in the fifth century CE.

63. Translated in Sato, *Sword and the Mind*, 105; *HK*, 109–111.

64. According to Rogers, such family succession to the headship of sword schools did not exist in sixteenth-century Japan and developed in the early Tokugawa period. Rogers, "Military Profession," 148. The Yagyū New Shadow school as it survives today descends from the school's Owari branch founded by Munetoshi's grandson Toshitoshi (1570–1650). Rogers, "Arts of War" (1991), 173.

65. Quoted in Katō Takao, "Tairon," 6, from *Heihō hyakushu*.

66. In *Kage mokuroku*, Hidetsuna also occasionally transcribes *shinkage* using the character for shadow, silhouette, or trace, read *ei* in Sino-Japanese. Ibid., 6.

67. Quoted in Imamura, *Yagyū ichizoku*, 1:51. Certain of these New Shadow school themes are echoed in Issai Chōzan's (1657–1741) *The Cat's Marvelous Skill* (*Neko no myōjutsu*, 1727), a text that examines swordsmanship through the parable of a master rat-catching cat. According to the cat, the secret to its art lies in being completely empty in order to avoid telegraphing anything to one's opponent and thereby avoiding any sort of artifice. "Only be selfless and respond naturally," the cat advises. "Swordsmanship is not just about striving for victory over others. It is, in a phrase, the art that looks upon the profound and clarifies life and death.... Thus one will adapt and respond spontaneously with change." Translated by Friday in "Beyond Valour and Bloodshed," 10.

68. Friday, "Off the Warpath," 251. Friday cites such galloping archery duels as an example of the "peculiar light cavalry tactics" of the time, which he compares to the tactics of the individualistic dogfighting aces of World War I. Friday's articles cited in the bibliography offer an excellent overview of samurai combat and its history, symbolic and actual, in Japanese warfare and martial arts culture.

69. The widespread use of *ashigaru* seems to date from the period of the Ōnin war. See Sansom, *History of Japan*, 2:125 .

70. Rogers, "Military Profession," 22. Suzuki Masaya, *Katana to kubi tori*, 151. Elsewhere Rogers states that it is possible gunfire did not alter the ultimate outcome of battles in late-sixteenth-century Japan. "Military Profession," 69. For the key role of guns, cannon, and explosives at the Osaka winter campaign (1614), see Taniguchi, "Military Evolution or Revolution?" 176–183, 186. The importance of guns in sixteenth-century Japanese warfare is still a matter of debate among military historians. See Friday, "Off the Warpath," 254.

71. Besides the capture or killing of the enemy, deeds of valor included such acts as rescuing a wounded comrade from the battlefield, being the first to

advance on the enemy lines, killing the enemy general, guarding the rear of the army as its troops withdrew, and so forth. See Suzuki Masaya, *Katana to kubi tori*, 172–173; Taniguchi, "Military Evolution or Revolution?" 184.

72. See Suzuki Masaya, *Katana to kubi tori*, 75–86. Unless otherwise indicated, the following brief discussion of the use of the sword in battle and the emergence of the martial arts sword schools in late medieval and early Tokugawa Japan is based on ibid. and on the articles and essays by Friday, Rogers, Bodiford, and Taniguchi listed in the bibliography, along with Rogers' unpublished doctoral dissertation.

73. Suzuki Masaya, *Katana to kubi tori*, 79–80. Suzuki's figures are based on *gunchūjō* concentrated largely in the period 1379–1380, toward the close of the civil war (1337–1392) between the Southern Court, headquartered at Yoshino, and the Northern Court, in Kyoto, the latter represented by the ultimately victorious Ashikaga forces.

74. Friday cites similar figures for the fourteenth through sixteenth centuries compiled by Thomas Conlan in Conlan's "State of War: The Violent Orders of Fourteenth Century Japan," Ph.D. dissertation, Stanford, 1998. See Friday "Off the Warpath," 253–254.

75. Suzuki Masaya, *Katana to kubi tori*, 91, 175–176.

76. Ibid., 6–69.

77. Although later associated with the Tokugawa samurai as a symbol of their warrior status, the wearing of the two swords was permitted to all classes of Japanese men in Takuan's day and was above all a public safety measure. Even when specific rules were issued by the bakufu in the late seventeenth century, forbidding commoners to carry other than short swords, exceptions were made for individuals who felt endangered or were able to bribe the authorities. See Rogers, "Military Profession," 16–22; and Suzuki Masaya, *Katana to kubi tori*, 198–199. Suzuki states that those samurai directly employed by the bakufu were also forbidden to carry long swords. Ibid., 200.

78. Ibid., 101. For the sword's structural problems, see also ibid., 93–108.

79. Ibid., 114–115.

80. Rogers, "Military Profession," 415. Rogers states that once the heads had been displayed, identified, and recorded, they were either exhibited as trophies, returned to the enemy force, or simply discarded.

81. Suzuki Masaya, *Katana to kubi tori*, 164.

82. Ibid., 185.

83. Ibid., 185–186. Rewards were thus calibrated not only according to the status of the victim but according to the risk involved in removing his head. Suzuki Masaya suggests that many of the "samurai" heads submitted for rewards after the siege of Osaka castle (1614) were probably taken from dead coolies, servants, and attendants. Ibid., 195.

84. Ibid., 58–59.

85. Rogers, "Military Profession," 150–153.

86. See, for example, the passage in *The Sword Taie* in which the text compares what happens when "two skilled warriors cross swords and fight to a draw" with the Buddha's acknowledgment of Mahākāshyapa's enlightenment, a famous legend associated with the origin of Zen.

87. Suzuki Masaya, *Katana to kubi tori*, 119, 121.

88. As Friday observes, a blurring of the distinctions between the two traditions occurred during the Tokugawa period. This resulted at times in an effort to free the sword schools' curricula of "excrescences" related to self-cultivation and to concentrate instead on practical techniques related to killing and maiming, which Tokugawa critics alleged to have formed the true core of sixteenth-century swordsmanship. In fact, Friday concludes, development of the martial arts sword schools, the *bugei ryūha*, was far more "linear" than appreciated in the past, and practitioners of both Tokugawa and modern postwar martial arts have more in common with their sixteenth-century prototype, the early martial arts master, or *bugeisha*, than the actual helmet-and-armor samurai warrior of the 1500s. See Friday, "Off the Warpath," 257–259.

89. For Neo-Confucian influence on the spiritual aspects of martial arts training in early modern Japan, see Bodiford, "Religion and Social Development," 493–495. Bodiford observes that Takuan's Buddhist approach in *Record of Immovable Wisdom* is something of an exception and that most teachings on the martial arts from the Tokugawa period are based in Neo-Confucian ethical notions of duty, reverence, and so forth. While conceding that *Record of Immovable Wisdom* was "the most influential of the Tokugawa-period martial-arts treatises," he finds in it a sound moral basis not unrelated to Neo-Confucian ideals. Bodiford, "Written Texts," 776.

90. Watanabe, *Kaisetsu, HK*, 162. Munenori's interest in Nō has been mentioned earlier. In 1601 Munetoshi produced a "pictorial catalog" of New Shadow techniques (*Shinkage mokuroku*) for the Nō actor Konparu Ujikatsu. Sato, *Sword and the Mind*, 12, n. 1. The manual, supplemented with comments by eighteenth-century sword masters, is included in ibid., 26–50.

91. Like other such secret transmissions for particular martial arts traditions, *Art of the Sword* remained a closed transmission document until modern times. See Bodiford, "Written Texts," 765. Rogers speculates that *Art of the Sword*, or some form thererof, was the "treatise on strategy" presented by Munenori to Iemitsu in 1632, according to the acount in *Tokugawa jikki* (Record of the Tokugawa [Shoguns]). Rogers, "Military Profession," 87.

92. Rogers argues that, overall, *Art of the Sword* presents a Daoist-centered philosophy aimed at clarifying the role of the new Tokugawa-age samurai, a warrior who fosters peace by the active avoidance of killing and war—except to suppress evildoers and protect the other classes of Japanese society from those who would disturb the peace. Ibid., 65–66, 82, 85–90, 137.

93. *Setsunintō.*
94. *Katsuninken.*
95. *Shinrikyō.*
96. *Byōki, yamai.* The term has the secondary meaning of "harm," "shortcoming," "error," "bad habit" and appears as such in Chinese and Japanese martial arts texts. I have, however, opted for the more comon definition of "disease" or "illness" here, given Munenori's Zen-influenced explanation of delusion in terms of attachment, which he considers the underlying illness of the mind, the latter an interpretation likely attributable to Takuan's influence.
97. *HK,* 51.
98. *Jaku; HK,* 54, 86.
99. *HK,* 71.
100. Translated in Sato, *Sword and the Mind,* 106; *HK,* 111–112. Munenori's comments in *Art of the Sword* on the importance of the mind "shifting with the moment" have been quoted previously in connection with Manorhita's poem.
101. Translated in Sato, *Sword and the Mind,* 106; *HK,* 115.
102. Munenori speaks of two stages in the warrior's mind practice aimed at removing disease, a beginning stage (*shoju*) and an advanced stage (*goju*). *HK,* 52–55.
103. *HK,* 61.
104. *HK,* 54–55.
105. Translated in Suzuki Daisetsu, "Zen and Swordsmanship" (2), in *Zen and Japanese Culture,* 165; *HK,* 53.
106. Kasai Akira, "Takuan zen to bugei," 647. Portions of Kasai's article deal with the New Shadow school and Munenori's teachings in *Art of the Sword.*
107. Following Hiroaki Sato's translations for the synonymous terms *tsune no kokoro, heizei no kokoro,* and *hyōjōshin.* The last of these, *hyōjōshin* (also *byōjōshin, heijōshin*), appears in various classic Chinese Zen texts and is often translated "ordinary mind" or "everyday mind"; but in the particular context of Munenori's work, Sato's rendering seems more apt.
108. *Dō; shigoku no koto.*
109. *HK,* 55.
110. *Honrai no menmoku. HK,* 57. A common Zen expression denoting original nature or consciousness.
111. Translated in Sato, *Sword and the Mind,* 75; *HK,* 57. Munenori's term for master, here, is *meijin.*
112. I have slightly altered Sato's translation here in accordance with the text.
113. Translated in Sato, *Sword and the Mind,* 86; *HK,* 72–73.
114. *HK,* 56.
115. Sato, *Sword and the Mind,* 108; *HK,* 115. For "no-mind," or "mindlessness," Munenori generally employs the Buddhist term *mushin,* occasionally substituting similar phrases in vernacular Japanese.

116. *Honshin ni kanau. HK,* 97.
117. Sato, *Sword and the Mind,* 75; *HK,* 56–58.
118. Some of these borrowings from Takuan have already been noted, such as Munenori's stress on the avoidance of attachment, on not allowing the mind to "tarry"; his contrasting of original mind and deluded mind in explaining the free functioning of wisdom; and his use of Takuan's metaphor of the cat on a leash for the constrained mind. Among examples not previously mentioned are Munenori's likening of the swordsman's instantaneousness of response to the lightning give-and-take of Zen dialogue (*HK,* 85); Munenori's discussion of reverence (*kei*) as a secondary stage in the quest for enlightenment (*HK,* 61–62); and his quotation of two *waka* (the classical thirty-one-syllable Japanese verse form) included by Takuan in *Record of Immovable Wisdom* to explain the workings of delusion: Saigyō's poem to the courtesan of Eguchi (*HK,* 111) and the poem on mind misleading mind (*HK,* 93).
119. *HK,* 103.
120. The emphasis on *bushidō* in this period was itself a distortion of Japanese social and military history, according to Rogers, who insists that the concept was never of particular importance to the Tokugawa samurai themselves. See Rogers, "Military Profession," 11.
121. For an overview of changing attitudes toward Buddhism, Zen, and the martial arts in modern Japan, including the impact of Western ideas on militant notions of Japanese uniqueness, see Bodiford, "Religion and Spiritual Development," 474–485; Bodiford, "Written Texts," 766; Taniguchi, "Military Evolution or Revolution?" 192; Suzuki Masaya, *Katana to kubi tori,* 54–56; and Victoria, *Zen at War.*
122. See, for example, the partial listing of books on Takuan in *TZI,* v and vi, including several titles dealing specifically with *Record of Immovable Wisdom.* Also the NACSIS Webcat Database of published Japanese books on Takuan (http://webcat.nii.ac.jp; accessed December 5, 2011), which lists some fourteen titles from the period 1937–1945; and Lishka, "Zen and the Creative Process," 139–140, n. 1. Takuan even appears as a character in Yamamoto Eiji's (1892–1962) historical novel *Miyamoto Musashi* (1939), where the Zen master serves as the famous swordsman's spiritual guide. The work appeared serially in *Asahi shinbun* from 1934 to 1939, when it was published in book form and became an instant bestseller.
123. Quoted and translated in Victoria, *Zen at War,* 102–103.
124. The NACSIS Webcat Database lists some eighteen titles in this period (accessed December 5, 2011).
125. See, for example, Hurst, "Samurai on Wall Street," 1–3, 8–13. Hurst challenges the view of the Japanese businessman as corporate samurai and finds in contemporary Japan a distinct neglect of works like Musashi's *Five Rings* (adopted by many U.S. managers as the "secret" to Japanese business success) and scant

corporate attention to the samurai heritage generally. See also Bodiford, "Written Texts," 765.

## Chapter 2: Translations

1. The fifty-two stages of the bodhisattva's (here, Buddhist practitioner's) path enunciated by the Tendai school based on the *Yōrakukyō* (*T* 24, no. 1485). The ignorance of attachment as the ground of delusion (*mumyō jūji bonnō*), however, is not associated with the fifty-two stages, or *gojūni-i*, but with the similar-sounding *gojūji* (or *gojūjiwaku*), the five kinds of fundamental ignorance that trap sentient beings in the realms of delusion and transmigration. A copyist may well have confused the two terms; *gojūji* certainly comports more precisely with Takuan's emphasis on attachment as the basis of delusion. The five kinds of fundamental ignorance are (1) wrong views common to the three worlds (i.e., desire, form, and formlessness, the realms of delusion) (*ken'issaisho jūji*); (2) attachment to the realm of desire (*yokuai jūji*); (3) attachment to the realm of form (*shikiai jūji*); (4) attachment to the realm of formlessness (*uaijūji*); and (5) the state of unenlightenment or ignorance in the three worlds that is the root cause of delusion (*mumyō jūji*) (following W. E. Soothill, *A Dictionary of Chinese Buddhist Terms* [London, 1937], 113a). The fifth and last (at times referred to as *mumyō jūji waku* or *mumyō jūji bonnō*) is viewed as original ignorance, sentient beings' powerful attachment to the insubstantial worlds of subject and object, self and other. It is discussed, for example, in the *Srimala Sūtra* (*Shōmangyō*), *T* 12:220a–b. See Nakamura Hajime, *Bukkyōgo daijiten* (Tokyo, 1975), 1:367a. Satō Rentarō's MS A-1, the Imperial Household manuscript, which he considers the earliest form of *Record of Immovable Wisdom*, composed in late 1636 and presented to the shogun Iemitsu, does not contain mention of the fifty-two stages. Satō, "Shohon," 276.

2. Referring to Yagyū Munenori, to whom the text is addressed. Satō Rentarō concludes that earlier versions of *Record of Immovable Wisdom* were presented to the Tokugawa shogun Iemitsu.

3. *Heihō* or *hyōhō*. Literally, the art—or teaching—of combat or of the warrior. By the Tokugawa period the term was synonymous with swordsmanship. See Friday, "*Budō, Bujutsu*, and *Bugei*," 58. In modern Japanese, the meaning of the term is simply strategy or tactics.

4. A phrase appearing in case 46 of *Blue Cliff Record*, "Jingqing's 'Sound of Raindrops.'" *T* 48:182b.

5. Munenori's school of fencing prided itself on its skill at *mutō*, or No-Sword, the technique of disarming and subduing a sword-wielding opponent with only one's bare hands. As noted before, such techniques were by no means exclusive to the New Shadow school, but, because of Munetoshi's particular

development of his teaching, the technique was closely identified with his school. Friday mentions an (apparently sixteenth-century) secret transmission for such a technique associated with the Kashima shrine. Friday and Humitake, *Legacies of the Sword*, 143.

6. Satō Rentarō ("Shohon," 276) observes that sections 1 and 2 of Takuan's text, including the sections' titles themselves, relate to the commentary portion of case 37 of the koan collection *Record of the Hermitage of Ease* (*Congronglu*)—specifically a passage from a commentary on the *Huayan Sutra*, *New Commentary on the Flower Adornment Sutra* (*Xin huayanjing lun*) by the Tang scholar Li Tongxuan (635–730/ 646–740). The passage, from the work's chapter 15, "The Ten Abiding Stages" (Shizu pin), reads: "The supreme teaching of Buddhism turns the original ignorance of attachment as the ground of delusion into the immovable wisdom of all buddhas, innately possessed by all sentient beings." *T* 36:833c. (The quote in *Congronglu* is slightly truncated.) In the *Record of the Hermitage of Ease* commentary by Wansong Xingxiu (1166–1246), a monk asks the master Yun'an Kewen (n.d.) about the above passage from Li's text. Yun'an responds by calling to a workman sweeping nearby who turns his head—an example, Yun'an observes, of "immovable wisdom." Yun'an then promptly demands of the same workman, "What is your Buddha nature?" and, when the man is unable to reply, remarks, "Isn't that 'attachment to delusion?'" *T* 48:252a. The commentary refers in turn to the main case, "Guishan's 'Karmic Consciousness.'" In the case, Guishan Lingyou's (771–853) disciple Yangshan Huiji (807–883) calls to a monk, who turns his head. *Record of the Hermitage of Ease* (1224) records comments of the Yuan master Wansong on *Songgu baize*, one hundred koans with verses compiled by the Song Caodong (J. Sōtō) master Hongzhi Zhengjue (1091–1157). See Miura and Sasaki, *Zen Dust*, 425–426.

7. A Sanskrit term signifying transcendental wisdom. The penetrating, intuitive wisdom of enlightenment.

8. Skt. Acala. One of the "kings of radiance" (*myōō*), wrathful deities who protect the Buddhist teaching. The most frequently represented of the kings, Fudō ("the Immovable") is especially prominent in Shingon iconography as one of the "angry" or "wrathful" forms of Mahāvairocana (J. Dainichi), the central deity of Esoteric Buddhism. In one hand he grasps a sword, symbolizing intrinsic wisdom, and in the other a snare of barbed rope to bind ignorance. He is often shown glaring fiercely, standing (or sitting) on a rock, with flames emerging from his body.

9. The teaching of the Buddha.

10. Takuan's discussion here has many elements in common with the ritual for Fudō Myōō in Japanese Esoteric Buddhism. As described by Pierre Rambach, "The devotee, as he identifies with Fudō Myōō in the course of the ritual, becomes aware of the innate and intrinsic Buddha-nature within him.

Fudō Myōō will give him the power to drive away evil spirits and to set aside the obstacles opposing the 'coming' of the Buddhas." Rambach, *The Secret Message of Tantric Buddhism,* 134.

11. The text here appears corrupt. I have taken the final verb *ugoku* (to move) to be a copyist's error for the very similar character *hataraku* (here, to act or function freely), which Takuan uses repeatedly in the sentences that follow.

12. Takuan's interpretation of Shinto *kami* as the original, enlightened mind, never attached to things, is noted below, p. 74.

13. Takuan is referring to the scale of twelve tones traditionally used in East Asia, where five- or eight-tone scales also were employed. In a note inserted into the text, Takuan lists the twelve tones, ranging from the the lowest (*ichikotsu*) to the highest (*kamimu*).

14. Kōhō Ken'nichi, son of Emperor Go Saga (r. 1242–1246) and teacher of the celebrated Zen master Musō Sōseki.

15. That is, Zen, swordsmanship, poetry, tea, and so forth.

16. These terms, *ri* and *ji,* have a long history in both China and Japan, and have been employed at one time or another in Daoism, Buddhism, and Confucianism. Generally speaking, *ri* (Ch. *li*) is used to indicate the absolute, the underlying basis of reality, and *ji* (Ch. *shi*), phenomena, the world of existence and multiplicity in which principle is manifested. Rather than dualities, *ri* and *ji* are generally regarded as mutually interpenetrating aspects of a single totality—its substance and its manifestation. Here, Takuan's meaning is somewhat more practical and specific, referring to the mind that is fundamental to expert swordsmanship (*ri*) and the swordsman's actual movements (*ji*), hence, "principle" and "action." Although somewhat at variance with this meaning, Takuan here may also have been alluding to a passge on the practice of *ri/li* and *ji/shi* in chapter 12 of *On the Meaning of the Mahāyāna* (*Dasheng yizhang*), a well-known outline of Buddhism by the priest Huiyuan (523–592). The passage mentions two sorts of practices with which students attempt to pursue the six *paramitas,* or spiritual perfections, by which a bodhisattva attains buddhahood: "The first, to practice according to particulars [*shi*], fails to lead to ultimate reality. . . . The second, the practice according to principle [*li*], leads to the ultimate reality of Dharma, demonstrating the perfection of the purity of self-nature." *T* 44:706a.

17. The five kinds of bodily stance (*migamae no goko*) apparently refers to one or another of the five correct bodily stances employed in the New Shadow school of swordsmanship and detailed by Yagyū Munenori in his *Heihō kadensho. Takuan zenji itsuwashū* identifies the five as (1) holding the body sideways to your opponent, (2) regarding your opponent's fists as equal to your shoulders, (3) making a shield of your fists, (4) stretching out your left elbow, and (5) placing your weight on the forward knee and stretching out your rear knee (p. 172). Translations are from Sato, *The Sword and the Mind,* 24.

18. The phrase is included in *Zenrin kushū* (Collected Phrases from the Forest of Zen), a late-seventeenth-century anthology of Chinese phrases that is frequently used in Rinzai Zen study in Japan. See Hori, *Zen Sand*, 167. The phrase also occurs in *Hongzhi Zhengjue chanshi guanglu* (Extensive Record of the Zen Master Hongzhi), a collection of teachings by the noted Caodong master Hongzhi Zhengjue compiled by his disciples. In chapter 3, Hongzhi quotes a dialogue involving the Caodong patriarch Dongshan Liangjie (807–809) in which the expression occurs (*T* 48:33c–34a), as it does in chapter 5 in the course of a talk delivered by Hongzhi: "For one of true determination when he pisses, it's all the way; when he vomits, he gets it all out—he doesn't hold back even a thread! There's not even space to insert a hair. The past mind cannot be grasped, nor the future mind, nor the present mind. Search every direction, scour the three worlds [of past, present, and future], and there's just this mind, just this Dharma." *T* 48:65c.

19. Takuan's metaphor refers to case 80 of *Blue Cliff Record:* A monk asked Zhaozhou, "Is a newborn infant endowed with the six consciousnesses?" Zhaozhou replied, "A ball hurled onto a rushing torrent." Afterward, the monk asked Touzi, "What does it mean, a ball hurled onto a rushing torrent?" Touzi said, "Flowing right along from one instant to the next" (*T* 48:206b). Zhaozhou Congshen is traditionally said to have lived from 778 to 897. Touzi Fazong's dates are 819–914. The six consciousnesses are the visual, auditory, olfactory, gustatory, tactile, and mental consciousnesses.

20. A familiar simile in Buddhist writings. See, for example, the *Record of Linji*, where Linji characterizes the superior Zen student as one whose "manifest power is swifter than a spark struck from flint or a flash of lightning" (*T* 47:501b). Translated in Sasaki, *Record of Linji*, 25. The phrase also appears in case 26 of *Blue Cliff Record*, "Pai-chang's 'Magnificent Peak,'" again describing the superior Zen student as one who "in a flash of lightning or sparks struck from stone retains the ability to change with circumstances" (*T* 48:167b). Cleary and Cleary, *The Blue Cliff Record*, 174. In premodern East Asia, fire was commonly produced by striking together two pieces of flint to create a spark.

21. 1118–1190. Saigyō was a celebrated medieval poet monk of the Shingon school known for his travels throughout Japan. In the popular Nō drama *Eguchi*, by Konparu Zenchiku (1405–1470), Saigyō seeks lodging at a house whose tenant turns out to be a prostitute. Feeling her home would be an inappropriate stopover for a monk, the prostitute tries to dissuade Saigyō from staying the night, but he assures her the situation poses no difficulty for him. In response, the prostitute offers the poem quoted here by Takuan. Hōshō, *Kasuga ryūjin, Funabashi, Eguchi*, 4 (pages internally numbered). The poem is also cited by Munenori in *Art of the Sword* (*HK*, 111).

22. Site in present-day Osaka. In medieval times it was a river port on the water route connecting Kyoto with the ocean and, like many active ports of our own day, was reputedly home to many successful prostitutes.

23. In classical Chinese Zen dialogues, raising one's fist was a typical nonverbal resonse to questions about Buddhism. See, for example, *Gateless Gate* (*Wumen guan*), case 11, "Zhaozhou Examines the Hermitage Masters": "Zhaozhou went to a hermitage master's place and asked, 'What have we here? What have we here?' The hermitage master raised his fist. Zhaozhou said, 'Such shallow water is no good for anchoring a boat.' He then proceeded to another hermitage master's place. 'What have we here? What have we here?' Zhaozhou repeated. This hermitage master too raised his fist. Zhaozhou said, 'You can seize or let go, kill or bring to life,' and bowed." *T* 48:294b.

24. The phrase appears as part of a couplet in *Zenrin kushū*: "The [white of the] plum flowers on the branch / Merges with the snow, [intensifying the blossom's] fragrance." Shibayama, *Kunchū zenrin kushū*, 99.

25. Reference is to *Gateless Gate*, case 37: A monk asked Zhaozhou, "What about the Patriarch's purpose in coming from the West?" (That is, what is the ultimate truth that Bodhidharma, the semilegendary founder of Zen, brought to China from India.) Zhaozhou said, "The cypress tree in the garden." *T* 48:297c.

26. Or Uemon. Munenori's early given name. Letters of 1619 and 1623 from the teenaged shogun Iemitsu to the middle-aged Munenori continue to address the latter as "Yagyū Mataemon." Quoted in *HK*, 172. Satō Rentarō states that the correct reading of the name is Uemon and argues that the name's first character (read *mata* in Japanese) is simply used here in the text adverbially, meaning something like "or again." However, in light of Iemitsu's letters cited above, I have opted for the Mataemon reading, also adopted by Rogers in his translation of *Honchō bugei shoden*. The work is the earliest survey of classic Japanese martial arts traditions and devotes particular emphasis to the New Shadow school and its development. Rogers, "Arts of War" (1991), 179–184. Munenori's full name is given by Hin'atsu, the author of *Honchō bugei shoden*, as Mataemon no jō Munenori, and Hin'atsu praises Munenori as "the greatest of all the swordsmen." Ibid., 183–184.

27. As noted previously, in Japan practitioners of meditation and the martial arts are often instructed to concentrate their energy and attention on the *tanden*, or lower abdomen, a point several inches below the navel, traditionally regarded in East Asia as the physical and spiritual center of gravity.

28. Referring to Mencius' belief that virtue, exemplified by an attitude of reverence, is innate in people and later lost. "Mencius said: 'Benevolence is the mind of man, righteousness man's path. To forsake that path and fail to follow it, to lose that mind and not know to recover it is pitiful indeed! If a man has a chicken or dog and loses it, he knows to recover it. But if he has a mind that is lost, he does not know to recover it. The Way of Learning is none other than to

recover the lost mind.'" *Mengzi* (The Book of Mencius), 6A:11. Chinese Text Project, http://dsturgeon.net. See also Takuan's comments below under the heading "Recover the Lost Mind."

29. *Honshin, mōjin.* Terms commonly used in Buddhism and Zen to emphasize the innate character of enlightenment and the illusory nature of delusion. The *Vimalakīrti Sūtra*, for example, speaks of "at once suddenly regaining the original mind" (*T* 14:541a), and the expression also appears in the *Platform Sutra of the Sixth Patriarch*, both as the above quote from the *Vimalakīrti Sūtra* and on its own. See Yampolsky, the *Platform Sutra of the Sixth Patriarch*, Chinese-character text pp. 13, 14, respectively. (The translation from the *Vimalakīrti Sūtra* is by Yampolsky, ibid., 141.) The term "deluded mind" appears in a number of Buddhist texts including *The Awakening of Faith in the Mahāyāna* (Ch. *Dasheng quxin lun*). A work thought to be of the fifth or sixth centuries and highly influential in all the Chinese schools of Buddhism including Zen, the *Awakening of Faith* expounds the dynamic interpenetration of the absolute ("suchness") and phenomenal, of the realms of enlightenment and delusion, through realization of emptiness (*śūnyatā*). "Since all unenlightened men discriminate with their deluded minds from moment to moment, they are alienated [from suchness]; hence the definition 'empty'; but once they are free from their deluded minds, they will find that there is nothing to be negated." *T* 32:576b. Translated in Hakeda, *The Awakening of Faith, Attributed to Asvagosha*, 42. In a comment on this passage, Hakeda notes the similarity between such statements in the *Awakening of Faith* and observations on emptiness by Takuan in *Night Talks at Tōkaiji*. Ibid., 100, n. 10.

30. *Ushin no kokoro, mushin no kokoro.* Again, common terms in Buddhism, used to express, respectively, the deluded mind of attachment and the original mind of enlightenment, which transcends all ignorance and attachment. See, for example, Wangsong Xingxin's introduction to case 18 of *Record of the Hermitage of Ease*, "Zhaozhou's 'Dog'": "A hollow gourd on a stream—hold it down and it immediately escapes. A gemstone glinting in the noonday sun—its appearance is ever changing. You cannot grasp this with the mind of nonintention; nor can you know it with the mind of intention. It takes a great man who's beyond ordinary understanding. If you're caught up by words and interpretations, how will you ever escape?" *T* 48:238b. *Mushin*, "nonintention" or "no-mind," has entered modern colloquial Japanese, where, among other meanings, it denotes a state of pure concentration, innocence, or absorption.

31. A Chinese expression used in Zen. See preceeding note. See also Komazawa Daigaku Zengaku Daijiten Hensansho, *Zengaku daijiten*, 1: 361b. Dried and hollowed gourds were commonly employed as containers in East Asia.

32. A celebrated line from the *Diamond Sutra* (*Kongōkyō*). *T* 8:749c. The phrase, also read *ōmushōjūni shōgoshin*, has been particularly revered in the Zen school. According to some traditions, this was the phrase that awakened the

Sixth Patriarch, Huineng (638–713), when, while selling firewood in the marketplace, he overheard the *Diamond Sutra* being recited. The *Taishō daizokyō* notes that this rendition of the story appears in the version of the *Sixth Patriarch Treasure of Dharma Platform Sutra* (*Liuzu dashi fabao tanjing*, J. *Rokuso daishi hōbō dankyō*) contained in the "Old Song" Tripitaka (published 1104–1108) in the possession of the Japanese Imperial Household Library. *T* 48:348, n. 3. The account also appears in a recently published second Dunhuang edition of the sutra (c. 733–801), first discovered in 1935. Its Chinese-character text is included in Red Pine, *The Platform Sūtra*. For the episode in question, see pp. 320–321; Chinese-character text on p. 4.

33. 1155–1225. Late Heian–Early Kamakura period literary monk, best known as author of the historical work *Gukansho*. I have been unable to locate the poem by Jien that Takuan cites here.

34. For a similar explanation of the *Diamond Sutra*'s phrase, see the comment to case 74 of *Record of the Hermitage of Ease*, "Fayan's 'Name and Substance'": "The *Diamond Sutra* says, 'Without attaching anywhere, let the mind manifest itself.' 'Without attaching anywhere' means not attaching to appearance or sound, to delusion or enlightenment, substance or function. 'Let the mind manifest itself' means that one manifests the mind in *every* place. If one manifests the mind attaching to virtue, virtue will be manifested; if attaching to evil, evil will be manifested. [In either case] original mind is immediately obscured. But abide nowhere at all, and mind alone fills the universe in every direction." *T* 48:273c–274a.

35. A celebrated phrase of the Cheng brothers, Cheng Hao (1032–1085) and Cheng Yi (1033–1107), prominent Song Neo-Confucians who stressed reverence as the essence of moral self-cultivation. Reverence, in turn, is conceived by the brothers as a practice linked with Mencius' "floodlike breath." Near the opening of "Entering the Gate" (Ch. *Ruguan yulu*), chapter 16 of the Cheng brothers collected works, appears the following: "Concentrating the mind in one place and not letting it stray—this is through reverence to rectify what is within and thus to obtain the floodlike breath." Kyūshu Daigaku, Chūgoku Tetsugaku Kenkyūshitsu, *Er Cheng quan shu*, vol. 1, 11.

36. *Keihaku no kane*. At Buddhist temples, this term often refers to a large metal bell suspended from a beam and struck with a wooden mallet to announce ceremonies; the bell is customarily struck in three increasingly rapid series of tones. The term *keihaku* itself may refer to the formulaic liturgical speech that opens the ceremony, a speech in which reverence is paid to the buddhas, the Three Treasures, and so forth.

37. *Isshin furan*. A Buddhist phrase expressing the idea of singleminded concentration. It is often associated with Pure Land Buddhism and faith in Amitābha Buddha, expressed in the practice of *nenbutsu*, the singleminded calling of Amitābha's name. In a 1644 letter to his patron the daimyo Koide Yoshihide (1586–1668), Takuan recommends the *nenbutsu* for those otherwise unable to

practice Buddhism (*TOZ*, 4:551). Various forms of Pure Land–Zen syncretism arose in East Asia. *Nenbutsu* practice was a prominent feature of Chinese Zen in Takuan's day and was also espoused by several of Takuan's Japanese contemporaries, including the Zen teachers Suzuki Shōsan, Ungo Kiyō (1582–1659), and Takuan's own student Isshi Monju (1607–1645).

38. The émigré Zen master Wuxue Zuyuan (J. Mugaku Sōgen, 1226–1286), founder of Engakuji, the famous Zen temple in Kamakura.

39. In 1269, when invading Mongol armies reached Wuxue's Chinese temple, one of the Mongol troops is said to have been prepared to kill him with a sword, when Wuxue calmly recited the following *gatha*, or Buddhist poem:

> In the vast universe
> Not even room to set down a single staff
> What joy—the self is empty, and things are empty, too
> The precious three-foot great Mongol sword
> Cleaves the spring wind in a flash of lightning

Taken aback, the soldier is said to have fled the scene. The story is cited in Tsuji, *Nihon bukkyōshi*, 3:167.

40. Possibly referring to the performance of Nō, the classical Japanese dramatic form of which Munenori was an amateur, if enthusiastic, practitioner.

41. Shao Kangjie, or Shao Yong (1011–1077), a Song Neo-Confucian scholar influenced by Daoism. A close friend of the Cheng brothers, he taught that the mind was the source of the universe and the universe the source of the mind, stressing the unity between heaven and man, things and self. See Bruce, *Chu-hsi and His Masters*, 30–38; and Wyatt, *The Recluse of Loyang*.

42. A similar verse appears in *Zenrin kushū*: "A gem, even in the mud, remains pure." Shibayama, *Kunchū zenrin kushū*, 214; Hori, *Zen Sand*, 419.

43. *Jōdan, gedan*. These are positions or postures, in Japanese swordsmanship. In *jōdan*, the superior, offensive posture, the swordsman's blade is raised over his head to strike at the opponent. In *gedan*, the inferior, defensive posture, the point of the sword is lowered.

44. The Yuan dynasty Zen master Zhongfeng Mingben (1263–1323). I have been unable to identify the source of the phrases attributed to Zhongfeng by Takuan.

45. Touzi's response in case 80 of *Blue Cliff Record*, referred to previously (note 19). Here Takuan employs what is apparantly an *ateji*, or homophone, a character with the same sound but a different meaning from the original. The final character of the original text is the character "to flow" (read in Sino-Japanese *ru* or *ryū*), but Takuan—or a later copyist or editor—has, deliberately or inadvertently, substituted the similarly read character meaning "to stop" or "to stay still."

46. *Zengo saidan*. An expression indicating reality's transendence of the conventional categories of time: past, present, and future.

47. The meaning of this passage is unclear, and the translation is tentative. It would appear to be a quotation from a Chinese work, but I have been unable to identify the source. Satō Rentarō suggests that the passage, which does not occur in other versions of *Record of Immovable Wisdom* and appears indecipherable, may be a copyist's error. He also speculates that the mention of "white clouds" in the final poem is intended as a reference to "white dew," a common symbol of impermanence in Japanese poetry. Satō, "Shohon," 270.

48. A poem from the twelfth chapter of *Ise monogatari*, a work by the poet Ariwara no Narihira (823–880). In the somewhat confusing story, a man is said to have run off with someone's daughter, taking her to Musashi Province, where they were pursued by the provincial governor. (Musashi is an old province now included in the Tokyo Municipal District and Saitama and Kanagawa Prefectures.) The man was arrested but first managed to hide the girl in the tall grass. Apparently unaware of the man's capture, passersby, noticing a figure concealed in the brush, assumed it was the kidnapper and prepared to burn him out. The horrified woman then recited this poem, begging them to desist, and was led away to the governor. See Yamada, *Ise monogatari*, 14. Takuan's reason for including the poem here and its connection with the paragraph heading above and the poem following are unclear. Like the Chinese poem that precedes it, these materials appear only in this version of *Record of Immovable Wisdom*, and Satō Rentarō suggests that they may have been inadvertently inserted in the course of transferring the document from woodblock format to movable type. Satō, "Shohon," 284.

49. A famous passage from the opening chapter of *The Mean*.

50. The ancestral Yagyū lands, in present-day Yamato Prefecture.

51. Apparently a reference to Jūbei Mitsutoshi, Munenori's eldest son and his heir in the New Shadow school. See Chapter 1.

52. *Naizen dono.* Mitsutoshi's younger brother, Munefuyu (1615–1675), also known as Naizen no Shō Toshinori. Honorary titles such as *naizen* were granted by the Tokugawa shoguns to prominent samurai retainers and their offspring. It is unclear in what year Munefuyu received the title.

53. The precise meaning of this line is unclear and the translation tentative. Sarugaku was an early form of Nō, but the term was used in referring generally to Nō during the medieval and early Tokugawa periods as well as to the farces known as *kyōgen*, generally performed in association with Nō. Munenori himself refers to Sarugaku in *Art of the Sword*, and Sato in his translation identifies it as a branch of Nō. Sato, *Mind and the Sword*, 66.

54. The same poem is included by Munenori in part 3 of *Art of the Sword*, with each appearance of the word "mind" accompanied by either the Chinese character for "original" (J. *hon*) or that for "false" (J. *mō*), indicating original mind or false mind and recalling Takuan's distinctions between the two in *Record of Immovable Wisdom*. Thus "(False) Mind itself leads (original) mind

astray. / Do not let (false) mind [mislead] (original) mind." Each line is also annotated by Munenori. *HK,* 93–94. The poem also appears in *Ikkyū hō no hanashi* (*Tales of Ikkyū's Dharma*), an undated Edo period woodblock publication. As such, it is included among Ikkyū Sōjun's religious poems (*dōka*) in Zen Bunka Kenkyūjo, *Ikkyū dōka* (Kyoto, 2008), 70, no. 12.

55. As noted in Chapter 1, the origin of the text on which Takuan comments here, composed in classical Chinese, is uncertain.

56. *Shinga.* A Buddhist term denoting the original self as opposed to the false, delusory self; hence, Buddha nature, the self revealed through enlightenment.

57. That is, the Himalayas, where the Buddha is said to have undertaken prolonged austerities in his search for awakening. "World-Honored One" (J. *seson*) is a common epithet for the Buddha.

58. The phrase "The blade that kills, the sword that brings to life" is derived from Wumen's verse in case 11 of *Gateless Gate,* "Zhaozhou and the Hermitage Masters": "His eye, a meteor / The workings of his mind, lightning / The blade that kills / The sword that brings to life." *T* 48:294b. The phrase also appears in *Zenrin kushū.* See Shibayama, *Kunchū zenrin kushū,* 80.

59. A phrase appearing in the *Record of Linji*: "Gain such discernment as this, and you are not turned this way and that by circumstances: making use of circumstances everywhere . . . you spring up in the east and disappear in the west . . . walk on the water as on land and walk on the land as on water. How is this possible? Because you have realized that the four physical elements are like dreams, like illusions." *T* 47:498c. Translated in Sasaki, *Record of Linji,* 201–202.

60. According to legend, the Buddha's words when he was born. The baby Buddha is said to have taken seven steps, raised his right hand, and repeated this phrase. *Long Agama Sutra* (*Dīrgha-āgama Sūtra*), *T* 2:4c.

61. That is, wisdom that is natural, intrinsic, and spontaneous (*mushichi*). Specifically, the wisdom of the Buddha, who realized enlightenment wihtout a teacher. The term appears, for example, in chapter 35 of the *Avatamsaka Sūtra* (J. *Kegonkyō*): "Those lacking the Buddha's wisdom are merely sentient beings who, being deluded, fail to recognize the Buddha's wisdom. This wisdom transcends illusion, giving rise to the wisdom that is all-knowing, the wisdom that has no teacher, and the wisdom without obstructions." *T* 9:623c. Toward the close of *The Sword Taie,* Takuan similarly speaks of "the Dharma you have to realize and attain for *yourself,* apart from any teacher's instruction."

62. *Shi igi.* In Buddhism, used as a comprehensive term for human physical activity.

63. Set phrases used in classical Chinese and Japanese that indicate simply "drinking" and "eating."

64. *Tenma.* Heavenly beings who seek to obstruct the Dharma; also used to refer to the king of the Paranirmitavasavartin Heaven, according to Buddhist cosmology the last of the six heavens of desire, or *kāmadhātu.*

65. Zen traditionally traces its "wordless transmission" to an incident in which the Buddha, during a sermon on the Vulture Peak (Skt. Grdhrakuta, J. Ryōzen), held up a golden lotus flower. Of all those present, only the Buddha's senior disciple Mahākāshyapa grasped the Buddha's intention and smiled, becoming the first Indian patriarch of Zen.

66. Phrases appearing in Yuanwu's introduction to case 1 of *Blue Cliff Record*, "Bodhidharma's 'Empty, Nothing Sacred,'" phrases used here as metaphors for the Zen master's instantaneous intuitive response. Yuanwu remarks: "Glimpse smoke over the mountains and already you know there's fire. See horns across the wall and right away you know there's an ox. When one thing is spoken of, understanding three things; with one glance detecting the slightest difference in weight—that's the ordinary activity of a student of Zen. When you've finally severed the streams of delusion, you'll freely pop up in the east, sink down in the west, meet all circumstances favorable or contrary, move forward or sideways, give or take. So when that happens, tell me: Who's the one that's doing it all?" *T* 48:140a.

67. The meaning of the phrase translated here as "cut his opponent into three" (J. *sandan*) is unclear. The term *sandan* may refer to a three-part movement by which an opponent can be swiftly dispatched with the sword. I have followed the interpretation of Sato Hiroaki, who renders the phrase as "cut up anyone into three pieces." Sato, *Sword and the Mind*, 124.

68. The statement that this occurred just prior to the Buddha's death does not appear in the usual versions of the story and seems to be an original addition by Takuan.

69. D. 532. The semilegendary first patriarch of Chinese Zen, who is said to have brought the teaching to China from India.

70. Dajian Huineng (638–713). The sixth patriarch of Zen/Chan, celebrated in the *Platform Sutra*.

71. The Five Houses were five Zen lines named after their founding teachers and said to have coexisted during the late Tang dynasty. They are Linji, Guiyang, Caodong, Yunmen, and Fayan. The Seven Schools refers to the five houses plus two prominent Song dynasty branches of the Linji school, the Huanglong and Yangqi.

72. The Song Chan master Xutang Zhiyu (1185–1269), whose Japanese Dharma heir Daiō Kokushi (Nanpo Jōmyō, 1235–1308) carried Xutang's line of Linji (J. Rinzai) Zen to Japan, transmitting his teaching to Daitokuji's founder, Daitō.

73. For "thirty years more study" see below, pp. 80–82.

74. Thus one *ryō* equals one hundred *shu*. *Shu, ryō, shi,* and *bu* are the Japanese readings of old Chinese units for measuring weight, used for precious metals and so forth.

75. A phrase from case 7 of *Blue Cliff Record*, "Guizong Asks about Buddha": "The great function manifesting itself immediately before you has nothing to do with fixed rules. Sometimes one takes a blade of grass and makes it a

sixteen-foot golden buddha; sometimes one takes a sixteen-foot golden bud-dha and makes it a blade of grass. Tell me: What is the principle that under-lies this? Have you really grasped it yet?" *T* 48:148a.

76. A phrase appearing in verse 35 of the *Song of Realizing the Way* (*Zhengdaoge*) by Yongjia Xuanjue (665–713), a disciple of the Sixth Patriarch, Huineng: "There are some who ask what teaching I expound. / I tell them: the power of great intuitive wisdom (*mahāprajñā*) / Whether affirming or denying, you won't understand / Moving freely as it does in all directions, even heavenly beings cannot fathom it." *T* 48:396b.

77. J. *Hakutaku*, literally "White Marsh," a legendary Chinese beast. According to the entry "Beast Baize" (no. 75) in "Treatises on Auspicious Omens" in the *Song shu* by Shen Yue (441–512/513): "When the Yellow Emperor went for an impe-rial tour of inspection and reached the eastern coast, the beast Baize appeared. It can explain and understand the essence of ten thousand things. It arrives as a warning to the people and, at appointed times, wards off calamities. It arrives when a wise ruler's virtue/potency reaches obscure and remote places." Trans-lated by Tiziana Lippielllo in *Auspicious Omens and Miracles in Ancient China*, 143. The Yellow Emperor is a legendary Chinese ruler of the third mil-lennium BCE. Images of the Baize were apparently displayed in early medieval China to ward off evil influences, and a particularly grotesque version of the creature became popular in mid to late Tokugawa Japan, with an oxlike body, manlike head with protruding horns, and eyes on its back.

78. Use of the Baize's image as an apotropaic device appears in two important Chinese Zen texts: *Collection from the Hall of the Patriarchs* (*Zutang ji*, 952, in the Korean Buddhist canon, K1503, 45:290a) and *Jingde Era Transmission of the Lamp* (*T* 51:331c). Both entries are identical and quote from a remark by the Zen master Luopu Yuan'an (834–898), a onetime student of Linji Yixuan and a figure who makes several appearances in the Linji record. The entry for Luopu in both *Hall of the Patriarchs* and *Transmission of the Lamp* records a series of koan-type exchanges, in one of which the master is questioned by a monk: "'A single hair completely swallows the ocean.' Is there anything more to be said about this?" Luopu replies, "A home displaying a picture of the Baize is sure not to have such goblins." This is followed in the texts with an alternate response by the Zen master Baofu Longzhan (d. 928): "Even a home *not* displaying a picture of the Baize won't have such problems." Takuan's reference is evidently to Baofu's alternate answer. *Zengaku daijiten* explains Luopu's original reply as indicating that for those with true aspiration to en-lightenment (*bodhicitta*), evil thoughts can never appear and notes that Luopu's phrase occurs as an interlinear comment in *Record of the Hermitage of Ease*, case 16, "Magu Shakes His Ringed Staff" (*T* 48:237b) (Komazawa Daigaku Zengaku Daijiten Hensansho, *Zengaku daijiten*, p. 19). A phrase in-cluded in *Zenrin kushū* offers a somewhat different formulation: "A home

with a picture of the Baize will have such goblins." See Hori, *Zen Sand*, 371. The information on the Baize and its appearance in Zen texts was kindly provided to me by Donald Harper of the University of Chicago (personal communication, July 2010; William Bodiford supplied to him the reference to *Zengaku daijiten*).

79. Gaozong (literally, "Eminent Founder"), the posthumous title of Liu Bang (d. 195 B.C.E.), who established the Han dynasty in 206 B.C.E. The text refers here to a passage in the last part of chapter 8 of Sima Qian's *Shiji*: "When Kao-tsung was fighting against Ch'ing Pu, he was wounded by a stray arrow and on the way back fell ill. When his illness continued to grow worse, Empress Lü sent for a skilled doctor. This doctor examined Kao-tsung, and in answer to his question, replied, 'This illness can be cured.' With this, Kao-tsung began to berate and curse him, saying, 'I began as a commoner and with my three-foot sword conquered the world. Was this not the will of heaven? My fate lies with heaven.'" Translated in Watson, *Records of the Grand Historian*, 1:116. For the original text of the passage, see Takikawa, *Shiki kaichū kōshō*, 1:84. The phrase "conquer the entire realm with a single sword" is included in *Zenrin kushū*. See Hori, *Zen Sand*, 374.

## Chapter 3: Happenings in a Dream

1. *Knotted Cords*, TOZ, 5:10.
2. Unless otherwise indicated, biographical information in this section is drawn from Takeno Munetomo's *Tōkai oshō kinenroku*. Traditional biographies of Takuan are referred to in the notes below by their Japanese titles.
3. The clan claimed descent from Miura Yoshiaki (1092–1181), a chieftain in the Genpei Wars, in which Yoshiaki fought as an ally of Minamoto Yoritomo, founder of the Kamakura shogunate.
4. That is, the Kanto, the area of present-day Tokyo.
5. *Manshō* (also *Banshō*) *soroku*, TOZ, 6:2 (page numbering in all *TOZ* works is internal.)
6. Also known as the "Takuan temple" (Takuan-dera or Takuanji). It is located in the town of Izushi.
7. Of Takuan's siblings, we know only that he had an older sister and a younger brother, Hanbei, who eventually assumed headship of the family. Hanbei's dates are unknown, and it is unclear if he had been born when Takuan was brought to Sukyōji in 1579.
8. *Kinenroku*, TON, 44.
9. Loosely modeled on Chinese prototypes, the system in Japan originated during the Kamakura period, when the five "mountains," or temples, indicated the five Kamakura Rinzai Zen establishments Kenchōji, Engakuji, Jūfukuji, Jōchiji,

and Jōmyōji. During the Muromachi period the rank of Gozan generally indicated the six Kyoto Rinzai temples Nanzenji, Tenryūji, Shokokuji, Kenninji, Tōfukuji, and Manjuji as well as the five Kamakura temples mentioned above.

10. See Tamamura Takeji, "Gozan sōrin no tatchū ni tsuite," in *Nihon zenshūshi ronshū*, 1:197–244.

11. See, particularly, Tamamura's essays "Nihon chūsei zenrin ni okeru Rinzai, Sōtō ryōshū no idō: rinka no mondai ni tsuite," in ibid., 2:981–1040; and "Zenshū no hatten," ibid., 1:992–1012. Also Tamamura's *Gozan bungaku*, 250; and *Engakuji shi*, 273–298. A brief overview of Muromachi Zen in the context of *sōrin* and *rinka* is included in my *Letting Go*, 6–7, and "Bankei and His World," 15–27. Takuan himself bridged the Azuchi-Momoyama period (late sixteenth century), which witnessed the triumph of the *rinka* organizations, and the Tokugawa period, when sectarian identities were administratively imposed by the bakufu and fostered by revivals within the Rinzai and, particularly, Sōtō temples. (See Haskel, *Letting Go*, 1–3, 18–21.) In his correspondence Takuan refers to "Sōtō and Rinzai monks," and so I have taken the liberty of using the terms myself even in describing the master's early life and associations in the Zen temples. Mention of the two Zen schools appears in a letter of 1644 to Koide Yoshihide. In the letter Takuan despairs of the current generation of Zen monks, "both Sōtō and Rinzai," whom he censures for wasting their days in the temples playing *go*, the popular board game originally imported to Japan from China. Formerly, Takuan remarks, if the abbot of Daitokuji caught any monks playing *go*, he would smash the board and toss the pieces into the kitchen fire. *TOZ*, 4:610–611.

12. Funaoka, *Takuan*, 9–10. According to Funaoka, Kisen's Myōshinji teacher was Chintei Shūhō (n.d.). During this period it was not uncommon for Zen teachers to succeed to separate temple lines (*garanbōkei*, here Kisen's position as abbot of the Tōfukuji branch temple Sukyōji) and teaching lines (*hōkei*, Kisen's position as heir to the teaching of a Myōshinji Zen master). In such cases, the temple line might constitute a Zen priest's public, institutional identity; the teaching line his private, "spiritual" identity. See Nōnin, "Kinsei zenshūshi sunkō," 152–158. Such dual identities were conspicuous in Gozan temples of the sixteenth century, where they often involved not the Daitokuji and Myōshinji lines but the Genjū-ha, a Japanese Rinzai lineage centered on an Esoteric Buddhist–style transmission of koans. Tamamura, *Engakuji shi*, 278–279; idem, "Hōkei no kenkyū hōhō ni kansuru ichi kenkai," 2:843–863; and idem, "Rinzaishū Genjū-ha," 2:865–926.

13. The suffixes *in* and *an* in Japan commonly refer to a retreat or subtemple (and by extension to the priest in residence), while the suffix *ji* refers to temples proper. Large headquarters establishments such as Daitokuji, Myōshinji, and the Gozan temples commonly included a number of subtemples on their grounds, referred to as *tatchū* and frequently containing

the pagoda of an eminent priest or patron connected with the subtemple's particular lineage.

14. By contrast, modern Japanese Zen priests typically retain their lay surnames and use these to precede their Buddhist names. For example, Sasaki Shigetsu, Yamada Mumon, and so forth. (See below.)

15. See the introduction to Takuan's *Hekigan kyūjūge* (1629), *TOZ*, 2:1.

16. *T* 48:139a–225c, and *T* 48:292a–299c, respectively.

17. The synonymous term *jakugo* (capping words), now standard in Rinzai monasteries, was also used, though less frequently, in premodern Japan.

18. All three phrases are from *Blue Cliff Record*, cases 69, 31, and 77, respectively. *T* 48:198c, 170b, 208c. The three are also included in Daitō's koan commentaries. For these and other examples of *agyo* used by Daitō, see Kraft, *Eloquent Zen*, 200–208.

19. Japanese scholars only began to study the *missan* system in the mid-twentieth century; many questions about its history and character remain, and research is continuing. A brief overview of *missan* history and modern scholarship on the subject is included in my *Letting Go*, 8–10, and "Bankei and His World," 48–91. In the Sōtō school, the term *missan* is often replaced by other, similar terms, such as *hisan, densan,* and *monsan.* The late Zen scholar Ishikawa Rikizan has published over one thousand pages of such documents dating from the thirteenth to eighteenth centuries in his *Zenshū sōden shiryō no kenkyū.* Ishikawa argues that the leadership of the mid-Tokugawa Sōtō school was mistaken in rejecting such materials as degenerate. Instead, he views the *missan* system as a positive, creative accommodation of Zen to the Japanese language and to deeply ingrained aspects of Japanese popular religious culture, an accommodation that allowed Zen's dissemination throughout much of rural Japan during the fifteenth and sixteenth centuries. See Ishikawa's article translated and introduced by William M. Bodiford, "Colloquial Transcriptions as Sources for Understanding Zen in Japan," 120–121, 132–140.

20. For a discussion of yin-yang and Shinto syncretism in premodern Sōtō secret transmision documents, see Ishikawa, *Zenshū sōden shiryō,* 2:893–932. On the absence of syncretic *missan* at Daitokuji and Myōshinji, see Andō, "Chūsei zenshū ni okeru Genjū-ha no missan zen ni tsuite," 612. There are, however, reports of current-day Myōshinji-trained Zen masters still transmitting sixteenth-century *missan* that incorporate yin-yang and Esoteric Buddhist interpretations, though to my knowledge no such instances have appeared in the scholarly literature.

21. Yanagida, ed., *Jikaishū,* 3.

22. Reference is to *Gateless Gate,* case 37, the koan "Zhaozhou's 'Cypress Tree,'" noted previously. *T* 48:297c.

23. Yanagida, ed., *Jikaishū,* 367. The koan is discussed below, n. 35.

24. Kaneda's listings for *missan* materials in the Matsugaoka Library include *missan* documents by a number of seventeenth-century Daitokuji abbots. See Kaneda, *Tōmon shomono to kokugo kenkyū*, 138–141.

25. A *missan*-type interview is described in a commentary on the *Record of Linji* said to have been copied by Takuan. It is among the *missan* materials cited by Kaneda Hiroshi in ibid., 143. See also Bodiford, *Sōtō Zen in Medieval Japan*, 148.

26. *Yunmen lu*, the record of Yunmen Wenyan (862/864–949). *T* 47:544c–576c.

27. *Daitō kokushi hyakunijissoku no agyo* (National Master Daitō's Agyo for One Hundred Twenty Cases). The work remained in manuscript till 1927, when it was published by Suzuki Daisetsu, based on a copy from the early sixteenth century. An edition by Hirano Sōjō, based on various versions of the text, appears in his article "Daitō kokushi agyo no kenkyū." Kenneth Kraft has translated a selection of *agyo* used by Daitō in his koan commentaries, including the *One Hundred Twenty Cases*, in *Eloquent Zen*, 192–219.

28. *Manshōsoroku, TOZ,* 6:71.

29. Named for the Song Zen master Hongzhi Zhengjue (J. Wanshi Sōgaku, 1091–1157). The suffix *ha* signifies a group or lineage. Bunsei was teacher in a celebrated branch of the Wanshi-ha centered in the Kyoto Rinzai headquarters temple Kenninji.

30. Gyokuho Shōsō (d. 1613), the temple's 130th-generation abbot, and Un'ei Sōi (n.d.), its 141st-generation abbot.

31. *Zenjū Daitoku Myōhō Kokan zenji Ittō oshō gyōjitsu, TON,* 189–193. The work was composed in 1649 by Takuan's student and biographer Takeno Munetomo, probably in tribute to Takuan as Ittō's principal heir.

32. Ittō's handwritten poem is preserved at Shōunji, a Sakai temple erected for Takuan in 1634 by a wealthy merchant follower. The language of the poem is rather cryptic, and my tentative translation follows Funaoka's reading in *Takuan*, 6–17. For Ittō's poem as Takuan's *inka*, or sanction of enlightenment, see *TZI*, 16–17. My translation of the term *goryō* (realizing enlightenment) follows the definition in Ui Hakuju, ed., *Bukkyō jiten* (Tokyo, 1938, new edition 1977), 1107b.

33. Similarly the honorifics *oshō* (Buddhist teacher) or *zenji* (Zen master) were generally appended to the formal name. Rules on use of the two names were not, however, ironbound. Takuan, as seen below in his letter to his younger brother, would occasionally sign his name "Takuan." And two generations after Takuan, the Myōshinji-line master Bankei Yōtaku would refer to himself in his sermons as "Bankei" and sign many letters the same way as well; at other times he would sign with his Dharma name, Yōtaku, or even with both names combined. See the letters section of Akao, *Bankei zenji zenshū*, 526–544. In 1872 the Meiji government urged Buddhist priests to marry and required them to retain their

secular family names, then as now generally placed Japanese style before their particular (Buddhist) names (e.g., Sawaki Kōdō, Yamada Mumon).

34. *Kinenroku, TON,* 59.

35. *Manbō furyō.* A famous koan derived from a question posed by the layman Pang (Pang Jushi, d. 808) to the Zen master Mazu Daoyi. The layman went to visit Master Mazu and asked him, "Who is it that does not accompany the ten thousand things?" Mazu said, "Swallow all the waters of the Western Lake in one gulp and I'll tell you." *Pang Jushi yulu, Zokuzokyō,* 2:25, 1:27. The koan appears to have been popular in the Daitokuji line, and its use is alluded to by Ikkyū in a previously cited passage in *Jikaishū.* Mazu's answer was also used in the New Shadow sword school to refer to concentrating the power of *ki* in the *tanden* and, by extension, to remaining unwavering in the face of trying circumstances. Katō Takao and Yagyū Nobuharu, "Tairon," 7.

36. Part of a celebrated passage from the *Record of Linji*: "Followers of the Way, mind is without form and pervades the ten directions: In the eye it is called seeing, / In the ear it is called hearing. / In the nose it smells odors, / In the mouth it holds converse. / Fundamentally, it is one pure radiance; divided, it becomes the six harmonoiusly united spheres of sense." *T* 47:497c. Translated in Sasaki, *The Record of Linji,* 165.

37. *Zentai sayū.* Another well-known phrase appearing in the *Record of Linji.* My translation follows the interpretation by Yanagida Seizan in his *Rinzai roku,* 146.

38. Mazu's answer to the question posed by Layman Pang in the famous dialogue referred to earlier. The copyist has used the homophonic character for "lake" (J. *kō*) in place of the character "river" (J. *kō*) found in the original koan. The Western Lake, Xi Hu, usually refers to a scenic lake outisde Hangzhou in Zhejiang Province. The dialogue also appears in the *Record of Mazu.* See Iriya Yoshitaka, ed., *Basō no goroku,* 85.

39. *Gyōjō, TON,* 152. In the text of the dialogue, as elsewhere in the *Gyōjō,* Shun'oku is usually referred to by his honorary national master (*kokushi*) name, Enkan (Mirror of Perfection), and Takuan simply as "the Master" (*shi*).

40. *Kinenroku, TON,* 59.

41 *Wuwei zhenren* (J. *mui no shinnin*). A term coined by Linji, appearing in the *Record.* "The Master said, 'On this living flesh is a true man of no rank who is always going in and out the faces of each one of you. Those of you who have not yet confirmed this, look! look!'" *T* 47:496c.

42. At Daitokuji, the imperial abbacy is referred to as *shusse* or *juin.* The emperor's awarding of the purple robe to Daitokuji abbots was begun in 1463 under Emperor Go-Hanazono (r. 1429–1464). The temple's highest rank, "National Teacher" (*kokushi*), was also awarded by the emperor (with some masters receiving the title posthumously), as was the second highest, "Zen master" (*zenji*), both titles being accompanied by new, honorary Buddhist names. These titles were followed, in descending order, by *zenjū* and *zendō,* both signifying Zen

teacher, except that the former was a teacher who had received the purple robe and was referred to as *oshō* (master) or *chōrō* (venerable elder). For a description of abbacy and priestly ranks at Daitokuji in the Tokugawa period, see *Manshōsoroku, TOZ,* 6:8–10; and Funaoka, *Takuan,* 20–21.

43. *Manshōsoroku, TOZ,* 6:8.

44. Funaoka, *Takuan,* 24.

45. *Kinenroku, TON,* 62–63. The Zen monk's life of complete nonattachment is commonly likened to drifting clouds and flowing streams—hence the Zen monk's sobriquet of *unsui,* "cloud and stream." "Red dust" is a metaphor from classical Chinese literature, the delusions of worldly life being compared to the swirling dust stirred up on the streets of the busy capital city.

46. The other major branch, the "Southern" line, was centered in the subtemple Ryōgen'in. Charts of succession in the two lineages during the late sixteenth and early seventeenth centuries and of succesion in a third branch, the Ryōsen-ha, appear in Funaoka, *Takuan,* 202–205.

47. Taniguchi, "Military Evolution or Revolution?" 177. Taniguchi places the total number of combatants at Osaka at some 400,000, as compared with 150,000 to 160,000 who participated in the Battle of Sekigahara, the 1600 battle that confirmed Tokugawa dominance of Japan. See also Sansom, *A History of Japan,* 2:395.

48. *Manshōsoroku, TOZ,* 6: 32.

49. In 1616 Yoshichika was appointed daimyo of Sonobe (Kyoto Municipal District), and Yoshihide was made daimyo of Tajima, headquartered in Takuan's hometown of Izushi.

50. A subtemple on the grounds of Myōshōji, a Kyoto temple founded by Daiō Kokushi.

51. A restored version of Tōenken was erected at Sukyōji in 1969. In Takuan's day Sukyōji and Tōenken were located in the village of Irusayama, within the town of Izushi.

52. The "wall notice" (*hekisho* or *kabegaki*) is included in *Knotted Cords, TOZ,* 5:36–37.

53. *Manshōsoroku, TOZ,* 6:51.

54. Funaoka, *Takuan,* 34.

55. *Manshōsoroku, TOZ,* 6:51.

56. *TOZ,* 2:1–29. The work itself bears no date. The 1621 (Genna 7) date is given in *Kinenroku (TON,* 85). The text is composed in *kana majiri.* A version in *kanbun* is collected in *TOZ,* 1. Ogisu speculates that the latter is the original version, but there seems to be no way to make a final determination. *TON,* 85, n. 1.

57. For an examination of Takuan's views on *ri, ki, shō,* and their interaction as presented in *On the Distinction between Principle and Activity,* see Kasai Tetsu's article "Takuan ni okeru 'ki' no shisō ni tsuite." Bodiford considers Takuan's short work to be dominated by Neo-Confucian thought, a kind of

"introduction" by the master to the teachings of Neo-Confucianism's leading exponent, Zhu Xi. Bodiford, "Japanese Swordsmanship Reconsidered," 74–75. According to Bodiford, the text was extremely popular among students of jujutsu during the Tokugawa period. Ibid., 75.

58. *Riki sabetsuron, TOZ,* 2:22. Takuan's diagram is similar to many of the diagrams in early- to mid-seventeenth-century Sōtō school secret transmission documents published by Ishikawa in volume 2 of his *Zenshū soden shiryō no kenkyū.* See, for example, those on 2: 536, 686, 923, and 944.

59. *Riki sabetsuron, TOZ,* 2:22.

60. Ibid., 24.

61. Ibid., 29.

62. McMullan, *Buddhism and the State in Sixteenth Century Japan,* 41, 55.

63. Sansom, *History of Japan,* 2:394–395. Ekei's temple was in Aki (Hirohsima Prefecture). We have only the date of his execution, 1600.

64. *Chokkyō shie hatto.* The text appears in Amakuki, ed., *Myōhsinji roppyakunen shi,* 297.

65. *Manshōsoroku, TOZ,* 6:33–34.

66. Monbushō Shūkyō Kyoku, ed., *Shūkyō seido chōsa shiryō,* 6:54. The thirty-year figure does appear in the 1615 code for the Sōtō school, though not the stipulation regarding seventeen hundred koans. Ibid., 12.

67. Iriya Yoshitaka, ed., *Zengo jiten,* 160.

68. See, for example, case 4 (*T* 48:144c), case 20 (*T* 48:161b), and case 87 (*T* 48:212c). In this regard, Funaoka cites a 1613 succession dispute at Sōken'in, an important Daitokuji subtemple. In an appeal to Sūden, one of the contending parties accuses his rival of possessing a merely literary education owing to his background at a "Gozan" temple (Tōfukuji) and of consequently lacking the number of years of training traditional at Daitokuji. "Even in *Blue Cliff Record,*" the priest, Gesshin Sōin (n.d.), laments to Sūden, "it says, 'Study thirty years more!' But nowadays such determination is lacking. If you don't study twenty years night and day, it will be impossible to fully realize the Dharma." Quoted in Funaoka, *Takuan,* 46. For the Sōken'in dispute, see ibid., 42–50. Takuan also refers in his letter of protest, cited earlier, to the twenty years necessary to complete the curriculum at Daitokuji.

69. *T* 48:295b.

70. Takuan cites these facts in his letter to the bakufu. *Manshōsoroku, TOZ,* 6:66–67. See also Miura and Sasaki, *Zen Dust,* 352.

71. The Yuan Zen master and poet Qinghong (1272–1352), for instance, invokes the phrase in one of his poems, "For the Monks of the Haidu Temple." Red Pine, *The Zen Works of Stonehouse,* 84 (Chinese-character text).

72. Ogisu, *TON,* 17.

73. We know from his diary that, in drafting the 1615 decrees, Sūden had consulted with senior priests of the particular Zen temples involved. At Daitokuji these

included three leading abbots (among them Takuan's colleague Gyokushitsu), whose discussions with Sūden included the subject of koans. See Funaoka, *Takuan*, 53.

74. Cited in ibid., 54.

75. For an extended treatment of the Purple Robe incident, see Tsuji, *Nihon bukkyōshi*, 8: 230–231, 235–260, 271–273.

76. *Manshōsoroku, TOZ*, 6:64–75. Takuan's letter bears the heading "Regarding the Five Articles of the Daitokuji Decree [Issued] at the Command of His Venerable Lordship [i.e., Ieyasu]." However, the letter is sometimes referred to as the "Refutation" (Kōbensho) or "Vindication" (Benmeiron).

77. A tradition recorded in *Manshōsoroku* states that the authorities were nettled by the letter's use of *kana majiri*, mixed (*majiri*) *kana* and Chinese characters (*kanji*), and that, when asked why he did not compose a more formal (and erudite) response that used *all* Chinese characters, Takuan replied that had he done so, it was likely no one would have been able to read it—further incensing the authorities and ensuring that his punishment would be severe (*TOZ*, 6:81). The editor adds, however, that this is merely a tradition preserved in his domain and that he cannot vouch for its accuracy. In fact, another description he offers of the episode is more neutral, with Takuan explaining simply that he used *kana majiri* in his letter to be sure everyone understood it (ibid., 64).

78. Tamamura Takeji has argued that the references to seventeen hundred koans and thirty years' training in the 1615 decree reflect the lingering influence of *missan* practice, in which each Japanese Zen line maintained its own "schedule" of koans to be mastered over an extended period of study (see Tamamura, "Takuan Sōhō"). Much of the controversy surrounding the codes, he hypothesizes, centers on the repudiation of *missan* Zen at Daitokuji by Takuan and his supporters. As a product of the late-sixteenth-century Gozan, where *missan* practice was pervasive, Sūden, Tamamura reasons, would have sought to promote *missan* Zen. In doing so, he roused the opposition of reformers like Takuan, who were struggling to revitalize practice at Daitokuji and to leave behind the baggage of late medieval Japanese Zen. Tamamura's evidence for all this is slim, and his reading of the admittedly complex circumstances of the Daitokuji *hatto* seems unconvincing. Takuan's actual views on *missan* remain ambiguous. While in his letter to the bakufu he is critical of the quantitative approach to koan study associated with *missan* Zen, Takuan may have accepted certain aspects of *missan* practice in his own teaching, even while opposing the system's worst excesses. Takuan's description of a hypothetical Zen dialogue in *Record of Immovable Wisdom*, for example, is similar in style to surviving secret koan manuals, or *missanchō*, with their emphasis on capping phrases employed as fixed responses. Passages from several undated *missanchō* whose "answers" echo the responses

in Takuan's example appear in Suzuki Daisetsu, *Zen shisōshi kenkyū,* 4:26. The *missanchō* attributed to Takuan has been noted earlier.

79. I can find no independent source for Takuan's statement here regarding the number of koans passed by Daitō and Tettō, figures Takuan conceivably derived from traditions current at Daitokuji.

80. The passage appears above, p. 64.

81. *Manshōsoroku, TOZ,* 6:67.

82. As noted earlier, the koan method appears to have reached its fullest development during the Song dynasty. Takuan may be alluding here to the Linji master Dahui Zonggao (1089–1163), a celebrated exponent of koan practice, especially of concentration on the "Wu" (J. "Mu") koan, which Dahui recommended to various lay officials who were his students.

83. Buddhist teaching is often compared to a raft, a means to cross the "stream" of birth and death to reach the "other shore" of Nirvana.

84. *Manshōsoroku, TOZ,* 6:70–72.

85. Ibid., 73.

86. The text of the 1629 letter of apology appears in Funaoka, *Takuan,* 62, along with a photograph of the original document in Takuan's hand, in the possession of Tōkaiji (ibid., 63).

87. *Manshōsoroku, TOZ,* 6:78–80.

88. *Hosokawa keki,* quoted in Funaoka, *Takuan,* 63. The *Keki,* mentioned previously, is an unpublished document in the Tokyo Daigaku Shiryō Hensanjo.

89. *Manshōsoroku, TOZ,* 6:110. To place Naoyori's feat in context, some fourteen thousand heads were listed as taken after Osaka castle's fall in 1615, many, according to Suzuki Masaya, removed from unresisting victims, preferably corpses. Suzuki Masaya, *Katana to kubi tori,* 113. As noted earlier, a head's worth was valued according to the status of the victim, and Suzuki avers that cheating was rampant, with many heads claimed to be those of enemy generals or samurai actually belonging to their coolies, servants, or attendants. Ibid., 195.

90. Literally "my teacher of the Law" (*nori no shi*), law here signifying the Dharma, the Buddha's law, or teaching. *HK,* 63. *Art of the Sword* has been discussed above. Munenori's koan study with Takuan is noted in *Kintōshō,* an undated work included in *TON,* 123.

91. Funaoka quotes a passage in a 1636 letter from Takuan to Ogawa Kyūeimon (n.d.) to the effect that Munenori, at the time of the Purple Robe Affair, was a close acquaintance who had been coming to Daitokuji for many years (*Takuan,* 64). But the letter to Ogawa, as transcribed in volume 4 of *TOZ* (no. 82), does not contain the lines quoted by Funaoka, and I have been unable to locate them elsewhere in the letters volume of the *Zenshū. Manshōsoroku* claims that Munenori's Zen studies with Takuan predate 1600, when Munenori left Yamato to serve Ieyasu (*TOZ,* 6:121), but it fails to offer convincing proof for this assertion.

92. Letter to Ogawa Kyūeimon, *TOZ*, 4:179.

93. Ibid., 179–180.

94. As noted earlier, each year Zen temples observe two such ninety-day retreats, or *kessei ango*. The retreat Takuan participated in at Kōtokuji was the so-called *geango*, or summer retreat, lasting usually from the sixteenth day of the fourth month to the fifteenth day of the seventh month.

95. *TOZ*, 2:1–46. The number of poems, as indicated, is actually ninety-one, but in Zen literature round figures often seem to have been appreciated more than numerical precision. Given that the retreat was ninety days, it is unclear what the additional poem was intended for—perhaps an opening or closing ceremony.

96. *Hosokawa keki*, quoted in *TZI*, 34. See also Funaoka, *Takuan*, 67. *Manshōsoroku* states merely that Kogetsu apologized and was pardoned (*TOZ*, 6:81). Funaoka sees in Kogetsu's pardon evidence of a pattern of mutual understanding between Sūden and Kogetsu. But, as indicated in *Manshōsoroku*, the latter may simply have been let off after he agreed to apologize, perhaps by prearrangement with his comrades, as Kogetsu, though himself well into middle age, was still the youngest of the three.

97. See *TZI*, 34, including Takuan's statement in a 1631 letter to Kogetsu: "For the past three years you have gone back and forth between Kyoto and Edo, but since last winter you have settled in Edo, enduring countless sufferings. . . . True, we two received punishment while you did not. But these sufferings of yours are surely a hundred times worse." The letter, however, is not included in the letters volume of *TOZ*, and no source for it is indicated.

98. Letter to Yoshihide (1629). *TOZ*, 4:52–53.

99. *Hosokawa keki*, quoted in Tsuji, *Nihon bukkyōshi*, 8:259. "National Teacher" (*kokushi*) refers to Sūden's formal title, Honkō Kokushi (National Teacher of Original Radiance). The word "mountain," as noted before, is used frequently in East Asia as a metaphor for Buddhist temples and here probably refers to Sūden's Edo headquarters, the Nanzenji branch temple Konchi-in.

100. Tadatoshi's 1629 letter to his father, Tadaoki, is quoted in *TZI*, 33.

101. Quoted in Tsuji, *Nihon bukkyōshi*, 8:258. The verse adds the pejorative "muddy" (*nigori*) to the characters for "river and moon" that make up Kogetsu's name.

102. Ibid., 8:260.

103. A cautionary example is the case of Takuan's colleague Shōgaku Jōchō (n.d.), related in *Manshōsoroku*. Jōchō, Daitokuji's 137th-generation abbot, had been among the senior masters who consulted with Sūden on the Genna decree. Like many Daitokuji abbots, Jōchō was known as a skilled calligrapher, and he had once obliged a request to produce a copy of Daitō's calligraphy. The result was so convincing that, after leaving his hands, the copy became mistaken for Daitō's original brushwork. As such, it came into the shogun's possession and was

presented by him to Takuan's patron Hosokawa Tadaoki, daimyo of Buzen. When Takuan, Gyokushitsu, and Kogetsu joined Tadaoki in his tea hut, where the work was displayed, Tadaoki was puzzled that the priests failed to admire it. Informed by them that it was only a copy by Jōchō, Tadaoki was furious and complained to the shogun, who in turn was mortified that his retainer's gift had turned out to be merely a facsimile. Jōchō, as the unwitting cause of the shogun's embarrassment, was ordered expelled from Daitokuji in 1617 and died in seclusion at the Tendai temple Miidera on Lake Biwa. *Manshōsoroku, TOZ,* 6:45.

104. Takuan describes his quarters in a letter of 1630 to his brother Hanbei. *TOZ,* 4:64–65.

105. *Manshōsoroku, TOZ,* 6:89.

106. Letter to Hanbei (1630). *TOZ,* 4:64–65.

107. Ibid.

108. Unaddressed letter (1630). *TOZ,* 4:90.

109. Letter to Hanbei (1630). *TOZ,* 4:68.

110. Letter to Hanbei (1630). *TOZ,* 4:71.

111. Letter to Naoyori (1629). *TOZ,* 4:59–60.

112. *Sangai.* The worlds of desire, form, and formlessness. The expression is often used, as here, to indicate the realms of transmigration.

113. Unaddressed letter (probably 1629–1630). *TOZ,* 4:62–63.

114. Biographical information on Isshi is based on *Honchō kosoden,* in Suzuki Gakujutsu Zaidan, ed., *Dai Nihon bukkyō zensho,* 63, 276–277; *Butchō kokushi nenpu,* T 81:185b–189b; and Amakuki, *Myōshinji,* 362–372.

115. Quoted in Amakuki, *Myōshinji,* 362.

116. *Manshōsoroku* states that it is unclear how long Isshi remained with Takuan in Dewa (*TOZ,* 6:102). Ogisu agrees but feels Isshi probably stayed about one year (*TON,* 95, n. 2). Funaoka believes Isshi joined Takuan in Dewa for a somewhat shorter period, from winter 1629 to summer 1630 (*Takuan,* 80).

117. According to *Manshōsoroku,* Matsumoto had been a retainer of the Dewa daimyo Torii Tadamasa (1567–1628) but following Tadamasa's death became a *rōnin,* or masterless samurai. He eventually traveled to Edo and became lance instructor to a succession of feudal lords. In 1651 he was summoned by the shogun to demonstrate his art, but owing to illness he was unable to appear. *TOZ,* 6:89–90.

118. *Manshōsoroku, TOZ,* 6:89. The term *kan,* sometimes translated as "fascicle" or "volume," indicates the sections or divisions of a document.

119. Ibid., 90. In Yoshikawa Eiji's 1930s blockbuster historical novel *Miyamoto Musashi* and the Inagaki Hirose film it inspired, titled in English *Samurai Trilogy* (Tōhō, 1956), Takuan instructs another famous martial arts master of the day, Miyamoto Musashi. The story, however, is entirely fictional. There is no evidence that Takuan ever taught or even met the noted swordsman.

120. Unaddressed letter (1630). *TOZ*, 4:89. In 1630 Takuan was actually fifty-seven by Western reckoning. Japanese in the premodern period were considered one year old at birth; hence, ages here are one year older than their modern Western equivalents.

121. According to *TZI*, Kogetsu waited to greet his companions at Kōtokuji, and the three produced a joint set of poems to commemorate the occasion (42). A dated scroll with the three poems, in the calligraphy of Kogetsu, Gyokushitsu, and Takuan, respectively, is still preserved at Ryūkōin, the Daitokuji subtemple founded by Kogetsu. (For a photograph of the scroll and transcription of the verses, see ibid., 42–43.) No mention of the reunion, however, appears in the traditional Takuan biographies, and Funaoka suggests that Takuan and Kogetsu were probably reunited the following month, when Kogetsu visited the shogunal castle to express his thanks for his colleagues' pardon (*Takuan*, 84).

122. Takuan's dated farewell letter to Yoriyuki, quoted in Funaoka, *Takuan*, 84, is not included in the letters volume of *TOZ*.

123. *TOZ*, 6:90.

124. Letter to Yoshihide (1634). *TOZ*, 4:121–122.

125. Letter to Yoshihide (1634). *TOZ*, 4:130–131.

126. Funaoka, *Takuan*, 89.

127. Iemitsu's 1634 sojourn was the last time a shogun would stay in Kyoto and make use of Nijō Palace till 1836. Papinot, *Historical and Geographical Dictionary of Japan*, 446.

128. Letter to Yoshihide (1634). *TOZ*, 4:133.

129. Tani Shōan (n.d.). Shōan later became a priest, receiving his Buddhist name from Takuan. Funaoka, *Takuan*, 90.

130. Azabu, now a fashionable residential district of Tokyo, was in Takuan's day on the outskirts of Edo.

131. For Munenori's appointment as *sōmetsuke*, see Rogers, "Military Profession," 87.

132. Samurai stipend and status were calculated in terms of a measure of rice equivalent to approximately 5.2 US bushels, sometimes said to be the amount of rice necesary to feed one person for one year.

133. Apparently referring to case 89 of *Blue Cliff Record*, "Yunyan's 'The Whole Body Is Hand and Eye'": Yunyan asked, "How does the Bodhisattva of Compassion [Guanyin] use all his hands and eyes? . . . The whole body is hand and eye." *T* 48:213c. This reference, in *Tōkaiji yakusha shojō*, an undated document probably compiled in the eighteenth century, may also allude to Takuan's discussion of Kannon's thousand arms in *Record of Marvelous Immovable Wisdom*. Yunyan is the Tang Zen master Yunyan Tansheng (780/782–841).

134. *Taiyūin dono gojikki* (64), quoted in *TZI*, 48; *Tōkaiji yakusha shojō*, *TON*, 236–237; *Manshōsoroku*, *TOZ*, 6:120–121.

135. No such specific age requirement appears in the Daitokuji *hatto*, though the decree does raise the issue of abbots with insufficient years in the priesthood.
136. *Hosokawa keki*, quoted in Funaoka, *Takuan*, 94, and Tsuji, *Bukkyōshi*, 8:458. The *Keki's* account is based on a letter to Hosokawa Tadaoki from his son Tadatoshi, who was in Edo at the time of the audience.
137. *Manshōsoroku, TOZ*, 6:63–64.
138. The practice, known as *junshi*, considered an extreme demonstration of loyalty by a retainer to his lord, was banned by the bakufu in 1663.
139. Letter to Yoshihide (1636). *TOZ*, 4:188–189. As noted earlier, Satō Rentarō argues that the document Takuan refers to here was the original version of *Record of Immovable Wisdom*.
140. Letter to Yoshihide (1636). *TOZ*, 4:197.
141. That is, Tajima, Takuan's native province.
142. Letter to Yoshihide (1637). *TOZ*, 4:211–212.
143. Ibid.
144. The two daimyo were, respectively, Matsukura Shigeharu (d. 1638) and Terazawa Kataka (1609–1647). The Amakusa islands are in present-day Kumamoto Prefecture.
145. Letter to Six Persons Outside Sukyōji (1637). *TOZ*, 4:243–244.
146. Letter to Tadatoshi (1638). *TOZ*, 4:252–253.
147. Letter to Six Persons Outside Sukyōji (1637). *TOZ*, 4:235–247.
148. Ibid., 237. Formal Japanese seated posture involves tucking the legs under, with the knees extended in front, the buttocks placed on the heels, and hands resting on the thighs—hence Takuan's reference to the space between his knees and those of the shogun. For anyone, even a samurai retainer, to share the shogun's dais, and to do so at such proximity, would have been an honor and a rare expression of the ruler's confidence.
149. Scrolls of calligraphy are frequently displayed in tea huts. Because of Daitokuji's historical connection with the tea cult, scrolls of calligraphy by Daitokuji masters were particularly popular in the Edo period, and samples of Takuan's own brushwork were sought after for use in tea huts even during the master's lifetime.
150. Letter to Six Persons Outside Sukyōji (1637). *TOZ*, 4:236–238.
151. Ibid., 240.
152. *Hosokawa keki*, quoted in Funaoka, *Takuan*, 150.
153. Letter to Yoshihide (1638). *TOZ*, 4:273.
154. Takuan describes in detail the circumstances surrounding his temple's founding, including his various discussions with Iemitsu and Munenori, in two letters to Yoshihide (*TOZ*, 4: nos. 115 and 121) written while Tōkaiji was under construction.
155. Letter to Yoshihide (1638). *TOZ*, 4:274–275.
156. Ibid., 275–277.

157. Ibid., 276.
158. Those present were Ii Naotaka (1590–1659), Doi Toshikatsu, Abe Tada'aki (1602–1675), Sakai Tadakatsu (1587–1662), and Hotta Masamori.
159. Letter to Yoshihide (1638). Quoted in Funaoka, *Takuan*, 115.
160. Nihonbashi, in modern-day downtown Tokyo, was the fifty-third station, but in fact Shinagawa was the first station on the highway for Kyoto-bound travelers leaving Edo and the final stop for those arriving from Kyoto at the shogunal capital. Shinamura Izuchi, ed., *Kojien* (Tokyo, 1969), 1000; and Melinda Takeuchi, in Singer et al., *Edo Art in Japan: 1615–1868*, 324.
161. *Daiō Kokushi goroku*, *T* 80:127:a–b.
162. Letter to Yoshihide (1638). *TOZ*, 4:281.
163. Following Funaoka's analysis in *Takuan*, 115–116. Based on the dates in Takuan's correspondence, Funaoka concludes that Takuan did not leave Edo till the seventh month of 1638 and believes *Kinenroku* is mistaken in asserting that Takuan attended Ittō's memorial, held in Kyoto late in the fourth month of that year (*TON*, 107).
164. *Kinenroku*, *TON*, 108. The entire document is included in ibid., 107–111.
165. Ibid., 109–110.
166. Ibid., 111.
167. *Tōkai yakusha shijo*, *TON*, 241.
168. Letter to Mitsunao (1643). *TOZ*, 4:528.
169. Letter to Yoshihide (1644). *TOZ*, 4:606. *Tō* and *shō* were old units of measure for rice. Ten *tō* equaled one *koku* (approximately 5.119 bushels), and ten *shō* equaled one *tō*.
170. Ogisu, historical addendum in *TON*, 250.
171. *Tōkai yakusha shijo*. *TON*, 242.
172. Letter to Yoshihide (1639). *TOZ*, 4:372–373.
173. Letter to Yoshihide (1634). *TOZ*, 4:132.
174. Letter to Hata Chūan (1641). *TOZ*, 4:421.
175. Letter to Yoshihide (1640). *TOZ*, 4:408.
176. The full text of the bakufu's decision, bearing the joint signatures of Takuan, Tenyū, and Kogetsu, is included in Funaoka, *Takuan*, 127–128. A dated 1641 statement by Takuan describing the decision to Daitokuji's elders is included in *Manshōsoroku*, *TOZ*, 6:173.
177. Tsuji, *Nihon bukkyōshi*, 8:479.
178. Letter to Kōkō Shuso (1641). *TOZ*, 4:432–433. Kōkō's dates are not known. The term *shuso*, "head monk," refers to Kōkō's priestly rank.
179. Letter to Yoshihide (1641). *TOZ*, 4:438.
180. *Gyōjō*, *TON*, 165.
181. See the background information included in *Manshōsoroku*, *TOZ*, 6:177–185.
182. Buddhism conceives of three stages of the Buddha's teaching, or Dharma: the true, the reflected, and our present age, the decayed (J. *mappō*). While Takuan's

explanations to Iemitsu invoke the standard view of Hōnen and Nichiren's teachings as accommodations to the present degenerate age, elsewhere Takuan offers a more nuanced, pragmatic interpretation of the popular three stages theory: "As to the three stages of the Dharma," Takuan writes in *Night Talks at Tōkaiji*, "these are to be found in people, not in the age in which they live. Even in the Buddha's day there were those [among his followers] who were dissolute and shameless, who drank wine or ate during restricted hours, and that was precisely why the Buddha promulgated precepts and monastic rules, to restrain them and put an end to such behavior. . . . In the same manner, nowadays are still to be found men of faith, whether they follow the scriptures or a teacher, men who practice in a pure, simple, courageous, and diligent manner, striving to discern the Way and realizing the peerless and subtle truth of the teaching. Are not these men of the true law?" *Tōkai yawa, TOZ*, 5:76.

183. *Manshōsoroku, TOZ*, 6:176–177.

184. Ibid., 177.

185. Letter to Yoshihide (1640). *TOZ*, 4:373–373. For details on the Koya dispute, see also Tsuji, *Nihon bukkyōshi*, 8:489.

186. The four other Tōkaiji subtemples were Genshō-in, erected in 1640 by Hotta Masamori; Chōshō-in, erected in 1641 by Sakai Tadakatsu; Unryō-in, erected in 1643 by Koide Yoshichika; and Shun'un-an (date of completion unknown), erected by Tosa Yorikyuki.

187. Letter to Mitsunao (1642). *TOZ*, 4:514–515. Keishitsu did in fact become Daitokuji's 187th-generation abbot ten years later in 1652. Two other letters from Takuan to Mitsunao, both written in 1642, also include the statement, "I have no disciples [*deshi*]" (*TOZ*, 4:509 and 524); and a 1635 letter from Takuan to Yoshihide similarly observes, "As you know I have no disciple or supervisory monk [*in'o*]." Ibid., 155.

188. Before coming to Daitokuji to study under the temple's founder, Daitō, Tettō had trained at the Kyoto Gozan temple Kenninji. Where Shun'oku had originally studied is unclear.

189. *Tōkai yawa, TOZ*, 5:48–49.

190. Letter to Yoshihide (1645). *TOZ*, 4:663.

191. Letter to Chūan (1641). *TOZ*, 4:422. Chūan's dates are unknown. It is unclear what Takuan means when he refers here to "thirty years." The time may roughly allude to the decades since 1607, when Takuan became a Daitokuji Zen master.

192. Quoted in Funaoka, *Takuan*, 173, from *Isshi goroku*, Isshi's posthumous record, published by his disciples in 1667. Because Isshi clearly refers here to Tōkaiji, the letter can be dated to sometime between the temple's 1639 founding and Takuan's death in 1645.

193. Teacher of Men and Devas is one of the epithets of the Buddha and is sometimes applied to Zen teachers. *Deva*s are divine beings, and the category includes, among others, virtuous men, sages, and bodhisattvas.

194. A practitioner who has freed himself from the bonds of birth and death. The term is often used, as here, pejoratively, to refer to those who live isolated from others, content with a lesser, selfish realization, in contrast to the fully realized bodhisattva, who returns to the world to save all sentient beings.

195. Takuan received Ittō's *inka* in 1604, making this approximately 1644, or shortly before Takuan's death. It is unclear what Takuan is referring to by "a single koan," possibly the "Mu" koan or some particular koan emphasized in Takuan's teaching line.

196. *Manshō goroku, TOZ*, 2:24–25. Quoted in Funaoka, *Takuan*, 176–177.

197. Funaoka, *Takuan*, 179–180.

198. *Manshō goroku, TOZ*, 2:25.

199. *Kinenroku, TON*, 130–131.

200. *Kinenroku, TON*, 138.

201. An interlinear note in *Kinenroku* (*TON*, 138), included with the account of Takuan's meeting with the retired emperor, states that Takuan's former student Isshi Monju was especially revered by Gomizuno'o, who sought to have Takuan appoint Isshi as his successor. (A similar account appears in *Manshōsoroku, TOZ*, 6:81–82.) While this may well have been true at an earlier period, by the time of Takuan's 1644 audience with Gomizuno'o, the retired emperor had probably completed the arrangements for Isshi to receive transmission from another Zen teacher he patronized, the celebrated Myōshinji master Gudō Tōshoku. Isshi's *inka* from Gudō, by which Isshi became his Dharma heir and a member of the Myōshinji teaching line, bears the same date, the fourth month of 1644 (no day is given), as Takuan's interview with the retired emperor, making it unlikely that Gomizuno'o was still trying at this point to engineer Takuan's adoption of Isshi as his successor. The *inka* is included in Isshi's biography, *Butchō kokushi nenpu, T* 81:187c. Although Isshi had studied under Takuan, Gudō's *inka* makes clear that Isshi's enlightenment was independent and without a teacher.

202. Yanagida, ed., *Jikaishū*, 378. Ikkyū's criticisms in *Jikaishū* of indiscriminate bestowal of koan transmission at Daitokuji have been cited previously. *Jikaishū* remained in manuscript till its publication in the twentieth century but was familiar to Japanese Zen monks of the seventeenth century. *Jikaishū*'s attacks on *missan*-style practices at Daitokuji are referred to, for example, in *Mukai nanshin* (A Compass in the Foggy Sea; 1672) by the Rinzai master Chōon Dōkai (1628–1695). Yamada Kōdō, ed., *Zenmon hōgoshū*, 3:164. There is evidence that use of *inka*-style sanctions at Daitokuji, and Myōshinji as well, did not predate the early fifteenth century. Katō Shōshun concludes that at Daitokuji the earliest *inka* is that given by Ikkyū's teacher, Kaso Sōdon (1352–1428), in 1414 to Yōsō Sōi, Ikkyū's Dharma brother and one of his principal targets in *Jikaishū*. Katō Shōshun, "Kanzan no inkajō," 54.

203. *Rōsō yuikai no jōjō. Manshō goroku, TOZ,* 2:185. *Rōsō yuikai* is the longer of the two surviving versions of Takuan's last admonitions. See below, n. 229.
204. Ibid., 188.
205. *Tōkai yawa* (2), *TOZ,* 5:75.
206. *Tenshin.* An expression drawn from Daoism, used in Zen to indicate original nature.
207. *Hekigan kyūjūge, TOZ,* 1:11. Cited by Funaoka, *Takuan,* 175. Such *ge,* or Buddhist religious poems, are often, as here, primarily didactic in nature, and I have therefore chosen to render them in prose.
208. Referring to the thirty-four legendary patriarchs said to have transmitted the Zen teaching "from mind to mind" in an unbroken line from the Buddha Shakyamuni. These include the twenty-eight Indian patriarchs, from the Buddha's disciple Mahākāshyapa, who received the master's "wordless teaching," to Bodhidharma (d. 532), who carried the teaching from India to the east; and the six patriarchs of Zen in China, from Bodhidharma to Huineng, the "Sixth Patriarch" celebrated in the *Platform Sutra.*
209. *Hekigan kyūjūge, TOZ,* 1:10–11. Cited by Funaoka, *Takuan,* 175.
210. *Tōkai yawa* (2), *TOZ,* 5:81–82.
211. An area named for a bridge erected in 1602 across the Sumida River, referred to previously as the fifty-third station of the Tōkaidō. In premodern Japanese cities, bridges and, when dry, the riverbeds beneath them, were often gathering places for beggars. Not all the Nihonbashi beggars were displaced farmers and victims of rural famine. As Takuan indicates in a 1643 letter to Gyōja (Practitioner) Motonari, many seem to have been professional mendicants, drifters, and the sorts of problematic homeless who cluster in our own modern cities. "Nihonbashi," Takuan writes, "offers many examples of wretchedness. Everywhere one turns one is moved to pity. Offer the beggars rice gruel, and some will actually throw it away, saying it's cold or whatever. Give them five or ten coppers, and they'll immediately set up a lottery with their friends. At other times they'll have sumo matches, wrestling with each other, then stop when they're tired and fall down. There are beggars who weep and those who cause others to weep. In such a time as ours, to be a beggar is indeed a punishment from heaven. Truly their situation is desperate. Yet their attitude is that so long as today things are all right, that's all that matters." *TOZ,* 4:540–541.
212. Letter to Mitsunao (1643). *TOZ,* 4:534. Similar accounts of the Nihonbashi beggars occur in a letter of the same year to Yoshihide (ibid., 537).
213. *Gokoku.* In Japan, the term commonly indicates wheat, rice, beans, glutinous millet, and Chinese millet.
214. Letter to Munenori (1634). *TOZ,* 4:142.
215. Letter to Yoshihide (1644). *TOZ,* 4:587.
216. Letter to Hanbei (undated). *TOZ,* 4:80–81.

217. Tsuji, *Nihon bukkyōshi*, 8:476–477. Takuan's visit to Nikkō is mentioned in a 1639 letter to Yoshihide. *TOZ*, 4:372. Such pilgrimages to Nikkō were incumbent not only on the Tokugawa shoguns but also on the daimyo, who would travel acompanied by their samurai retainers. Taniguchi, "Military Evolution or Revolution?" 171.

218. Letter to Isshi (1645). *TOZ*, 4:666–667.

219. *Gyōgoki, TON*, 169.

220. Title of case 87 of *Blue Cliff Record*, "Yunmen's 'Medicine and Illness Cure Each Other.'" *T* 48:212a.

221. *Manshōsoroku, TOZ*, 6:198–199.

222. While there are recorded instances of Chinese Zen masters using drawn circles, the oldest painted circles that survive in a Zen context are Japanese. The empty circle that represents the eighth stage of the Ten Ox-Herding Pictures (J. *Jugyū zuju*), a product of the Song dynasty, may have served as a prototype for the Japanese examples. Shibayama notes that among Zen priests in Japan, however, the circle (J. *ensō*) served not so much as a teaching device as an independent calligraphic art form. The earliest surviving example is a circle dated 1455 painted by the Daitokuji abbot Yōsō Sōi, mentioned previously as Ikkyū Sōjun's bête noire. The painted circle became particularly popular during the Edo period, and Takuan's circles are among the earliest examples. Shibayama Zenkei, *Zenga no ensō*, 9–12. Another Takuan circle cited by Shibayama (ibid., 18) is undated and inscribed with a passage referring to Wumen's poem in *Gateless Gate*, case 21, "Yunmen's 'Dried-Shit Stick'" (J. "Unmon kanshiketsu"): "Swift as a flash of lightning / Or a spark struck from flint / If you so much as blink an eye / You're already off!" *T* 48:295c. That is, Shibayama remarks, thought and discrimination interfere with the immediacy of one's response, a theme emphasized by Takuan in *Record of Immovable Wisdom*.

223. *Yuikai, Manshō goroku, TOZ*, 2:186.

224. *Kinenroku, TON*, 140; *Manshōsoroku, TOZ*, 6:240–241. Fire in premodern Japan was an ever-present danger, as most buildings were constructed largely of timber, and flames could spread quickly between neighboring structures. Takuan's fears were realized in 1694, when Tōkaiji caught fire from a nearby building. The temple was rebuilt in 1698.

225. Transcribed in *TZI*, 75, from Takuan's handwritten death verse, in the possession of Tōkaiji. The translation of the second line is tentative.

226. *T* 8:752b.

227. Letter to Munenori (1645). *TOZ*, 4:655.

228. *Ketsujōshū, TOZ*, 5:13.

229. *Kinenroku, TON*, 141. *Rosō yuikai no jōjō* (My Final Instructions), a second, longer set of last instructions in possession of Tōkaiji, offers several further provisions, in particular Takuan's statements, quoted earlier, that he has no Dharma heirs and his demand that the painted circles substitute for any

official portrait. Additional burial and postburial instructions contained in the document include the following:

> Since I have no disciple who has succeeded to my Dharma, how can there be anyone who assumes the role of chief mourner, receiving guests who arrive to pay their respects? People will probably come from our own and other Buddhist schools to chant sutras. The head priest of the temple here should go out alone in front of the main gate and, in accordance with my rule, tell them to go home. Whatever you do, don't ask them in!
>
> During my lifetime I brought back the robe and bowl [emblems of the Zen transmission] to my teacher's pagoda, so I'm just a useless monk with a plain black robe.
>
> No memorial tablets for me are to be installed in the main temple's [i.e., Daitokuji's] founder's hall. Should anyone set one up on his own, somebody should secretly take it and burn it. That person is the one who will be closest to me.
>
> My body is not to be cremated. In the middle of the night, secretly carry my corpse out of the temple and find a place no one knows in the fields. Bury me deep in the ground, and plant grass over the spot to conceal it. Don't leave any trace of a mound, but let the spot appear undisturbed; I want to be sure that afterward no one can find it. . . .
>
> Once I've stopped breathing, take me out in the fields that very night. If it's still daylight, don't announce that I'm dead, but wait till dark and carry me out in secret. . . .
>
> No stone monument is to be erected for me inside or outside the temple. Our ancestor Shunpo's *gatha* says:
>> The original body has no relics
>> These stinking bones are just a pile of dust
>> When you dig up the earth, bury me deep
>> Then the green hills will be free of even a speck of ashes.
>
> Remember this!

*TOZ*, 2:185–188. A photograph of the handwritten document appears in Funaoka, *Takuan*, 137. Shunpo is Shunpo Sōki (1416–1496), an heir of Yōsō Sōi and fortieth-generation abbot of Daitokuji. It was his line that became the main Daitokuji lineage and the line from which Takuan descends.

230. The grave can still be seen at Tōkaiji. For a photograph, see Funaoka, *Takuan*, v. Takuan's efforts at self-effacement were also resisted by Nanshūji's monks, who installed in the temple's founder's pagoda a wooden statue of the master commissioned by his Kyoto followers. And at Takuan's other Sakai temple, Shōunji, a memorial stupa was erected in 1650 with an inscription contributed by Takuan's longtime student Munetomo, offering a brief outline of the master's career. (The Shōunji stupa inscription is by the Nanzenji abbot Saigaku

Genryō [n.d.] but was commissioned by Munetomo, who probably supplied the details of Takuan's biography. The text appears in *TON*, 185–186.) Two years earlier, in composing *Account of the Life of Master Takuan*, Munetomo had already contravened Takuan's injunction against biographies, though only, he confessed, after wrestling earnestly with his conscience. At the close of the work, Munetomo explained his decision: "Because I served at the master's side over many years, I have recorded the bulk of his words and deeds. Once the master declared that if any student, in violation of his command, recorded his biography, that student would be perpetrating a crime against him. Yet, I wondered, should I adhere strictly to the master's prohibition and allow the record of his life to perish? Or shall I violate his last wishes and so forever preserve the facts of his life? Who is to judge which is right and which is wrong? . . . What crime is there in this?" *Gyōjō, TON*, 172.

231. Titles have been added by the anthologists.
232. *Manshōsoroku, TOZ*, 6:124–125.
233. *TZI*, 104–113; *Manshōsoroku, TOZ*, 6:192; *TON*, 30. This popular variety of pickled radish is still generally refered to in Japan as *takuanzuke* (Takuan pickles), or simply *takuan*.
234. *Manshōsoroku, TOZ*, 6:122 The *soroku*'s author, Kudō Yukihiro (n.d.), was a samurai in the Numata domain (present-day Gumma Prefecture).
235. *TZI*, 119–121.
236. *Manshōsoroku, TOZ*, 6:186.
237. In present-day Fukushima Prefecture.
238. N.d. A famous horseman of the early seventeenth century, proclaimed by Iemitsu to be the best rider in Japan. His feat at Mount Atago is said to have occurred in 1634.
239. 1568–1595. Nephew and heir of Toyotomi Hideyoshi.
240. *Anjō hito naku, anka uma nashi*. The eight-character phrase is included in *Zenrin kushū*. See Hori, *Zen Sand*, 313.
241. *TZI*, 129.
242. *TZI*, 121–123.
243. *TZI*, 147–149. Adapted from *Kōshi yawa*, an Edo period miscellany in the collection of Toyō Bunko.
244. *TOZ*, 149–150. Adapted from *Yassui zuihitsu*, an Edo period miscellany.

# Bibliography

Akao Ryūji. *Bankei zenji zenshū*. Tokyo, 1970.

Akashi Mariko and Tad Tohen, trans. "Fudōchi shinmyōroku." *Traditions*, vol. 1, no.1 (1976): 12–34.

Amakuki Setsunan, ed. *Myōshinji roppyakunen shi*. Tokyo, 1935.

Andō Yoshinori. "Chūsei zenshū ni okeru Genjū-ha no missan zen ni tsuite." *Indogaku bukkyōgaku kenkyū*, vol. 50, no. 2 (March 2002): 611–617.

Bodiford, William M. "Religion and Spiritual Development: Japan." In *Martial Arts of the World: An Encyclopedia*, edited by Thomas A. Green, 472–505. Santa Barbara, 2001.

———. *Sōtō Zen in Medieval Japan*. Honolulu, 1993.

———. "Written Texts: Japan." In *Martial Arts of the World: An Encyclopedia*, edited by Thomas A. Green, 758–773. Santa Barbara, 1975.

———. "Zen and Japanese Swordsmanship Reconsidered." In *Budo Perspectives*, edited by Alexander Bennett, 69–103. Auckland, 2005.

Bruce, J. Percey. *Chu-hsi and His Masters*. London, 1923.

Chan, Alan K. L. "A Matter of Taste: *Qi* (Vital Energy) and the Tending of the Heart (*Xin*) in Mencius 2A2." In *Mencius: Contexts and Interpretation*, edited by Alan K. L. Chan, 42–71. Honolulu, 2002.

Chan, Wing-tsit. *A Source Book in Chinese Philosophy*. New York, 1969.

Cleary, Thomas. *Soul of the Samurai*. North Clarendon, 2005.

Cleary, Thomas, and J. C. Cleary. *The Blue Cliff Record*. Boston, 1992.

de Bary, William T., ed. *The Buddhist Tradition*. New York, 1969.

——— et al. *Sources of Chinese Tradition*. Volume 1. New York, 1970.

——— et al. *Sources of Japanese Tradition*. Volume 2. New York, 2005.

Friday, Karl F. "Beyond Valor and Bloodshed: The Arts of War as a Path to Serenity." In *Knight and Samurai*, edited by Rosemarie Deist, 1–13. Copenhagen, 2003.

———. "*Budō, Bujutsu*, and *Bugei*." In *Martial Arts of the World: An Encyclopedia*, edited by Thomas A. Green, 56–59. Santa Barbara, 2001.

———. "*Kōryū Bugei*." In *Martial Arts of the World: An Encylopoedia*, edited by Thomas A. Green, 301–305. Santa Barbara, 2001.

————. "Off the Warpath: Military Science and Budō in the Evolution of Ryūha Bugei." In *Budo Perspectives*, edited by Alexander Bennett, 249–268. Auckland, 2005.

Friday, Karl F., with Seki Humitake. *Legacies of the Sword: The Kashima Shrine and Samurai Martial Culture*. Honolulu, 1997.

Funaoka Makoto. *Takuan*. Tokyo, 1988.

Haga Koshirō, ed. *Daitokuji to chadō*. Kyoto, 1972.

Hakeda, Yoshito S. *The Awakening of Faith, Attributed to Asvagosha*. 2nd ed. New York, 2006.

Haskel, Peter. "Bankei and His World." Ph.D. diss., Columbia University, 1988.

————. *Bankei Zen*. Edited by Yoshito S. Hakeda. New York, 1984.

————. *Letting Go: The Story of Zen Master Tōsui*. Honolulu, 2001.

Hirano Sōjō. "Daitō kokushi agyo no kenkyū." *Zen bunka kenkyūjo*, no. 3 (October 1971): 47–60.

Hirose, Nobuko. *Immovable Mind*. Rockport, 1992.

Hori, Victor. *Zen Sand*. Honolulu, 2003.

Hōshō Shigefusa. *Kasuga ryūjin, Funabashi, Eguchi.* . . . Tokyo, 1929.

Hurst, G. Cameron, III. "Samurai on Wall Street: Miyamoto Musashi and the Search for Success." *UFSI Reports*, no. 44 (1982): 1–15 (reprinted 2001).

Ichikawa Hakugen. *Takuan: Fudōchi shinmyōroku, Tai-a ki*. Zen no koten, 7. Tokyo, 1982.

Imamura Yoshio, ed. *Shiryō Yagyū Shinkageryū*. 2 vols. Tokyo, [1962] 1995.

————. *Yagyū ichizoku*. Tokyo, 1971.

Iriya Yoshitaka, ed. *Basō no goroku*. Kyoto, 1985.

————, ed. *Zengo jiten*. Tokyo, 1991.

Ishikawa Rikizan. "Colloquial Transcriptions as Sources for Understanding Zen in Japan." Translated and with an Introduction by William M. Bodiford. *Eastern Buddhist*, new series, vol. 34, no. 1 (2002): 120–142.

————. *Zenshū sōden shiryō no kenkyū*. 2 vols. Kyoto, 2001.

Kaneda Hiroshi. *Tōmon shomono to kokugo kenkyū*. Tokyo, 1976.

Kasai Akira. "Takuan no shūgyōron." *Indogaku bukkyōgaku kenkyū*, vol. 47, no. 1 (December 1998): 185–189.

————. "Takuan to chadō." *Indogaku bukkyōgaku kenkyū*, vol. 49, no. 97 (December 2000): 246–250.

————. "Takuan zen to bugei." *Indogaku bukkyōgaku kenkyū*, vol. 45, no. 2 (March 1997): 646–652.

Kasai Tetsu. "Kenzen ichinyo no shisō no genryū: Takuan to Yagyū Shinkageryū." *Indogaku bukkyōgaku kenkyū*, vol. 55, no. 1 (December 2007): 230–234.

————. "Takuan ni okeru ki no shisō ni tsuite." *Indogaku bukkyōgaku kenkyū*, vol. 58, no. 3 (March 2010): 730–740.

Katō Shōshun. "Hakuhō Eryō to shie jiken." *Zen bunka kenkyūjo kiyō*, vol. 9 (1977): 391–435.

——. "Kanzan no inkajō." *Zen bunka,* no. 186 (Fall 2002): 43–54.

Katō Takao and Yagyū Nobuharu. "'Tairon': Yagyū shinkageryū no sekai: kiriai no gi to tetsugaku." Yagyūryū official internet site, 2003.

Komazawa Daigaku Zengaku Daijiten Hensansho, ed. *Zengaku daijiten.* Tokyo, 1985.

Kraft, Kenneth. *Eloquent Zen.* Honolulu, 1992.

Kyūshu Daigaku, Chūgoku Tetsugaku Kenkyūshitsu. *Er Cheng quan shu.* 2 vols. Tokyo, 1979.

Lippiello, Tiziana. *Auspicious Omens and Miracles in Ancient China: Han, Three Kingdoms and Six Dynasties.* Monumenta Serica Monograph Series, vol. 39. Sankt Augustin, 2001.

Lishka, Dennis. "Zen and the Creative Process: The Kendō-Zen Thought of the Rinzai Master Takuan." *Japanese Journal of Religious Studies,* vol. 5, nos. 2–3 (June–September 1978): 139–158.

Matsuta Bugyō. *Takuan.* Tokyo, 1943.

McMullan, Neil. *Buddhism and the State in Sixteenth Century Japan.* Princeton, 1984.

Milburn, Olivia. *The Glory of Yue: The Annotated Translation of the Yuejue shu.* Sinica Leidensia, vol. 23. Leiden, 2010.

Miura, Isshū, and R. F. Sasaki. *Zen Dust.* New York, 1966.

Monbushō Shūkyō Kyoku, ed. *Shūkyō seido chōsa shiryō.* Tokyo, 1977.

Morinaga Sōkō, ed. *Zenkai ichiran.* Tokyo, 1987.

Murai Sanae. "Shie jiken go no chōbaku kankei." *Kinsei bukkyō shiryō to kenkyū,* vol. 6, no. 1 (March 1983): 1–11.

Nagata Hōjō. "Takuan." In *Kōza zen,* edited by Nishitani Keiji et al., 4:275–288. Tokyo, 1967.

Nishikatsu Osamu. "Keichō, Genna ki ni okeru jiin hatto." *Bukkyōshi kenkyū,* vol. 9 (March 1979): 1–18.

Nōnin Kōdō. "Kinsei zenshūshi sunkō." *Zen bunka,* no. 189 (Fall 2003): 152–158.

Ogisu Jundō. *Takuan oshō nenpu.* Kyoto, 1983.

Papinot, E. *Historical and Geographical Dictionary of Japan.* Tokyo, 1976.

Rambach, Pierre. *The Secret Message of Tantric Buddhism.* New York, 1979.

Red Pine. *The Platform Sūtra: The Zen Teaching of Hui-neng.* Translation and commentary. Berkeley, 2006.

——. *The Zen Works of Stonehouse.* San Fancisco, 1999.

Rogers, John M. "Arts of War in Times of Peace: Swordsmanship in 'Honchō bugei shoden.'" *Monumenta Niponica,* vol. 45, no. 4 (1990): 413–445; and vol. 46, no. 2 (1991): 173–202.

——. "Development of the Military Profession in Tokugawa Japan." Ph.D. diss., Harvard University, 1998.

Sansom, George. *History of Japan.* Vol. 2. Stanford, 1961.

Sasaki, R. F. *The Record of Linji: Translation and Commentary by Ruth Fuller Sasaki.* Edited by Thomas Yūhō Kirchner. Honolulu, 2009.

Sato, Hiroaki. *The Sword and the Mind.* New York, 1986.

Satō Rentarō. "Takuan Sōhō 'Fudōchi shinmyōroku' ko shahon sanshu, 'Tai'a ki' ko shahon isshu." *Hokkaidō daigaku bungaku kenkūka kiyō*, vol. 103 (2001): 24–139.

————. "Takuan Sōhō 'Fudōchi shinmyōroku' no shohon." *Indō tetsugaku bukkyōgaku*, vol. 15 (2000): 269–288.

Sawada, Janine Anderson. "Religious Conflict in Bakumatsu Japan: Imakita Kōsen and Confucian Scholar Higashi Takashi." *Japanese Journal of Religious Studies*, vol. 21, nos. 2–3 (June–September 1994): 211–230.

Shibayama Zenkei, ed. *Kunchū zenrin kushū*. Kyoto, 1952.

————. *Zenga no ensō*. Tokyo, 1969.

Singer, Robert T., et al. *Edo Art in Japan: 1615–1868*. East Greenwich, 1998.

Suzuki Daisetsu. *Zen and Japanese Culture*. New York, 1959.

————. *Zen shisōshi kenkyū*. Vol. 4. Tokyo, 1968.

Suzuki Gakujutsu Zaidan, ed. *Dai Nihon bukkyō zensho*. Tokyo, 1970–1973.

Suzuki Masaya. *Katana to kubi tori: sengoku kassen issetsu*. Tokyo, 2000.

Takakusu Junjirō et al., eds. *Taishō shinshū daizōkyō*. Tokyo, 1914–1922.

Takeno Munetomo. *Takuan dai-oshō gyōjō*. In Ogisu Jundō, *Takuan oshō nenpu*. Kyoto, 1983.

————. *Takuan oshō kinenroku*. In Ogisu Jundō, *Takuan oshō nenpu*. Kyoto, 1983.

Takeuchi Genshō. "Isshi Monju to Takuan Sōhō." *Zen bunka*, no. 162 (Fall 1996): 38–46.

————. *Nihon zenshūshi*. Tokyo, 1989.

————. *Shin Nihon zenshūshi*. Tokyo, 1999.

Takeuchi Yūriyo. "Hachimanshi Honmyōji no Kogetsu Sōgan ude Takuan Sōhō shojō ni tsuite." *Zen bunka*, no. 164 (Spring 1997): 40–45.

Takikawa Kametarō, ed. *Shiki kaichū kōshō*. Tokyo, 1934.

Takuan Oshō Zenshū Kankōkai, ed. *Takuan oshō zenshū*. Tokyo, 1928–1930.

Tamamura Takeji. *Engakuji shi*. Tokyo, 1964.

————. *Gozan bungaku*. Tokyo, 1955.

————. "Gozan sōrin no tatchū ni tsuite." In *Nihon zenshūshi ronshū*, 1:197–244. Kyoto, 1976–1981.

————. "Hōkei no kenkyū hōhō ni kansuru ichi kenkai." In *Nihon zenshūshi ronshū*, 2:843–863. Kyoto, 1976–1981.

————. *Nihon zenshūshi ronshū*. 2 vols. Kyoto, 1976–1981.

————. "Rinzaishū Genjū-ha." *Nihon zenshūshi ronshū*, 2:865–926. Kyoto, 1976–1981

————. "Takuan Sōhō: shie jiken ni taisuru ichi kenkai." *Zen bunka*, no. 70 (September 1973): 106–111.

————. "Zen to Gozan bungaku." *Nihon zenshūshi ronshū*, 1:1025–1038. Kyoto, 1976–1981.

Taniguchi, Shinko. "Military Evolution or Revolution? State Formation and the Early Modern Samurai." In *Knight and Samurai*, edited by Rosemarie Deist, 169–155. Copenhagen, 2003.

Tsuji Zennosuke. *Nihon bukkyōshi.* Tokyo, 1992.

———. *Takuan oshō shokanshū.* Tokyo, 1942.

Tucker, John Allen. "Quiet Sitting and Political Activism: The Thought and Practice of Satō Naokata." *Japanese Journal of Religious Studies,* vol. 29, nos. 1–2 (2002): 107–146.

Uozumi, Takashi. "Research of Miyamoto Musashi's 'Gorin no sho' from the Perspective of Japanese Intellectual History." In *Budo Perspectives,* edited by Alexander Bennett, 45–68. Auckland, 2005.

Victoria, Brian. *Zen at War.* New York, 1997.

Watanabe Ichirō, ed. *Heihō kadensho.* Tokyo, 1985.

Watson, Burton. *Records of the Grand Historian.* New York, 1961.

Wilson, William Scott. *The Unfettered Mind.* Tokyo, 1986.

Wyatt, Don J. *The Recluse of Loyang.* Honolulu, 1996.

Yamada Kiyoshi, ed. *Ise monogatari.* Tokyo, 1979.

Yamada Kōdō, ed. *Zenmon hōgoshū.* Tokyo, 1921.

Yampolsky, Philip B. *The Platform Sūtra of the Sixth Patriarch.* New York, 1967.

Yanagida Seizan, ed. *Jikaishū. Shinsen Nihon koten bunko,* vol. 5. Tokyo, 1976.

———. *Rinzai roku.* Tokyo, 1972.

Zen Bunka Kenkyūjo. *Ikkyū dōka.* Kyoto, 2008.

———. *Takuan zenji itsuwasen.* Kyoto, 2001.

*Zokuzokyō.* Kyoto, 1902-1905.

# Index

# About the Author

PETER HASKEL received his doctorate in Japanese thought from Columbia University. An accomplished translator, author, and editor, he is author most recently of *Letting Go: The Story of Zen Master Tōsui* and coeditor (with Mary Farkas and Robert Lopez) of *Original Nature: Sokei-an's Translation and Commentary on the Sixth Patriarch Platform Sutra.* He lives in New York, where he has for many years been a practitioner of Zen Buddhism.

Production notes for Haskel | *Sword of Zen*

Cover design by Julie Matsuo-Chun.

Text design by inari with display type in Warnock Pro
   and text type in Warnock Pro

Composition by inari

Printing and binding by Sheridan Books, Inc.

Printed on 55 lb. House White Hi-Bulk D37, 360 ppi.